SNAKES IN MY DREAMS

A Mental Health Therapist's Odyssey from Hardship to Healer

A MEMOIR

DR. MIKE DENINGER

A Division of Health Communications, Inc.
www.unrivaledbooks.com

Library of Congress Control Number: 2011934401

© 2011 Mike Deninger
ISBN-13: 978-1-61360-109-9
ISBN-10: 1-61360-109-3
ISBN-13: 978-1-61360-110-5 (e-book)
ISBN-10: 1-61360-110-7 (e-book)

All rights reserved. Printed in the United States of America. No part of this publication may be reproduced, stored in a retrieval system or transmitted in any form or by any means, electronic, mechanical, photocopying, recording or otherwise, without the written permission of the publisher.

Unrivaled Books, its logos, and marks are the trademarks of Health Communications, Inc.

Publisher: Unrivaled Books
          3201 SW 15th Street
          Deerfield Beach, FL 33442

Cover design by Justin Rotkowitz
Inside book design and formatting by Dawn Von Strolley Grove

DEDICATION

FIRST AND FOREMOST, to Michael Mayes, my partner of thirteen years, for his steadfast love, his abundant patience and his support as I painstakingly composed this book for as long as we have been together.

To my children Renee Deninger Alsop and Kurt Deninger for their love, and for making me a proud father each and every day.

To my siblings and extended family, especially the individuals who believed me from the start. A special thanks to my sister Ann Weber and my nieces Marilyn Mogenhan and Jackie Conte, who read an early draft of this book and gave me permission to cry.

To my parents Margaret and Lester, who loved me as they knew how, and whose contentious life together serves as the backdrop for this unfolding story.

To Ned Geraty, a gifted mental health professional, who confirmed my worthiness week after week and who guided me through recovery with kindness and with care.

To my good friends Elaine Lowry, Becky Sadler, and Phil Mackall, and also to my brother Dan Deninger and my sister Pidge Wienecke, for reading earlier drafts and providing valuable feedback.

To Carlene Thumann-Prezioso, my close friend and compatriot, for listening attentively as the mystery unfolded, for sitting on the bleachers with me while I cried and for reading every draft of this book she could get her hands on.

To "D," my first AA sponsor, for listening to my fourth step and for modeling serenity.

To my editor Barbara McNichol, who wisely encouraged me to soften my tone when I had the urge to preach and whose skill and insight greatly enhanced the quality of this book.

To my fellow survivors of all types who know what it's like to stand in my shoes.

To our dog Mikey who nudges me out of bed each morning and makes me get on with the day.

TABLE OF CONTENTS

Foreword vii
Prologue ix

CHAPTER 1	Neighborhood Images 1
CHAPTER 2	Ancestral Infractions 15
CHAPTER 3	Coming Attractions 39
CHAPTER 4	Lester's Transgressions 53
CHAPTER 5	Drawn to the Action 71
CHAPTER 6	Anxiety Personified 95
CHAPTER 7	Aching to Learn 118
CHAPTER 8	Missing Pieces 132
CHAPTER 9	Cosmic Connection 154
CHAPTER 10	On the Brink of Insanity 164
CHAPTER 11	Showdown at the Cemetery 173
CHAPTER 12	Descent Into Madness 191
CHAPTER 13	Spoiled 216
CHAPTER 14	The Unthinkable 223
CHAPTER 15	A Seat at the Back of the Bus 243
CHAPTER 16	Rebirth of Wonder 265
CHAPTER 17	Full Circle 287

About the Author 311

FOREWORD

If you are a survivor of childhood sexual abuse, this carefully crafted memoir, more than a decade in the making, will have you feeling ill at ease, but oddly comfortable in Mike Deninger's shoes. He "speaks" the language of survivors, and he does it quite well. Although his story will prove once again that you are not alone, you will also be reminded of the problems associated with standing in those shoes. While reading this book, I empathized with Mike. I laughed. I cried. I hurt. And I was haunted—terrified really—not for him, but by my own nightmares that were triggered by his recollections. As disturbing as this story is at times, in the end, it is a tale that will inspire hope in all of us and the confidence that we really can mend the fractured pieces from the wounded individuals we once were.

The author sets the stage by drawing the reader's attention to seemingly insignificant but repetitive memories from his childhood, laying down markers along his path to discovery. These signposts guide the reader back and forth, up to, and finally through the traumatic events of his working class boyhood. By painstakingly recording his memories, dreams, and details of his life, and revealing their interconnectedness, the author formed a base from which he could work in pursuit of his truth. It is the same base from which we all have to work, if we are to heal.

Survivors and their allies will not be surprised by the unexpected twists and turns that complicated his adult years. Only those of us who have had similar experiences will fully understand how bizarre the connections can be that trigger the recall of incidents your mind had blocked from conscious memory a long, long time ago, because they were too much for you to handle. Thus, are shocking realities sometimes hidden from view, not maliciously, but in order to help you survive that day, that hour, and at that very moment when you were violated.

The author's forthright and entertaining style will appeal to every man. His truth feels authentic and real, even if his childhood experiences, cast of characters, and his particular "slow burn" in adulthood are vastly dissimilar from your own story. His painful peeling back of the layers, leading to more twists, more outrageous recollections, more pain, and more faltering may seem very familiar; so like your own history that you might believe you could have written the same story—to a point—about yourself. And finally, his ultimate triumph will leave you hoping that your story could end just as well as his.

Jorge Ramirez, PhD
President
Male Survivor: The International Organization
Against Male Sexual Victimization

PROLOGUE

It's not like I had a choice. I had to write this book. Failure to do so would have gone against what I had come to believe. I thought about writing a memoir for years, but a nasty inner voice kept warning me to keep my mouth shut. I'd been hearing his negative chatter since I was a boy, but his carping became downright ruthless and vulgar whenever I sat down to write. Sebastian, my soul's intermediary, explained during a meditation that the voice was unusually angry and insecure, because he had been conceived in degradation. For as long as I had fears, I would need to console him.

I first became aware of Sebastian during a meditation several months after I had my last drink of alcohol. No name came to me, just a presence. For several days thereafter, the name Sebastian arose in my thoughts. Then I met a young man named Sebastian. I read about a church named St. Sebastian. I was prompted to research the name and found that St. Sebastian was a third-century Christian and Roman guard who had been condemned to death for his beliefs, tied to a stake, and shot with arrows. He was left for dead, but a woman nursed him back to health.

I thought about recovery. When I encountered the presence in my next meditation and asked if that is how he was known, it was confirmed with a tingling in my neck. His insights (which come to me as thoughts) are often accompanied by physical sensations—a chill or a shudder in my back or shoulders. These are not hallucinations, and I don't believe I have extraordinary psychic abilities. It's a connection to a higher level, spiritual and uplifting.

I wrestled with a secret for four decades that nearly crushed me. But that was nothing compared to what was yet to come. When I was in my forties, I recorded every dream I could remember and filled a dozen journals with everything else about my life I could recall. A number of the dreams and journal entries are included in this book, more or less as they were recorded over time. The journal entries need no explanation. Readers are encouraged to explore the dream content, imagery, and emotions in relation to the unfolding story. I believe that dreams are instructive and not randomly generated output—"readouts" of internal impressions and emotions that relate to our experiences.

I had hoped that dedicated introspection would make me feel more at home in the world. Unfortunately, another decade passed before I began to find my way. It was on my fiftieth birthday that I got serious and committed to writing this book.

By then, my internal critic was on me like a drill sergeant, dressing me down with harsh subliminal diatribes.

"No one's going to believe this shit. And it's shamefully depraved. Don't make a fool of yourself, for Christ's sake. It probably never happened anyway!"

It probably never happened....

As soon as I began writing about the memories, that thought started bouncing back and forth in my head like the ball in Pong, from one temple to the other. But if what I had remembered never really happened, where would that leave me? How could I understand the direction my life had taken?

I once conducted an imaginary test for the truth. I pictured myself leaning over a rickety-old pinball machine, pulling back the plunger and launching it from between my thumb and forefinger. A silver ball of doubt raced up the chute and leapt onto the game board of my consciousness. Lights flashed and bells rang as the ball was jostled from post to post. My life-long fears and insecurities made so much sense in light of what I had remembered. "Yesssss!" I hissed to myself. Thousands of points were racked up in my favor. *Brrrring, da ding, ding, ding!* It was all true. "I wasn't nuts after all, not the emotional jellyfish some had made me out to be. *Clicka, clicka, ding, boing.* And the memories . . . they couldn't be figments of my imagination . . . they just couldn't . . . *rat-a-tat-tat-tat, flash, buzz-flash!* Or could they . . . ?"

"Shit!" I cursed up at the ceiling. Whenever I got close to accepting these memories as real, that malignant voice thundered into my consciousness from a place just behind my forehead . . . . *"NONE OF THIS EVER HAPPENED. You would've remembered it all along. You just want attention. Stop squawking like a friggin' baby!"*

A tidal wave of doubt breached my protective barriers and flooded the surface of the game. The ball was swept down a hole and into the depths of my unconscious. The score plummeted by the thousands, and my vital signs skyrocketed into the danger zone. *Zoink, sputter, sputter, ker-PLUNK!* The machine went dark. Nausea swelled in the pit of my stomach.

"Why are you writing about this? Jesus, Mike! Let it go."

But I couldn't. After the images returned, they kept agitating from the wings of my awareness. Each vivid scene replayed like background noise to the current events in my life, threatening my equilibrium and undermining my self-confidence. Through trial and error, I learned to cope with the devastation they caused, to override the insecurities they fed.

During my fifty-first year, I began compiling all I'd remembered in earnest—the new memories and the old, the entire account. Each time I clicked open the file on my computer, my critic struck with venom. Only after I *vowed* to complete the work did the noise in my head lose steam. Sebastian suggested I might have been called to this task in the name of others terrorized by similar demons. I believe that. I always felt this work was an important part of my journey, a higher calling, a duty I had to fulfill before my time was up.

"Bullshit! Higher calling? What the hell is that? You bet your sweet ass I'll be wailing at you."

Sebastian hinted that the voice was born at a time when my self-concept was being shaped, and when I was tragically confused about why certain things were happening to me—a time when two and two made three and I was less than whole.

I struggled to understand the workings of the universe for much of my life, always in search of a belief system that would provide a source of comfort. I longed to be secure in what I knew. I was doused in religion from the first time my pudgy, little fingers groped a crucifix on my mom's lap, so I had about as much chance of escaping indoctrination as a fox pup on the run from the royal hounds. My Catholic upbringing made life difficult, given the man I was to become in the world, and I can't say I escaped without any resentments.

But in spite of all the trouble I've had with "people of faith," I wouldn't say my birth religion is any worse than the others. In that respect, I would be wrong to lay all the blame for my misfortunes on the cathedral doorstep. Now, at age sixty-five, I've concluded that each of my earthly experiences was part of a grander scheme. Each was purposeful, each a marker on the trail of my personal odyssey.

And this is the tale I'm now convinced I'm here to tell.

> RECURRING DREAM—1953
>
> *A swarm of snakes is writhing under my bed. I hide under the covers to protect myself. I dare not dangle my legs over the side. A witch lingers outside the house at night, ready to rush in. I keep her out by placing two garbage cans inside the glass patio doors before dark.*

1

NEIGHBORHOOD IMAGES

When I was five years old, my world was only four blocks long. It stretched from St. Monica's School at one end to our family's tiny house on Cottage Street at the other in Rochester, New York. I loved scampering along behind my four older siblings as we made the daily trek from school to home for lunch. Nothing pleased me more. That was how I learned about life. I studied how they moved and talked, securely locking their mannerisms into my memory. They took good care of me; although they did protest each time my mother insisted they let me tag along.

Every day at noon, my sister Ann picked me up from kindergarten at the south end of the school building, and I would beg her to stop at Shackleford's Confectionary straight across Genesee Street. For a penny, you could buy a narrow strip of shiny white paper lined with candy buttons, a large Tootsie Roll, or a caramel crème. No matter how much my mother preached that sugar would rot my teeth, the cravings ruled.

Black tooth decay was already eating away the surface of my front teeth. Mom called them "soft." This imperfection was a source of embarrassment I would have done anything to change. However, when Ann assured me that I'd get a second set of teeth when I was six or seven, I gave in and surrendered to the cravings.

Ma and Pop Shackleford were too old to keep an eye on the droves of kids who crowded the store and manhandled their treats every day. Ma was a sweet but fretful old lady with a clump of white hair wound tightly in a bun on top of her head. Pop was a blustery curmudgeon who glared sternly at us kids over his wire spectacles. Cranky as a hornet in a heat wave, Pop shouted, "If you touch that candy, you pay for it!" Every few weeks someone got caught stealing. The next day Sister Rose Catherine intoned a somber warning over the school PA system: "Children, if the stealing at Shackleford's does not stop, the store will be off limits before and after class." More than twelve hundred baby boomers were crammed into that school in 1951, about fifty in a class, and three classes in each grade.

> Dream—July 15, 1990
>
> *Ghouls are chasing me down a road, right at my heels. My legs are too heavy to lift off the ground. Worse, I have no voice and can't yell for help. A scream is stuck at the back of my throat until I finally wail out in my sleep, an involuntary reaction to exorcise the demons. I'm breathless and drenched in sweat when I come to. I was greatly relieved it was all a dream.*

After elbowing our way out of Shackleford's, we joined a herd of kids five abreast, moving silently in front of the massive-wooden doors of our church. We could never pass the building without some super-pious classmate shaming us for not making the sign of the cross. Those jerks were more annoying than salt on a canker sore. They blessed themselves *and* genuflected as if they were actually inside the sacristy.

These were the same kids who boasted that their aunts were nuns, their uncles were priests, or their fathers were ushers—those men who wore brown suits and collected change in wire baskets attached to the end of wooden poles at Sunday Mass. Even at that young age, I believed my schoolmates' exaggerated displays of religion were sanctimonious, Christianity taken much too far. I learned to lunge, bring my right knee down to the sidewalk, cross myself sloppily, and rush on. I was reluctant to succumb to peer-pressure, but I also didn't want to end up in that place called hell that the nuns threatened us with in kindergarten.

At the corner of Seward Street, we often peered into Alex Brothers' Restaurant, the greasiest of spoons, run by Greek siblings. They were a local anomaly, derided by the men of northern European descent who controlled the west side of town.

At any hour, one of the Greeks could be seen hunched in the window flipping cheeseburgers and dressed in a white T-shirt, sleeves rolled to the shoulders. A twenty-foot rubber tree with limbs suspended from the grey, tin ceiling by lengths of hemp arched its way across the plate-glass storefront. A film of grease from the grill clung to the window, warning of the cholesterol served within. At daybreak, men from the neighborhood gathered there to sip coffee, argue politics, and smoke their Lucky Strikes to the tips. After the bars closed at two the next morning, the same men reconvened there to bitch about their wives before lumbering home and disturbing their households.

On the near side of Sawyer Street, we usually ogled the sides of beef hanging in the meat market window, blood oozing from flesh and dripping onto white butcher paper spread below. Then, after we rushed across the street at the traffic light, I squeezed between my sisters' hips and pressed my palms and forehead against the window of Brint's Pharmacy. Young Mr. Brint, the subject of our interest, seemed as vain as a starlet on Oscar night. He postured behind the chest-high counter, dressed meticulously in a white, druggist's jacket with a fountain pen clipped into its breast pocket. But his lopsided, dime-store toupee, fastened in place with black bobby pins, stood out like a corset on a cowboy. Ann liked to rap on the window and shout, "Nice rug, Mr. Brint!" Our rough-and-tumble crew screamed and stomped in a circle before running on.

We trotted past the hardware that smelled of lubricants and paused to gawk at the girls with money who took weekly ballet lessons at Francine's School of Dance. Then our moods turned serious as we approached the infamous Madison Grill, the tavern where our dad spent too much of his time.

> Journal Entry—August 22, 1990
>
> *Dozing off at midnight, I heard someone at my bedroom door. "Who is it?" I asked. I called out my son's name. No response. There was no one in the dimly lit hall. Kurt was asleep in his bed. I know what I heard—an agitated rattle demanding my attention.*

Because I was the runt of the litter, I was out of breath and hobbling several paces behind when the five of us tiptoed past the Grill. On one of those days we cut down the alley between the bar and Levinson's Grocery. At the rear entrance to the Grill, my sister Joan yanked the screen door open. "Shotgun! Windy Blow! Boom-Boom!" she shouted like a ruffian through the door. We erupted into a chorus of snide laughter and then high-tailed down the alley and clung to the bricks on the back of the grocery. The drunken customers, who were sipping Jenny Cream Ale in the smoke-filled back room, must have thought our antics seemed bizarre. And that's what made it so funny. They had no idea my sister's chant was actually about the three different kinds of farts people make.

The first was the Shotgun—a single, loud ka-pow of a fart that can rock the walls of any room. Shotgun farts have no conscience. Fat-witted cretins who care nothing about bystanders uncork Shotgun farts with gusto, even lifting a leg like a dog at a hydrant with decided flair.

Second was the Windy Blow, a fart that eases its way out with a silent whooshing sound. Although it's inaudible, a Windy Blow is the foulest smelling and most flagrant—silent but deadly. Matrons of society let out Windy Blows. Following a muted discharge, a lady will fan the back of her dress with an open hand while flitting across the room to escape the odor.

Third was the Boom-Boom, a crisp, two-shot emission. It neither boasts nor makes any apologies. People with a healthy attitude about farts will casually drop a Boom-Boom and nonchalantly move on.

This flatulence code was admittedly boorish, but it became a jewel among our family traditions, a treasure to be passed from eldest to youngest, presumably preserved throughout eternity.

One time, Dad's Windy Blow at home gave us a rare opportunity for monkeyshines. As soon as the stench registered, we let out a cacophony of complaints: "Who squeezed the cheese?" "Who puffed out that air biscuit?" "Oh, my

God!" and "Somebody laid a fart!" Dad feigned disgust (as he always did) and asked in turn, "Who dropped that cookie?" After staunch denials from us all, he turned and spoke disparagingly to our dog. "Queenie! What did you do?" Poor Queenie, our obese, black mongrel who already suffered from extremely low self-esteem, shook with nervousness, her chestnut eyes darting from left to right, searching to understand what she'd done wrong.

> Journal Entry—November 15, 1990
>
> *I awoke from a sound sleep last night. A man's voice demanded my attention. "Mike! Mike!" he shouted. I sat up and answered, "Yeah?" The call came from my bathroom mirror. It sounded like my own voice calling to me. What am I being asked to do?*

When it came to dinnertime at our house on Cottage Street, each of us siblings coveted two items: the "birdie plate" and the "Hawkeye spoon." The plate, edged in gold with a peacock hand-painted on its face, was the family's only piece of decorative china. The spoon, with "Hawkeye" engraved on its stainless handle, had been swiped from the cafeteria at Kodak's camera division. Before each meal we battled over who would get to use those treasures. Each had to yell "I get the birdie plate!" or "I get the Hawkeye spoon!" The first to yell out could use the item for that meal only. Mom told me years later that she smashed the plate and tossed the spoon into the trash when she grew weary of the squabbles. No one hearing the pandemonium at each meal would have blamed her.

When I was four, my mother caught me swiping safety matches from a wall dispenser in the kitchen. She looked crazed as she dragged me over to the stove. She lit a gas jet and threatened to shove my hand into the flame. I had seen her that angry at my sisters, but I had never been the focus of her wrath. I screamed "Nooo!" to get her to stop. When her eyes widened at the sight of what she was doing, she released her vice-like grip on my hand. Her anger was understandable. A fire would have gutted our tinderbox of a house in a matter of minutes. I had to be watched closely after that. My siblings became spies who reported my whereabouts at all times.

I don't remember lighting the fire behind the TV set that family members have blamed on me. I can, however, recall the thrill surrounding the combustion of a match. I have a faint memory of my tiny hand scraping the white head across the brown striker panel on the side of a matchbox. With ignition, the scene comes to life in slow motion, accompanied by physical sensations: chills, a burst of adrenalin, and the sweet smell of sulfur as the head explodes into flames.

My love affair with the match was orgasmic. I learned that pent-up emotions could be cleansed from my consciousness, torched from my troubled mind with the combustion of a match. I never understood my insatiable attraction to fire until years later when I learned it was connected to quite another matter.

That same year, I clobbered my big brother in an upstairs

bedroom, an unforgettable achievement. It was a sultry August evening. The room's knee-high window was open, and the green, wooden frame of the screen was hooked shut at the bottom. After Joe and I were laced into our new boxing gloves, we danced on our parents' creaky double bed as if we were the main event at Madison Square Garden. Joanie and my youngest sister Pidge played our managers. Ann announced the fight: "Lay-dees and gentil-men . . . in this kornuh . . . the challenger . . . weighing in at twentee-sevin power-packed pounds . . . in the black trunks . . . the one . . . the only . . . Mighty Mike Deninger!" I grasped the headboard with a gloved hand, bounced like Joe Louis on a corner of the mattress and pumped the other glove in the air. The girls cheered and pounded the plaster walls. Then my nemesis was introduced: "And in this kornuh . . . in the white trunks . . . weighing thurtee-five pounds . . . introducing . . . the HEH-vee weight cham-peen of the world . . . the Kruncher . . . the Destroyer . . . Jumpin' Joe Deninger. Ding, Ding!"

Early in the round, my brother landed a stiff punch to my gut and knocked the wind out of me. I heard my sister react: "Whoa! A solid shot to the solar plexus." I paused for a second of woeful self-pity before a rage exploded inside my head. KABOOM! I tore into him like a stevedore in a dock brawl. I connected a stiff left jab to his shoulder and slammed my right glove into his belly button. He hurtled ass first off the bed and onto the window sill. The wire screen bulged out with a ripping sound but held his doubled-up torso like a bass in a fishnet.

The chatter in the room was snuffed out in a second, like a candle thrust into water. We all froze. The look of terror on Joe's face was unlike anything I'd ever seen. Once he was rescued from his predicament, the room filled with nervous, tittering laughter. Joan snapped at me. "You almost killed him. Joey almost died, you dope!" My experience with death was limited to the bugs I had squashed on the sidewalk. When I thought about crushing my brother like a spider under my sneaker, I could not stop the vengeful grin that crept across my face. I was never violent like that again . . . until I was infuriated by someone else four decades later.

Being the baby in a large family has advantages, but it can also be agonizingly unpleasant. One evening I begged to go with my brother and sisters as they were leaving for a Tarzan movie at the Madison Theater. When my mother insisted I was too young, I staged a meltdown in the front hall. "I wanna go!" I screamed. Outbursts like that had worked before, but her answer was still no.

I rushed up the front stairs and forcefully and rhythmically stomped one foot on each step as I went. The idea was brilliant, but the tactic backfired. I could hear Ann chiding me from below: "Thumper, Thumper! That's right! Go ahead, you big baby!"

I pounded harder on every step. What followed was my first insight into the uselessness of rage. After I disappeared into the dark at the top of the stairs, I was alone. I had nowhere to go. My anger flipped quickly to sadness. The thumping failed to get me what I wanted. Even worse, I had been called a baby, and nothing diminishes a four-year-old's self-esteem more than that word.

> Journal Entry—December 6, 1990
>
> *I'm nervously shifting my St. Christopher medal back and forth on its box chain while grimacing with pain. Psychic pain. Going dancing to rid myself of the jitters. Several drinks might help.*

In the summer of 1950, our family took the only vacation we ever had as children. By mail, my dad booked a cottage at Humphrey's Harbor, a fishing enclave in The Thousand Islands just south of Cape Vincent on Lake Ontario. Humphrey's was a dilapidated sheep farm on an inlet that led out to the lake where it merged with the St. Lawrence River. Cape Vincent's official status among sportsmen as "The Home of the Gamey Black Bass" was undisputed in barroom discourse.

I enjoyed the adventure, although I was only allowed in the rowboat with my dad once. I remember feeding weeds to the sheep through a barbed-wire fence. I recall the smell of the outhouse and an image of us as we snagged crayfish with bacon tied around a stone. We swam in front of the cottage in brand-new life preservers with pictures of naked kids on them. We talked about the family vacation for years to come, especially what happened on the drive home.

My parents waged a silent war after the family's 1931 Oldsmobile Coupe stopped dead in a downpour near the town of Mexico, New York. After he worked under the hood for a half hour, Dad concluded that water from the road must have splashed into the engine. He wanted to build a fire in the carburetor to evaporate the moisture. Mom became hysterical. "I won't have you starting a fire under the hood with the children around," she screamed. "You'll blow us all to bits!"

The stalemate lasted a long time. As this was the final day of our vacation, we had little money left for a mechanic.

We sat in silence as a cold war between the family's super powers chilled the front seat. Not a time to intervene and risk the deflected wrath of a parent. Begrudgingly, Dad conceded victory and left on foot. He returned an hour later with a mechanic from town. Mom must have felt infinitesimally small when she heard the mechanic give this diagnosis and cure: "Yup, I'd say you've got water in that carburetor of yours. I'd start a small fire in there and see if that doesn't dry it out." After he did that, the car started on the first try and we went on our way. The temperature was ice cold in the car for the rest of the drive home.

Dad was sober enough one Sunday evening to take the five of us to watch the passenger trains on the tracks next to Hinchey Road. The speed and the sound of the engine roaring past were supposed to be thrilling. This was the first time I'd come along. My sisters were filled with an anticipation that puzzled me as we drove out of town. They were acting weird, carrying on about the wind on your face as the train whooshed by. I could tell something wasn't right. When Dad parked the car, and we climbed the hill, I was already scared.

My sisters promised I had nothing to worry about, a sure sign I was about to be duped. Pidgey and Joan squeezed my hands so hard, I felt pain. As the train rumbled in the distance, and the tracks trembled, I tried to pull loose from their grips. They scrunched my hands even tighter. Their eyes mocked me as they delighted in my discomfort. Dad was looking down the line and oblivious to my plight. If I had possessed the power, I would have vaporized them all on the spot.

As the train's horn blared at a nearby crossing, my sisters turned in that direction and screamed like crazies. I pried my hands free and bolted back down the hill as fast as my stumpy little legs could carry me. I curled up in the back seat of the car and cupped my hands over my ears until the train roared passed. No one had told me about the noise.

When they returned, I glared at each of them in turn, putting them on notice that they would pay dearly for that betrayal. Oddly enough, though, after my younger brother Dan came along, I had no qualms about duping him eight years later when he went to Hinchey Road for the first time.

When we lived on Cottage Street, I often visited Uncle Vin in his room while everyone else remained downstairs. My dad's brother, a reticent bachelor, preferred the solace of his room to mingling with the family. He would have lived on his own if he'd had the money. Being around kids made him nervous, but, for some reason, I was an exception. The fact that he allowed me to visit was conclusive evidence. Vin frequently found glossy ads in popular magazines and cut out color photos of refrigerators filled with mouth-watering foods for me. (Color photography was rare at the time.) I'd toddle back downstairs armed with these treasures and gloat in front of my envious siblings.

Ann and Joan were leading me around the neighborhood after dark one summer evening when they dragged me into the backyard and crouched behind Uncle Vin's rose garden. They shouted, "Uncle Dunkle, Uncle Dunkle!" until he stared down at us from his open second-floor window. I glanced up to see Vin's eyes trained on me as they pulled me across the lawn and through the back gate. For days, I worried that my sisters' buffoonery might mess up the special relationship I had with the man.

My kindergarten graduation photo showed me smirking and close-lipped. The surfaces of my front teeth were spotted with decay, damage irreversible. Dental care was a luxury for working class families, so my baby teeth would continue to rot until they fell out. When I first went to a dentist in the summer after eighth grade, I had twenty-six cavities in my permanent teeth. The side of one incisor was badly decayed, evidence that I didn't brush my teeth, and I still gave in to the sugar cravings. I was relieved to get it repaired, so I could enter freshman year without looking like a hooligan. It took a year to fill all my cavities and to extract one dead molar, a record even in our neighborhood. With such a bad start, I endeavored not to show my teeth much until I had them cosmetically improved at age forty-seven.

In our neighborhood, we played baseball on a dirt lot at the foot of Cottage Street. A large crowd of kids met there every evening for a lively game that lasted until dusk. My sister Joan taught me how to ride a bike on that lot when I was five. I can still feel what it was like to have her panting into my ear as she held onto the seat and trotted beside me, her sneakers slapping a rhythm into the dirt as I pedaled. She helped me practice for two nights without much success. On the second night, the handlebars wobbled and the bike toppled over each time she let go of the seat. But on the third night, when I finally found my balance and pedaled across the lot under my own power, I felt for the first time what it meant to be truly free.

2

ANCESTRAL INFRACTIONS

I was born Michael Lester Deninger on May 4, 1946 and named after my maternal grandfather. I was the fifth of six children born to Margaret Helen Cahill and Lester Allen Deninger in Rochester, New York. The older children, in order of birth, were Ann, Joan, Margaret (Pidgey), and Joe. My younger brother Dan arrived when I was seven.

Our working class family had barely enough money to meet all financial obligations, but we never went to bed hungry. I do remember a time when my mother had me paw through thick layers of dust in the cold-air returns to scrounge up 17 pennies for a loaf of bread, but that was an exception.

Our family always sat down to dinner without the man of the house. Dad was either at work or at the bar. Although none of us left the table unsatisfied, we were all known to complain about the monotonous menu. My mother's ability to stretch cream chipped beef on toast or tuna casserole rivaled that of Jesus with the loaves and fishes at the Sermon on the Mount. She argued that we did just fine and didn't want for anything. But no matter what she said, we all privately wished for more.

GRANDPA MIKE

Grandpa Mike Cahill, the fifteenth of eighteen children, was born on July 3, 1875, in the Parish of Coolcappa, Ireland. By the turn of the century, eleven of the eighteen children and their mother, Honora, had immigrated to the United States. Grandpa Mike's father, Patrick, died in the old country before he could make the trip over. Grandpa probably arrived at the Rochester Pier on Lake Ontario sometime during 1898. According to his citizenship certificate that hangs on my office wall, he was given the oath on August 3, 1903.

> Journal Entry—Christmas, 1990
>
> *I didn't understand why the movie* Field of Dreams *was my eleven-year-old son's favorite until we watched it together tonight. The story occurs in the context of a baseball tale, but it's actually about missed opportunities, unfulfilled dreams, and connections between a father and a son.*
>
> *In the last scene, the main character chats with his dead father while playing catch. I cried at that sight. Kurt surreptitiously observed my reactions from behind a pillow at the end of the couch. I tried to explain why I was sad, but he became uncomfortable. I wish I could help him talk about his feelings. I want to understand his discomfort. It took me most of my life to understand mine. Now we sit in bedrooms at opposite ends of the house with our doors closed. The movie was a gift from him, the only way that he could tell me he loved me.*

Mike was an exceptional man who worked as a streetcar foreman for the New York State Railway System until his retirement at age seventy-eight. Grandpa was personable and innately intelligent, and everybody in the family agreed that he had a photographic memory. I can remember him sitting in his corner chair beside a brown, console radio, his eyes smiling through wire-rimmed glasses. A filter-less cigarette always hung from the left side of his mouth. To the right of the chair was an ashtray stand with a push-button trap door through which he dumped the butts. The edges of the tray were caked with black tar. I was repulsed the one time I rubbed my finger in that residue and put it up to my nose.

I can also vividly recall Grandpa drinking beer and dancing a jig at his eightieth birthday celebration. But my very last image of him alive was in a hospital bed later that year, dying of colon cancer. He was always known as Mike, and so am I.

GRANDMA CAHILL

Grandma Cahill was a second-generation Irish American whose parents (Thomas Brown and Bridgett Connors) had emigrated from the old country. Like the Cahills of Coolcappa, the Browns had left Ireland to escape the carnage of the potato famine. Margaret was the middle of their three children.

"Maggie" Brown Cahill was a strong, maternal figure, deeply religious and completely devoted to her family. Of the eight children that she and Grandpa Mike had, only six survived to adulthood. Veronica Virginia and Bonnie Eileen both died in childhood.

A gardener of some talent, Grandma Cahill lived to be seventy-six, but her health and mental faculties deteriorated a few years before her death. I spent time with her while she was failing, weeding her garden and mowing her tiny lawn. She taught me a lot about how the elderly fade and pass over.

MY MOTHER MARGARET

Margaret, the fifth-born of the Cahill children, was a bright and capable young woman when she graduated from Nazareth Academy, a Catholic high school run by the Sisters of St. Joseph. She had the ability to further her education, but not the resources. Only a few of Mom's friends could afford to continue their education beyond Nazareth. She was eighteen years old when the stock market crashed and, like many young adults of the time, she helped provide support at home during years of financial devastation.

An attractive woman with jet-black hair and classic Irish features, she was, after all, pure bred. Following graduation, she worked as a secretary to an architect in the Lincoln Alliance Building in downtown Rochester. My dad was a uniformed elevator operator who rode her up to her floor every morning.

Surprisingly, my mother never even told me how the two had met until she was eighty-seven, and my father had been dead for fifteen years. We children were discouraged from asking questions about how our parents fell in love. I tried asking her one time at dinner when I was about ten. "You don't need to know that," she said with finality. "Now who wants more potatoes?" Her reluctance to divulge that information definitely aroused curiosity, but we learned not to probe. That could have been my first indication that she regretted her marriage. But, for her, wedding vows were irrevocable, a life sentence imposed by her religion without the possibility of parole.

My parents married when they were in their mid-twenties. Because they never discussed their courtship, I didn't learn why their wedding anniversary remained a secret until Mom was near death in the hospital at the age of eighty-nine. My sister Ann pulled me aside and whispered that our mother had conceived her out of wedlock. She *had* to get married—a fifty-year cover up.

My mother was the one who bound our family together,

a single, strong, continuous fiber woven through the fabric of her children's lives. In a letter she wrote when I was a college student, she commented that her children had been her life, a calling just as sacred to her as a religious vocation. She managed what money the family had, did the shopping, prepared the meals, looked after the house, and raised her kids almost single-handedly. Some considered her a saint. She would have scoffed at the suggestion, as humble as she was. But I think there was saintliness in the way she looked after her family when one considers the suffering she endured through so many harrowing years with an abusive husband.

MY FATHER LESTER

Dad was seldom at home and of little support to the family, because he spent most of his non-working hours in bars. He was a product of a sexist era when husbands and fathers got away with abusiveness. Men of that time believed family obligations were satisfied when they brought home a paycheck at the end of the week. Euphemistically called "good providers," these troublesome men had this one major virtue—a term that was meant to cancel out all of their faults.

Alcoholism, gambling, womanizing, domestic violence, mental illness, and pigheadedness crippled their lives. No matter what the problem, their families bore the burden. Even when acknowledging their deficiencies, these men argued that their shortcomings were of no consequence, simply because they brought that check home every week. They'd justify and brag about their drinking and philandering at Alex Brothers' Restaurant. Their tirades could be heard through Cottage Street windows when they shouted down their wives on hot summer nights. "I keep a good roof over our heads and plenty of meat on the table!" they'd bellow, as if that was all one should expect of any father. In every one of these households, a heap of misery was plopped down on the kitchen table along with that regular paycheck.

Dad was normally a quiet, sheepish man who had little to say unless his nerve was bolstered by a few belts of whiskey. When he was sober, he was uncomfortably introverted yet well mannered. He had a zany sense of humor and could be hilarious, but only when drunk. At his retirement dinner from his job as a machine operator at Eastman Kodak in 1973, he proved his muster. He worked for weeks on a farewell speech, determined to impress his co-workers. His boss introduced Lester this way: "So, Punk (his nickname since childhood), now that you're about to begin your retirement tell us about your plans."

He stood, paused for dramatic effect, and with all seriousness, said: "I've thought a lot about this. I don't have any fancy travel plans. No particular hobbies. There's nothing special I want to do. Maybe simple things that tickle my fancy. You know what I'd like to do? And this would be interesting. I'd like to do nothing more than sit at the kitchen table and pick fly shit out of pepper."

A smattering of nervous laughter broke the silence before a thunderous reaction spread through the crowd like canyon fire fanned by a gust of wind. In a short time, all those present were on their feet with shots of liquor raised in Lester's honor. He could have that effect on people but only when he was both drunk and hilarious. And that was a rare thing indeed.

Dad was intelligent, but the fact that he was a ninth-grade dropout must have bothered him. In an honest moment, my mother revealed how insecure he had been about his lack of formal education. His low self-confidence gave rise to paranoid reactions when he accused others of taking advantage of him. When drunk, he often complained about people "making a pineapple out of him." He drank every day until he staggered—something that didn't change until he inexplicably stopped drinking before turning seventy.

Every family member feared that dark, pickled side of him. His mood was unpredictable when he stumbled through the back door after a night of boilermakers. He could erupt into violence, chairs flying and doors slamming. Those of us at home might have to flee in the middle of the night if he were to charge my mother or begin destroying things.

Even though Ann told me Dad wasn't like that during *her* younger years, this is what I remember.

> Dream—January 2, 1991
>
> *My surroundings are unclear. I'm being tossed and buffeted, bumped and battered by nondescript forces. Is this an unconscious expression of all that my life is right now?*

GRANDPA JOE

Dad was one of two sons (Vincent and Lester) born to Anna McAndrew and Joseph Deninger. Grandpa Joe was one of six children born in Germany to a Bavarian stonemason and his wife. Joseph's parents died young, leaving four boys and two girls to fend for themselves. Without any relatives in the area, the children were placed with nearby farmers. The oldest child, who came to be known as Aunt Trace, arrived in America as a young woman in the 1890s. A few years later, she brought her sister Marie, her two youngest brothers, Joe (my grandfather) and Matt, and her brother John's two youngest sons to the States.

Grandpa Joe was a reserved, patient man who had the respect of family and friends. Some said he was nice to a fault. A tailor by profession, Grandpa Joe died of asthma in his fifties.

GRANDMA DENINGER

Anna was born Canadian of English (Allen) and Irish (McAndrew) descent. She had one sister and three brothers. According to Uncle Vin, Anna and her siblings were also orphaned as children. She and her sister Lillian were "sold" across the border to work on farms in upstate New York. The sale of orphaned children as indentured servants was illegal, although my uncle reported it was common in those days.

Two completely different perceptions of Grandma Deninger were passed on to me, one reported by my dad and the other by his brother. In Dad's version, she was a nagging, acerbic bitch who took pleasure in ridiculing her soft-spoken husband. Dad described how, as a young man, he would pound on his bedroom wall at night to get his mother to stop berating his father in the next room. According to Uncle Vin, Anna was a kind-hearted, religious woman who valiantly struggled with the problems she faced in life and a generous soul who took in the homeless.

Mom described Anna as a strange woman with weird beliefs, someone who "dabbled" in non-mainstream religions. I surmised there was much more to the story than any one person knew or was willing to share. Anna suffered from thyroid disease. Because no effective treatment for the illness was available, a large and painful goiter grew on her throat and aggravated her already sour disposition. The tumor, which eventually took her life, was so unflattering that she refused to allow photos of herself. For that reason, no likeness of Grandma Deninger has survived.

Both of my paternal grandparents passed away before I was born. I still wonder what Dad's childhood was like—information that might have shed light on his behavior as an adult.

UNCLE VIN

If someone were to say my father's brother was merely an odd gentleman, they'd be grossly underestimating his eccentricities.

Uncle Vin lived in the past, predictably ignoring every modern convenience that came on the market. He refused to get a telephone until he was so old and feeble that his life literally depended on it. He said he'd rather be "tarred and feathered" than own a TV, calling it "the work of the devil." But every time he called something the work of the devil, he'd burst into hearty laughter, making me wonder if he meant a single word he'd just said.

Uncle Vin dressed as oddly as he lived. All his clothes came from the army surplus store—black, ankle-high, lace-up boots, khaki pants, canvas belts with shiny, brass buckles, regulation-green army boxer shorts, and tank tops. All his clothes were scrubbed by hand on a washboard with Fels Naptha bars and dried on lines hung in the basement. His affinity for army dress was practical, not shaped by a love of the armed forces. He had hated every minute of his military service.

In ninety years of life, Vin never ventured outside of Rochester, except to serve in the Great War effort. He was stationed in Oklahoma, Georgia, and at a German POW camp in Louisiana. Those experiences proved too much for him. Following his discharge, he suffered a nervous breakdown back home. After having crude oral surgery to remove all of his teeth, he remained locked in his room for weeks. He ignored messages from his employer and refused to talk with my parents. He even stopped contributing to the household expenses. Because Dad wouldn't confront his brother, Mom slipped a threatening note under Vin's door. That and a final warning from his boss got him back to work.

Vin probably suffered from social phobia, a condition that Dad most certainly shared. He rarely traveled more than a few miles from home except to go to work, and he avoided crowds whenever possible. Because he never learned to drive, he took public transportation or traveled on foot wherever he went. On rare occasions, he allowed my dad to drive him to family events.

After we moved to Brooks Avenue, Uncle Vin stayed in the Cottage Street house. We could count on him showing up at our new house twice a year, once for Thanksgiving dinner and again for a visit on Christmas Eve. That was when he left his nephews and nieces ten dollar bills in individually addressed money cards.

Because he had no phone, we never knew when he would arrive. He was certain to come, however, because he always did. He never personally handed out our Christmas money. Sometimes, he would give the cards to Mom for distribution. Although he never said so, we all knew he didn't trust Dad with the money. Usually, though, he waited until no one was looking and then placed the stack of envelopes beside a lamp in the living room. As soon as he departed, one of us would scream, "He's gone!" and a mad dash for the cash would ensue.

Uncle Vin, who didn't drink, never spoke disparagingly about his brother, but it was clear how he felt from the condolences he offered Mom for Lester's indiscretions. Dad spent most Christmas Eves planted on a bar stool, so he and Vin were not likely to cross paths when Vin made his holiday visit.

> Dream—January 3, 1991
>
> *A co-worker and I are jogging in the woods. Rats scatter at our feet. I rappel down a steep hill, using vines to ease my descent. It's dangerous, life-threatening. Hostile, faceless people surround me. I can see buildings that were part of my past in the background, a dorm at my college—large, multi-storied structures.*

I visited Uncle on Cottage Street every Saturday for several years after we moved to Brooks Avenue. No formal agreement or expectation. I just showed up, like Vin did on Christmas Eve. I would arrive late in the morning, after my Frosted Flakes and Mighty Mouse cartoons, and stay until sundown.

Uncle made no changes in the house after we moved out. To do so would have been frivolous. The linoleum was badly worn in all the first-floor rooms, the wallpaper pocked with grease stains and peeling at the edges, the lace, living room curtains peppered with holes, yellow with age, frayed and torn. The only furniture in the house, other than a few inexpensive side tables for his array of cactus plants, consisted of a porcelain kitchen table and chairs, his bed, a single dresser, and a smelly, worn living room set. The Salvation Army would have rejected all this furniture as unusable. However, that same decrepit living room set held a lucrative attraction for me.

I somehow discovered coins lodged deep in the recesses of the sofa and chairs. I can't recall how. Uncle had me believing the money fell from his pockets and into the furniture, but the logic behind that premise was clearly faulty. He never sat in the chairs, and I never found coins in the sofa.

I came to understand that I should avoid retrieving the change while he was watching. I was sure he wanted me to have the money, because we always discussed how much I had "found" at the end of a visit. I also knew that the money was a gift that should go unrecognized, just like the money cards at Christmas. Some days I found upwards of three dollars, a lot of cash for a boy of seven.

I also got to sample Vin's unusual cuisine during my visits. Lean meats were poached with unseasoned vegetables and served on metal plates with bread and butter. Each experience was more like a cookout than a dinner. After lunch, Vin led me into the pantry where I could select packs of Wrigley's Spearmint and Juicy Fruit gum from a private stash he kept in an empty Maxwell House coffee can.

We then retired to the living room where he reclined on the smelly-old couch and listened to a Yankee's game on the radio. I took my place in the overstuffed chair by the corner of the sofa. I popped several sticks of Juicy Fruit into my mouth and Uncle stuffed fingers-full of Beechnut Chewing Tobacco between his cheek and molars.

We settled in for the afternoon. On the floor next to him, Vin kept an empty, sixteen-ounce sauerkraut can that he used as a spittoon. Lifting it to his face every few minutes, he spat brown juice into the tin and returned it to the floor. When the flavor fizzled, he tongued the tobacco ball to the front of his mouth and dropped the cud into the can like a turd being pushed out of a horse's ass.

While he listened to the game with his eyes closed, I slipped my arm under the seat cushion, a pirate in search of buried treasure. I ran my fingers through dusty crevices, and scooted my body down until my head disappeared beneath the arms of the chair. The hours in that room with Uncle were peaceful and typically silent. I did most of the talking, if there was any. I talked about what I was learning in school, my friends, and my siblings. I could tell him anything—except how much my parents argued. He never got upset with me. He treated me with kindness and respect. He praised me for the things I did well. He was a surrogate father. I felt safe with him.

Letter from Uncle Vin—c. January, 1976

I got a "kick" out of that incident with the watering can, had forgotten all about it! Actually, you were a good boy along with Joe and little "Pidge," but those two Ann and Joan were "Hell Raisers." For God's sake don't tell them about what I wrote. Joan makes the most delectable pastry and always gives me some at Xmas. When I was digging in my garden, you were always pestering me to find you a worm. I always thought you would grow up to be an Entomologist!

The money I gave you was just a token; the truth is I'm tighter than a Scotch Jew when it comes to money. I'm "yacking" like an old "wash woman," so I had better call a halt before I have to start another page!

Yours,
Vin

P.S. I hate telephones, those mechanical devices frustrate me! Hope you can make out my "Hen scratching!"

I was naturally curious about Vin's personal life; whether he had friends; whether he'd ever had any romance in his life. He never talked about women except in response to my questions. Whenever I asked why he never married, he exclaimed, "Perish the thought!" Then he broke into a volley of laughter, effectively ending the conversation. Once I pressed him for an answer. He just drowned me out with loud guffaws until I stopped asking. That made me suspicious. I wondered what he might be withholding, but I never got an answer. Neither did anyone else who knew him.

Over the years, I talked proudly about Vin with friends. My thoughts about him didn't change until after he died at the age of ninety. No one informed me of his passing until it was too late to attend the funeral. One year later, Ann told me something my mother had wanted withheld from me. While cleaning out Vin's apartment after his death, my mother and Ann found a drawer full of pictures of prepubescent children, all of them fair and blonde, just like I had been. Many were of girls, but some were of boys. Among the assortment was a piece of cardboard with one word handwritten by Vin on it in large letters: PEDOPHILE. The photos were removed with his other belongings and placed in my mother's basement. Ann agreed to retrieve the pictures and the cardboard for me, but when she went to get them, they were gone. My mother must have destroyed them. The matter was never discussed again.

AUNT MARIE

Mom's oldest sister Marie held a professional position at Eastman Kodak where she was paid well for her work. Marie had a long-term relationship with a man we called Uncle Joe Maedar.

They never married, but they did live under the same roof with my grandparents on Kenmore Street. None of us understood how he could be allowed to sleep in Grandma's house without being married. My sister Pidge was sure they slept in separate rooms, but I thought she was naïve. I already knew they slept together at their summer cottage on Conesus Lake. I saw them!

Uncle Joe left Aunt Marie for another woman after many years together because of her incorrigible alcoholism. She was a binge drinker of the worst kind, and her behavior had become increasingly unmanageable. Marie never recovered emotionally from the rejection. A decade after their breakup, she was found dead in her bathroom, her hips wedged between the commode and the wall, a half-empty bottle of brandy at her feet. She was as undignified in death as when she drank in life.

The official cause of death on the coroner's certificate was acute alcohol poisoning, although the family did not divulge that information. All of my mother's five siblings who lived to adult age were more than casual drinkers, but Mom rarely took a drink herself.

UNCLE JOE

My other Uncle Joe, the oldest of the Cahill children, had a booming, annoying voice that people blamed on a hearing loss. A binge drinker like his sister Marie, he was out of work for days at a time when he couldn't control his addiction. He and his wife Irma had three attractive daughters, two of whom were the oldest of the grandchildren.

For six years, I delivered the morning paper to Joe's house on Sawyer Street. On Friday evenings when I came to collect payment, I walked quietly across Joe's porch and listened for any sound of trouble. Just like my parents, Joe and Irma squabbled over money, disrespect, and betrayal.

I could sometimes hear the sounds of domestic violence inside—yelling, slapping, furniture tipping over—as I approached the front door. I was well qualified to interpret such sounds. I took pleasure in using the doorbell to stop their arguments mid-course, like a secret power. I wished I could stop my own father with the ring of a bell.

One night I waited patiently for their feud to reach a crescendo, just before I imagined a plate being thrown or Irma being pushed against a wall. I punched the doorbell several times in a warning, like a cop who was about to raid the joint. The commotion stopped immediately. Someone shuffled quickly to the bay window and peeked through the sheer curtains. Whoever it was saw I was just the paperboy and not the authorities. My face was stone serious when Uncle Joe meekly opened the door. "Democrat and Chronicle," I said, flashing a toothy smile. When I left with a generous tip, I bounded down the porch steps two at a time, holding back laughter until I was across the street. I felt as strong as Atlas to have stopped the violence at my uncle's—because I was powerless to stop it at home.

Dream—January 8, 1991

I'm in a boathouse near the Genesee River. Several men enter. One reminds me of my father. Another is a mustached minister wielding a gaff. He pounds it menacingly on the floor near my father. Dad threatens him with a cocked fist. I've seen him do that to my mother. The cleric swings the gaff and I yell, "Don't hurt my father!" Dad lunges at the minister, yanks the gaff from him, and whacks him on the hip. Dad is clearly in control.

AUNT ELLEN

I witnessed my Aunt Ellen's drinking problem on a hot summer day when I was nine. Someone had let Mom know there was no food in her youngest sister's house. The conversation was grim as my Aunt Eileen drove my mother and me across town with a trunk full of groceries. This was my first exposure to the ghetto, a degree of poverty foreign to my experience.

Just like Aunt Ellen's marriage, her rented house on Barnum Street had very little life left in it. Used tires littered the grass-less back yard, rats scurried near the corners of the foundation, and a battered screen door hung off its hinges. Ellen's husband had not been heard from in days and was probably on a bender of his own. My male cousins Pete and Pat—at six and seven too young to be left unattended—were playing in the dirt. They rushed to the car as Eileen parked on the street.

When we got no response from our knock on the door, we entered the house and were accosted by the stench of human urine. Straight ahead, Ellen lay unconscious on the couch, her hair in oily strings, clad only in a stained white slip, an empty bottle of whiskey on the floor beneath her limp hand. My ten-month-old cousin Judy stood in a playpen strewn with soiled linens. Her yellow, pee-soaked diaper had slipped off her hips. Tears had dried into black rivulets on her cheeks.

She stretched out her arms in a sorry plea to be rescued from the cesspool.

When Ellen's husband didn't return, she and my cousins were housed temporarily with Grandma Cahill. One Sunday, Ellen deserted her three young children; just walked out of my grandmother's house and left them behind. The family never heard from her until Aunt Marie's estate was probated a decade later, and Ellen contacted the estate attorney for her inheritance.

My mother was livid that she would dare emerge to collect on her sister's death. She refused to allow that to happen. Withholding her share would be a fitting punishment for the worst sin a mother could commit against her natural-born children. She wanted a trust fund set up for Ellen's three offspring, arguing that her youngest sister should be disenfranchised for abandoning them. That didn't happen. Ellen got the money and disappeared with the cash as fast as she had reemerged, leaving the care of her children to others in the family.

Years later, in an unusual twist of fate, I came face to face with Aunt Ellen when I was jogging one evening. A block from my in-law's home, I noticed a woman sitting on her stoop who looked like my mother's double. When I slowed my pace and watched her drag on a cigarette, I recognized her immediately. I decided against speaking to her. After all, she wanted nothing to do with the family. She had even rejected her grown son's attempts to reconcile with her.

Long after her sister's disappearance, my mother received word that Ellen had gotten sober in AA—the only one of my mother's siblings who stopped drinking. She deserved some credit for that, but never got any. When she was never heard from again, that seemed fine with everyone . . . except her children, who ended up in foster care. She must be dead by now, but no one knows.

UNCLE TOM

My mother's older brother Tom was the only Cahill who achieved a harmonious relationship with a life partner. Tom and his wife Corrine were well suited to each other. Both were extroverts with a zest for life. They got on well and actively participated in their four children's lives. Tom's close-knit family loved to party, and they were usually center-stage at family celebrations. Although Tom probably drank just as much as his siblings, it didn't seem to interfere with his work or family.

AUNT EILEEN

Aunt Eileen was my favorite and I suspect I was hers. She also enjoyed her beer. Like Tom, though, her drinking did not cause serious problems. She was a positive spirit who encouraged the best in every one of her nieces and nephews.

I had not intended to write much about her, because I believed she might have been a lesbian. I was uncomfortable speculating about that, fearing I'd be criticized for tarnishing the memory of a pious Catholic woman.

Aunt Eileen died of an aneurysm in her early forties when I was twelve. She was a pleasant, peaceful soul whose passing was a great loss to the family. I'd intended to keep my thoughts about her sexual orientation to myself—until one night when Eileen appeared to me in a dream that was so vivid I had to turn on a light and record what I had seen.

> Dream—November 24, 1997
>
> *Aunt Eileen is wearing a flowing, peach-colored, cotton dress with a full skirt fitted at the waist. A thin, brown belt matches a beaded necklace adorning her neck. She's like a fashion model, an apparition, but larger than life, close enough to touch, and back-lit by an intense, white light. Her face is beaming a broad, joyful smile and her shoulder-length hair is billowing in the wind.*
>
> *I tell her that peach is definitely her color. She glows in response to the compliment. The celestial nature of the vision magnifies what she then tells me.*
>
> *She affirms that she wants me to write about her with kindness and love. She says I should be honest about my perceptions. If I do this, I will represent her memory well.*

Eileen had been quite the tomboy when she was young, much to the chagrin of her mother. Because of her flagrant boyishness, she was penalized when gifts were given. Her younger sister Ellen got fancier dolls and more expensive toys. Although Eileen found those insults humorous as an adult, they must have wounded her when she was young.

Eileen's disinterest in men and her pull toward women were obvious. She traveled frequently with her "girlfriends" to places such as Cape Cod, Washington, D.C., and Quebec. I wondered what it must have been like for her then and whether she had ever acted on her sexual attractions. As a fervent Catholic who attended mass and received Holy Communion every week (more frequently during holy seasons), she'd probably accepted her lot as a Catholic woman forced into celibacy by the laws of the church. Her lesbianism may even have remained a secret from *her*. Those were different times.

I thought of her often after this dream. I could see her in my mind's eye, feel what it was like to sit at her knee and look up into her eyes with admiration. I could picture her dragging on her Phillip Morris cigarette, deftly picking tobacco particles from her tongue between a thumb and pinkie, then dusting them delicately into an ashtray. She popped into my thoughts so often that I began to feel her presence at my side.

My preoccupation with her led to an even deeper connection a few days before Christmas in 1997. While browsing in a Barnes and Noble bookstore, I leafed through a book that caught my interest. I thought of buying it, but for some reason, I returned it to the shelf. I lingered in that section of the store, sensing that something was about to happen. Then a dark-blue book drew my attention. I had noticed the same text at Crown Books the day before, and a friend had recommended it to me. I picked it up and, as I read its table of contents, a tingling sensation traveled up my spine and moved across my shoulder blades. I immediately thought of Aunt Eileen and a black prayer book she had lent me when I was young.

I must sheepishly admit that there is still a spot of shame attached to this memory. You see, for two weeks in the sixth grade, I considered becoming a priest. Perhaps I was more attracted to the *idea* of the priesthood—the recognition and privileges of the church—than the reality. Parish nuns cleaned and ironed all the sacred vestments, a cook prepared the meals, housekeepers did the laundry, and I'd get to drive a recent-model luxury car. This life also appealed to me because male erotic images were invading my thoughts by then. The possibility of permanently "shelving" my sexuality in exchange for a white collar held a naïve attraction at that time.

After announcing my decision to my family, I quickly realized I'd need a sophisticated missal to support my future life of prayer. The one tattered prayer book shared by my entire household was only one inch thick—no way could it contain all the prayers I'd need to say at seminary. So I asked Aunt Eileen for help. Imagine my disappointment when she gave me a shabby, one-inch missal just like the one at home! When she handed it to me and praised my religious aspirations, I groused inside. "Come on! I can't become a priest with this piddling prayer book!" Unacceptable.

With the stealth and speed of a cat burglar, I rifled through my grandmother's china cabinet drawer and swapped the missal Eileen had given me for one that was two inches thick. I didn't know I had swiped her personal prayer book. The fact that this was *stealing* didn't occur to me until she confronted me the following week. Then, I felt no less ashamed than if the pope himself had caught me with my hand in the poor box.

Never again did I think about becoming a priest. But at the time, I was much too proud and ashamed to apologize to her. I wondered if she had ever forgiven me. While reading later that night in 1997, I was thinking of her. I found myself wishing I could travel back in time and make amends. The weight of those thoughts pushed down on my eyelids. As I began the descent from consciousness, my book lowered to a resting place on my chest. If Eileen were close by, I thought, perhaps she would accept an apology for the mistake I'd made when I was twelve.

Dreamland was calling me, and I was sailing over London to that never-never land of the lost boys. So peaceful . . . so calm. Until a disturbance from another dimension halted my descent.

Someone blew so hard on my left cheek that I was jolted

back to consciousness. Instinctively, I raised a hand to my face. Then I heard her voice in my head. "Yes to all of it, Mike: my presence with you, my forgiveness, and what you have written." Another chill tickled like static between my shoulders, marking the importance of the moment.

Eileen stayed with me after that, her presence confirmed each time I felt a run up and down my spine. We became companions across the divide; perhaps we always had been. Call her what you will—an apparition, a guardian angel, a friend. I loved having Eileen around. My connection with her heralded an emerging spiritual sensitivity that became refined with age and experience.

> Dream—January 13, 1991
>
> *Not sure where I am, but I'm searching for something. Someone else is there—a woman who's helping me. She has two lists or documents. One is being checked while the other is held for later. After both lists are checked, nothing new or interesting is found and she moves on, leaving the lists with me.*

I began to consider the role that Eileen and all my forefathers played in shaping me. Like many others who have studied their lineage, I realized how each of us is linked to those who came before us. In that respect, my persona was derived from my parents, my grandparents, my aunts and uncles. Markers from each of them pulsed through my arteries and helped determine who I was and how I would be in the world.

Because of this influence, I had a strong genetic predisposition to addictions. My preschool sugar cravings foreshadowed future substance dependencies. However, I also benefited from my forebears' intelligence, humor, drive, and ingenuity. Traces of my ancestors and relatives were contained in every gene, every cell, and every neuron. They were all part of me—like it or not.

As a young man, I was drawn to innovation, to progressive ideas, and to understanding the human experience. By adolescence, I could sense that I was different and the path my life took became a testament to that. My work, my avocations, and my relationships all bore that out. I was not *taught* to be different; it was in me.

After marrying, raising two children, earning two graduate degrees, building a successful career in higher education, and opening to a spiritual life, I was led to walk down the trail of my ancestors. Eileen heralded the way, but it was Grandpa Mike who shed the most light on my path. First, I was literally born with his image and likeness. More than that, we shared a determination to succeed, a strong work ethic and a lighthearted spirit. I hope I too will dance a jig on my 80th birthday. I carried more than just his name as I set out in search of my roots and my essence. It was as if I was pulling on an old pair of gloves lost in a corner of the closet for several seasons. I liked how they fit.

> Dream—January 14, 1991
>
> *I'm on the playing field with the football team at my daughter's school. One player of the eleven on the team is missing. I'm sitting on the ground, not wanting to get into the game.*

3

COMING ATTRACTIONS

It felt good to be combing Dad's hair while all seven of us watched *I Love Lucy* on TV one evening. My sixth birthday was approaching. I was perched on the back of the couch with my legs draped over his shoulders. His scent was a mix of body odor, tobacco, and alcohol. I had fun parting his hair one way, then messing it up and starting all over again—parting on the side, parting in the middle, combing straight back, or combing forward with no part at all.

This is the only pleasurable memory I have of being physically close to my dad. He never played or rough-housed with me. He never held me, tucked me in at night, or whispered affirmations in my ear. Except for one time when he dragged me by the hair from his vegetable garden for stealing carrots, I didn't remember Dad touching me at all—until memories slowly began to surface in my forties.

Dream—January 17, 1991

I'm among spies. A man and woman offer me a ride in a convertible. I sit on the trunk with my feet draped into the back seat. The couple is not to be trusted. I somersault backwards off the rear of the car and hide in the bushes behind a house where "the problem is." My ex-wife throws me a gun. I struggle with one of the spies. The barrel of the gun is pointed at my face. I twist it around and it discharges into his stomach. The struggle continues as I wake up with my arms flailing.

I was raised in an all-white, working-class neighborhood, and I felt like I belonged right there where Mom was my greatest supporter. She was proud of me. I could feel it. Proud of my intellect, my positive outlook, and my cooperative spirit. I also had four older siblings who watched over me and taught me what I needed to know. And I felt at home at school.

I was an "A" student at St. Monica's, quite a feat considering I never opened a book after school hours. The education I got provided a cornerstone in my young life. All of us were involved in extracurricular activities—scouting, cheerleading, and athletics. The quintessential "best little boy in the world," I was quiet and unassuming, but full of curiosity.

> Journal Entry—January 21, 1991
>
> *Two panic attacks this week. One at a reception for Supreme Court Justice Thurgood Marshall. I thought I was going to pass out. I took deep breaths and backed up to a chair for support. It passed. The second happened while driving across the Wilson Bridge to Virginia. I had thoughts about losing control and crashing through the guardrail. It's a good thing I didn't end up in the water. These episodes consume so much energy.*

Not that I was perfect, mind you. Once I got caught stuffing candy bars into my army fatigues at Carr Drug Store. The clerk let me go because it was my first offense. But the time my friends and I broke into the church hall the morning after a social and stole candy and sodas, I suffered serious humiliation. One of my buddies was the son of Mr. Gafney, our church janitor. The kid had swiped the key to the building, but his dad found out and reported us. Father Kane called us over to the rectory the next morning. I felt blessed when he decided not to inform our parents, but I couldn't escape the wrath of my teacher.

Sister Rose Gonzaga struck fear into every boy in her charge. A witch's wart grew on the top of her long, hooked beak. Her crooked, yellow teeth, her hairy, upper lip, and her squinty, brown eyes that glared at us over wire-rimmed reading glasses topped off her threatening demeanor. The sound of her name made every kid wince.

When I returned to class, she dragged me by the ear into the cloakroom, closed the door and motioned me to approach. I lost balance when she struck a lightning blow with her right hand across my left cheek. All forty-nine of my classmates, hands folded where they sat on the other side of the door, heard the whack. My eye was nearly impaled on a brass coat hook as I reeled from the force of the slap. Worse yet, my pride was sorely wounded. Her handprint marked the surface of my cheek for an hour, and my dizziness lasted the rest of the day. Ironically, Sister Rose reserved her harshest punishments for the boys she held in the highest regard. She expected more of me. That's for sure. She told me so before she hauled off and clocked me that day.

I was well respected at St. Monica's aside from those rare misdemeanors. When I was eight, Marty Moynihan and I were selected to serve as "page boys" at a celebration of Monsignor Lambert's twenty-fifth ordination anniversary— a dubious honor. On the one hand, Marty and I got to lead the religious procession up Monica Street to the front doors of the church. On the other, we had to wear these god-awful, red-satin pageboy costumes with yellow capes and white plumes sticking out of floppy-red berets. My only time in drag. Okay, technically it wasn't drag, but in retrospect I was just as embarrassed then as I would feel now in a tutu and boa with spiked pumps.

I also became the next-to-highest ranked altar boy in eighth grade when I rose to the position of Vice Supreme Grand Knight. I lost out in the running for the top spot to Marty Moynihan, because he had a brother studying for the priesthood and a father who was a cop (hence, honor by association). I had no comparably favorable connections. In fact, the committee may have known that my dad hung out at the beer joints two blocks from church. Losing that position was a major disappointment, because, in any parish, being named top altar boy was coveted.

Marty and I were as tight as blood brothers, so the competition never spoiled our friendship. The church fathers had no idea that the Supreme Grand Knight and the Vice Supreme Grand Knight went down to the tracks behind the liquor store after Mass on Sundays and smoked an entire pack of Springs. We practiced scratching our groins, spitting on rails, and shouting, "What the fuck!?" until we sounded as tough as the greasers from West High School.

Before my teen years, my close-knit circle of neighborhood friends and I engaged in innocent activities. We dug tunnels in the backyard and built forts in the rafters of the garage. We played softball in the Kodak Park summer league and built tree houses in the woods bordering Plymouth Avenue. And we spent much of our summers at the swimming pool in Genesee Valley Park.

After I turned ten, I was allowed to pack a lunch in the morning and head off to the pool for swimming lessons. At noon, I usually bought a drink from the snack bar and ate my PB&J sandwich in the shade. Back at the pool, I waited with my friends on a long, green bench to get into half-hour free swims throughout the afternoon.

While waiting, we played a game called "Movie Stars." It required that we take turns standing in front of the bench and calling out the initials of a famous person. Those on the bench would have to guess who it was and then try to tag you as you ran to and from a tree. I remember when I took my turn one day dressed in my army fatigues and a white T-shirt with the sleeves rolled up two times. I called out the initials "MM!" Kids shouted back, "Marilyn Monroe!" "Marilyn Maxwell!" "Mickey Mouse!" "Minnie Mouse!" "Mickey Mantle!" When I heard the Yankee star's name I darted for the tree. My chaser shot off the bench after me, but I psyched him out by circling several times. With a fake of the head, I broke away and hot-footed it back to base, leaving my challenger behind. I was hot . . . panting . . . out of . . . breath. A locust high in an ancient oak reported the sweltering ninety-degree temperature that July afternoon like an air raid siren. It was a time of freedom, of independence. No school. No parents arguing. Life was good.

Although we were forbidden to go near the river, we did anyway. The Genesee converged with the Erie Canal and Red Creek at the center of the park. Certain stretches of the river had a treacherous undertow. Every year some kid drowned while foolishly trying to swim across. I had a healthy fear of the river from the times I watched the police drag its bottom with an iron-grappling hook, snagging and dragging the body of a child up from the depths.

My favorite river spot was "Pie Rock," a flat, pie-shaped boulder that jutted out from shore. Just upstream and past the boathouses with green clapboard siding, a two-lane, concrete bridge spanned the river at Genesee Park Boulevard. For excitement, my friends and I explored its underbelly. We walked clear across the catwalk suspended beneath the bridge several stories above the river. If we were caught by the park police during their riverboat patrols, we would've been in trouble.

To gain access to the catwalk, we had to inch across a nine-foot ledge that was eight inches wide and twenty feet above the path below—not a task for the weak of will or the squeamish. Many a young boy stepped out onto that ledge only to be driven back by overwhelming terror. If that ledge is still there, odds are that boys are still earning their manly stripes by painstakingly sideling their way across.

One of the strangest sights I ever witnessed in the park happened on a breezy August afternoon. I was having lunch with the park's female playground director. Nearby, on the bank of the river, a Girl Scout troop was picnicking on the lawn. A dumpy, middle-aged man in a trench coat scurried out from underneath the bridge, threw open his coat, and started playing with himself less than 50 yards from where we were seated. I knew his behavior was shocking, but I didn't know what you'd call what he was doing. The playground director told me in a firm but calm voice to run as fast as I could to the park police downriver and tell them a man was "exposing himself" in front of the girls. "Exposing himself," I thought. "*That's* what they call it."

I'd never been asked to do anything courageous before. I ran all the way, even after I got a searing pain in my right side. The police were playing poker when I burst into the boathouse. My thoughts raced faster than my mouth could work. But I couldn't remember the term "exposing himself." The policemen never looked up from their cards until I pointed to my groin and shouted, "Some guy is jiggling his thing outside his pants near the bridge!"

Apparently, the flasher had vanished up the stairs beside the bridge by the time we returned. I knew what happened was serious, but the frumpy character seemed harmless enough. His head had tilted back in a daze as he flopped his limp penis up and down like a soft garden hose, never hurting anybody.

It would be years before I understood the significance of that afternoon.

One summer night the year I was ten, I woke to find myself standing in my underwear at the top of the second-floor stairs peeing full force down to the landing twelve steps below. The sound of the urine splattering like summer rain on the vinyl steps roused me from my delirium. "How could I have made that mistake when I was standing next to the open bathroom door?" I wondered. I breathed in the stench wafting up the enclosed stairwell like a disgusting cloud of shame. All the while, I could hear the muffled sounds of the weather broadcast from the first-floor TV room.

No one heard me leaking on the stairs that night. I can't remember cleaning up after myself; neither do I remember going back to bed. Although I wish it had been only a bad dream, I'm certain it happened just this way.

Because throngs of kids played in and around our house every day, a certain amount of mischief was common. I received a sex education lesson one day when I was six years old. The "classroom" was a shaded alley next to a garage behind the Third Baptist Church; the two pupils were Colleen McKay and me. All three of my sisters looked on. One of the older kids told Colleen and me to drop our pants to the ground. I can't recall having been forced or threatened in any way, and I may have been eager to learn. I was told to kiss her vagina, and she to lick my pee-pee. We did what we were told.

All the while, a group of neighborhood kids peered at us through thick vines and stared down from garage rooftops, like thousands of movie extras watching the scene. I heard their muffled snickers as we performed for the throng. I think "the lesson" felt good; well, at least I don't recall it feeling bad. I just know that, as a junior member of the gang, I was willing to go to great lengths to move up in the ranks. I never attached any particular trauma to that experience, although what happened would border on abusive behavior today. And I hold no resentment toward my sisters. They couldn't even remember the incident when I brought it to their attention in 2001.

I have a clear memory of the time sexual feelings first stirred inside me when I was seven. We were attending a wake on the

Cahill side of the family. I can recall seeing the old man in the casket against the back wall of the dining room. But what I recall most is how I sat on the floor and admired my second cousin's handsome father. I was feeling hot in the head while I fantasized about climbing onto his lap and nestling my face into his neck. He had a glow about him I found irresistible. I was surprised when my "worm" inched its way across the front of my Fruit of the Looms—and things started to get confusing.

My sister Pidgey once set free a garter snake I captured and I got pissed. But I got even with all of my sisters later when I gawked at their naked bodies through a secret peephole. You see, the only real bathroom in our house was on the second floor. A crusty commode stood by itself in a corner of the basement, but after a sewer rat was spotted behind the bowl, no one wanted to go down there.

The upstairs bath shared a window with our enclosed sleeping porch. To assure privacy (and in lieu of curtains), my mother covered the windowpanes with the same wallpaper used on the walls.

That's when I devised a plan for my own private viewings. I scraped the paper off the upper-right corner of the window, caring not to make the resulting hole obvious. From the dark porch, I could spy on my sisters while they undressed. This was the first time I had seen a naked woman—and so what if she was a sister! Although the experience never did anything for me, I did learn about women's breasts. (I would really be messed up if watching my own sisters got me excited.) I conducted this surveillance for months until I sneezed one night and the peephole was discovered.

If I really wanted to bother one of my sisters, I took a bobby pin and popped out the wad of toilet paper stuffed into the bathroom keyhole. Then I knocked on the door and said, "I'm coming in." There were times when I stuck my middle finger under the door and wiggled it back and forth until the occupant screamed. I then ran downstairs and pled ignorance when my behavior was reported to my mother. The one time I got caught, though, Ann avenged the insult by shrewdly turning the tables on me.

She quickly jerked the door open and caught me on the floor staring at her polished red toenails. I retreated down the steps to the landing and turned to mock her, just in time for the fresh bar of king-sized Cashmere Bouquet she'd launched from the top of the stairs to catch me right between the eyes. A bar of soap can do a lot of damage from that distance! For days I had to tell an intricate lie I fabricated about the golf-ball-sized knot on my forehead and how it got there.

Peeking at my naked sisters and flicking my finger under the bathroom door lost all appeal after that experience.

Dream—January 26, 1991

I'm looking through the front door of Loblaw's supermarket. A man is on his back in the produce department with his head to the wall. A word is flashing in my mind that I can't make out. My cat Muppet, who died a year ago, is dead, frozen stiff as a board. He's being held in the mouth of a much larger version of himself. This cat is thrashing Muppet up and down and back and forth, shaking him forcibly, violently.

Sex was never discussed in our household, and sex education at school was limited to the miracle of Mary's virgin birth of Jesus. My younger brother, Dan, was born when I was seven, but I didn't even know Mom was expecting. We never received information about sex as kids, because my parents were uncomfortable with the topic.

I can remember my mother standing before the hall mirror combing her black hair as if she were leaving on a trip. No one would tell me where she was going; just that she'd be gone for a few days. When I saw Danny carried through the front door in a laundry basket that Mom had painted powder blue, I understood the *miracle* of life but not the mechanics. When I asked where he came from, I got a host of flimsy stories. Ann told me not long ago that she was unaware of Mom's pregnancy until a friend told her. And she was in the eighth grade!

A lifeguard at the park pool was the object of my most intense fantasies. Broad-shouldered and corn-fed handsome, Gil had a narrow waist and Michelangelo muscles molded into his tall frame. I used to linger at the foot of his guard tower and gaze up at his bulging calves, his defined pectorals, and furry underarms. If I caught a glimpse of his jockstrap under his swim trunks, I tingled all over. My man was playful and allowed me to drench him with the back-splash from a cannonball. I would have eaten a bucket of worms to sit on his lap and look into his eyes. But I knew the price I'd pay if anyone discovered my lust for him. Being eight years old that summer and having just received my first communion, I was flirting with mortal sin.

Weekend camping trips with the church Boy Scouts afforded me preadolescent opportunities to explore my sexuality. Boys that age tend to compare their penis sizes out of curiosity, but I always hoped for more than just a look-see. I liked exploring the objects of my attractions, even if it left a stain on my soul. But no one had to tell me those urges had to be controlled. Going too far could earn me a dance with the devil, or, as I later learned, a freakishly embarrassing chat with a priest. For weeks after each "practice session," I feared being reported until the worry faded with time.

Boys attracted to other boys take care to avoid discovery, just as my fellow Scouts did in our tents long after dark. Flashlights lit the scene and made it both eerie and stimulating. A stream of verbal foreplay led up to the event. We took turns describing the biggest dick we'd ever seen or what it felt like to get a stiff one. No one wanted to go first, but one of us would eventually rub himself or show a rigid form in his underwear. The one who pulled it out first took the greatest risk.

I was among the most cautious and always last. The excitement and danger made the moment pleasurable and frightening at the same time. My face blushed a light crimson, my hands got clammy, and my heart pounded fervidly in my chest. Never mind how hard my hooter got! We were all only eleven years old and too young to orgasm. We never actually touched each other because that would label you a *queer*. The next day, we behaved like nothing had happened and went back to chopping wood and joking about pussy.

Two years later, my friends and I became acquainted with a volunteer scoutmaster named Bill Law. He was a bachelor in his late thirties who provided beer and drove us around on weekends, unknown to our parents. Clever and manipulative, Bill knew how to steer a conversation to stories about sex between men. He asked if we ever played with each other and then encouraged us to share details. One night, he told us how good it felt when his male cousin gave him a blow job. I had detected his trickery the first time he fed us alcohol, but my interest in the topic outweighed any concern. At age thirteen, my friends and I were learning life's mysteries as the dupes of Bill's sexual games. Whenever I went along, the talk was sexual and suggestive—but just talk.

Looking back, I'm not certain Bill actually took advantage of my friends, but I suspect he did. I considered the weekend outings warped and deceitful. Ironically, they also gave us the only information we ever got from an adult about sex. We learned the good old American way at the time—in the streets, and in this case, from a sleazy, middle-aged pedophile.

> Dream—January 28, 1991
>
> *Something to do with "pods." I'm transplanting azaleas and find a white, slimy snake two inches thick in the dirt. It's like a continuous cable and is stuck under a corner of the Brooks Avenue house foundation. I tell my folks, but Dad can't find it. I pull it up from the dirt, slice it open, and white fluid spurts all over the place. The juice creates a vast lake in front of the house. When I pull one end of the snake out of the dirt, it has a pulsing, penis-like head.*

The information I got about homosexuality at home, at school, and from church was condemning and incontrovertible. All that frightened me into constructing an elaborate system of denial. If I was as unclean as they said, what was I to do? The absolute need to hide my desire for males became clear when I confessed to a priest that I had played around with a friend. He became sexually charged while listening to my admission. His voice exuded a carnal tone like he was drooling for details behind the opaque screen: "How did it feel? You can tell me. Was he hard? Did you touch him? What exactly did you do?"

"Shit!" I thought, sweat forming on my brow. I couldn't speak!

I could feel him leering at me through the screen; even make out the smirk on his face. He was breathing heavily, just as Bill Law had when he talked about his cousin. I had to get out of there. This priest knew me. He knew my family. I shut down as he coaxed me to tell him more. "I can help if you give me specifics," he said. When I refused to talk, he finally let me go with a stern warning about hell.

I became suspicious of all priests after that. I still went to confession, but I began to fabricate venial sins I'd never committed. "I stole three times; I lied five times," sins no one would feel ashamed to confess. As fractured as that might seem, it was my way of maintaining my boundaries. I took no more risks.

For decades, I never spoke of my desire for men. I stuffed that shameful secret deep within me, a fatal carcinogen whose poison was slow in developing. The disease ate steadily away at my spirit. Anger, depression, anxiety, self-loathing, and other unnamed opportunistic infections fed on my life force until it could scarcely sustain itself.

4

LESTER'S TRANSGRESSIONS

Aside from routine exams, my siblings and I never saw a doctor except in dire emergencies. With eight mouths to feed on a machinist's salary, health care for the family was entrusted to Doc Cullinan whose office a few blocks north on Genesee Street was also his residence. He was a typical working-class physician of the time, making house calls, doling out pills from his worn, leather bag, and injecting the wonder drug penicillin through humongous needles.

I became Doc's patient once when I had a strep infection at the age of nine. My mom had seen the four older kids through all the childhood diseases and knew when to call for help. I needed help.

Doc showed up within the hour like he always did. I choked when he used a tongue depressor to inspect my raw throat and triggered my gag reflex. He whispered to my mom just outside the room, "It looks like strep. We'd better give him a shot."

I had learned all about cotton swabs and rubbing alcohol when we were immunized as part of the Salk vaccine trial at school the year before. But that day, something puzzled me.

Before Doc had opened his bag, I could already smell the alcohol. My confusion was cleared up a week later when I spotted Doc Cullinan through the front window at Kelly's Tavern straddling a barstool. That's when I learned he was a drinker, just like my dad. I realized when I thought about it that he didn't look like a real doctor. His clothes were disheveled, and he drove a rusty old car. When I told my mom, she said the doc had a big heart and would forgive a debt if a family had no money. She was enabling him the same way she did my father. How many others must have mistaken the smell of whiskey on Doc's breath for an antiseptic the way I had that day?

We celebrated on Brooks Avenue whenever one of us reached a milestone. Having plenty of beer on hand was every bit as important as the mounds of food prepared for these occasions. Mom did the cooking, and Dad bought and iced the beer. He began drinking long before the first guest arrived—so much, we were concerned he might embarrass us or disrupt the event. The extended family out to the second cousins came, and after a few rounds of drinks, adult conversations got so loud we had to shout across the room. The evening ended with the younger generation dancing to 45 rpm records in the garage, the women gossiping in the living room, and the men playing cards at the kitchen table.

When we turned eighteen, we were free to drink without restriction, as long as no one got violent or threw up. Mom always told us to be careful, but she never required moderation. Drunkenness was in the lineage, and, although Dad wasn't well schooled academically, he had earned an advanced degree in inebriation. He set up the perfect breeding ground for alcoholism. And in our family, those who weren't smoking by age fifteen fell shy of the standard set by their older siblings.

Vices were rights of passage in our house.

We'd have family sing-alongs as part of each celebration, when my parents had us harmonize old favorites like "You Are My Sunshine." Although we enjoyed performing, the Osmond Family we were not! Still, it provided opportunities to outshine our Cahill cousins, thought to be tone deaf.

After several drinks, Dad was coaxed into the living room to play his harmonica no handed, puffing out standards like "Oh, Susannah" by tilting his head back and sliding the mouth organ from side-to-side in his lips. His right foot tapped a syncopated beat. Old Queenie barked at his face, snapped at the air, and crooned her own tune in protest. We all cackled at the sight.

These celebrations brought our house to life and ushered in a quick thaw in the family's perpetual emotional winter. Then like the sweep of a low-pressure system, temperatures and feelings fell after the last guest departed. Even before cleanup, a blizzard would blow across our tundra and the turf would freeze solid again. We found ourselves back to our somber, uneasy existence.

Happiness was reserved for special occasions.

One summer my dad was offered half a ton of coal if he would haul it from a house near Irondequoit Bay. So on a muggy July afternoon, he took me, my brother Joe, and my cousins Pete and Pat to a woman's house across town. Two round trips with Dad's flatbed trailer required the better part of the day.

I have always had a clear memory of how the four of us shirtless boys unloaded the shiny coal back home that day, our sweaty upper bodies covered with a fine black dust that stuck like powdered sugar to greasy donuts. I can recall seeing our basement window hooked to the ceiling above the bin into which we shoveled the coal. Surrounding the window were bushes heavy with red berries, standing guard on each side of the opening. I can remember how we took turns tossing the coal through the window and into the darkness, each of us wanting to be judged the manliest of the crew. And I cringe when I think about how Joe swung his shovel around and nicked Peter above the eye. He only sustained a quarter-inch gash, but streams of beet-red blood trickled down his face and instigated a parental discussion about whether to head for the emergency room.

For some unknown reason images from that day frequently and persistently forced their way into my thoughts for the next forty years.

> Journal Entry—February 14, 1991
>
> *Unable to write for several nights. Blocked. I visited my friend Elaine. She told me how much pain she saw in my eyes. I burst into tears. I've been shut down ever since, holding back the sadness.*

My father had a buddy named Charlie Reuschel who owned riverfront property outside of town. He gave Dad permission to build a fishing dock on the shore during one of the summers when I was young. I tagged along to help him move stone from a quarry to fill the wooden frame.

Once, after working most of the day, we were invited into Charlie's house for a drink. He placed a cola on the coffee table in front of me along with two dollar bills. It could have been a test of my gumption. I looked to my father for a sign, but the host insisted that Dad not encourage me. I left the money where it was, afraid of being viewed negatively. I thought I saw maliciousness in the guy's face. It felt like kiddy torture. Who knows what he was out to prove? After the visit, we stopped at the Castle Inn, a dingy country tavern on Scottsville Road.

Dad drank Jenny draft beer, smoked one Pall Mall after another, and watched a Yankees game from his bar stool. I amused myself at the shuffleboard in a corner of the room. When I asked for a second cola, he scolded me for not grabbing the dollar bills, saying, "No, we have to go. We could've stayed longer if you'd taken the money." His words, meant to shame, burned like a yellow jacket's sting. I got angry inside my head and silently told him to shut up. I never went back to that dock with him again.

Journal Entry—March 1, 1991

Watched a TV movie tonight called Where Pigeons Go to Die. *It opened with aerial shots of the Monroe County terrain where I grew up. I'm startled alert in my family room rocker. Freaky feelings about Dad well up inside. He's been dead seven years.*

The story was about a young boy, his father, and his grandfather. The grandfather, who is near death, has helped the boy raise a homing pigeon. In the story, very little affection is expressed between the father and grandfather. The boy struggles to understand why.

Image: The grandson hiding in a closet, witnessing a tender moment when his father shaves his bedridden grandfather. (cont'd to page 58)

Journal Entry—March 1, 1991 (cont'd from page 57)

Image: Close-up of the father coiling two fingers in the grandfather's palm as the older man weakly tries to make a fist. In that moment, I recall my father's death several years ago. I wasn't afraid to ask for his love then.

Image: The pigeon escapes its cage. The movie camera flies the path of the bird south along the Genesee River. Through its eyes, I see bridges and trestles I've crossed on foot. From the woods below, a boy with a hunting bow spots the pigeon. He launches an arrow up at the bird. When the missile punctures its wing, it also pierces my psyche. I feel buzzing in my head. My emotions are getting away from me. It's a direct hit.

I'm overcome with grief. Sadness rolls up and out of me. A low, resonant groan trembles its way through my larynx, an eerie sound stretches to a complete thought. "Ohhhhh." It hurts. It's born on pain. It's fueled by guilt. It flashes a vivid memory of me beside his hospital bed after his stroke.

I remember: Ann says, "Dad, Mike's here from Maryland to see you." He utters the same word but as a question. "Ohhhhh?" She places his right hand into mine. I give it a squeeze. "Hi Dad," I say. Without opening his eyes, he moans that he understands. I squeeze harder. Weakened by the hemorrhage, he can only curl his fingers into my hand. I coax him out. "This is a hell of a way to get me to come visit you!" "Ohhh," he moans, a hint of levity in his syllable. That was the last contact he made with any of us.

I keep a vigil beside him all week. I talk as if we've always been close, like he was Uncle Vin. I speak tenderly to him for the first time in my life. After there is no change in his condition, I leave for Maryland six days later. I kiss his forehead and tell him I love him.

The road south from town hugs the shores of the river. I am travelling

> *the route of the pigeon but on land. An anxiety attack forces me off the road. Something is unfinished. I swallow an extra antidepressant and resume the seven-hour drive home. Thirty minutes after I arrive, the call comes that he passed on at dusk.*
>
> *Then I was back in my family room, transfixed before the television. The memories had flared one by one like sunspots in the foreground of my field of vision. When the movie credits rolled up the screen, I sobbed into my scotch and soda. I made a mental note to have the eulogy I gave at his funeral printed and copied as my mother had requested. I've put it off for years. I don't know why.*

Joe and I went fishing with Dad at The Thousand Islands when I was perhaps eight and Joe was ten. The night before we left, I soaked the back lawn with the garden hose and went hunting for earthworms after dark. You have to be quick to catch nightcrawlers, because the slightest tremor causes the critters to spasm back into a hole with amazing speed. The neatest thing about hunting for these night crawlers? Watching them copulate. I studied how their ends were grafted together in passion and envisioned how their vital bodily fluids were being exchanged. I even imagined them talking sweet as they spooned. Worms are easy to catch while they're locked together—like tackling a man with his pants down. I caught a shit-load of the buggers. You could say I was a major cause of *coitus interruptus* among the worm population that night.

> Journal Entry—February 27, 1991
>
> *My first appointment with a gay psychologist tonight. His name is Ned Geraty, and he runs a men's group I'm joining on Monday. I like the guy. He's had some of the same experiences I have, including depression and panic attacks.*

I remember a lot about that trip with my dad and Joe. The inside of the fishing cottage was divided into three rooms by curtains hung on overhead rods. Joe and I found a rotting sea tortoise beached down by the inlet and poked its eyes out. Most of all, I remember Mr. Humphrey's bait store with several large minnow tanks and the stalest candy I'd ever chewed. The man smelled as bad as the sheep that grazed in his pasture. Many years later, I recalled something else about the trip that triggered a landslide.

> Journal Entry—March 18, 1991
>
> *A good men's meeting. I was faced with how uncomfortable I feel when things get out of control. I was defending a group member but was taken to task for interfering.*
>
> *In exploring that topic, I explained how getting physical affection was rare when I was growing up. I mentioned that it hurts when someone touches me—makes me want to pull away. They were puzzled. It's like a twinge of physical pain, I explained, and it's more perceived than real. I've never felt comfortable admitting that.*

As the years passed, Dad's outbursts became more violent. The episodes destabilized everything. He bitched about the same perceived insults day after day. If one of us had told him to stop yelling or go to bed—even months earlier—you could count on him grousing about it for a good long while. The "elephant" we couldn't talk about had quite a memory.

My mother was always the target of his abusiveness unless one of us interfered with his assaults on her. Still, he took care not to seriously injure her. He pushed her around, but I don't think he ever struck her with a fist, as often as he threatened. Although Mom was never treated for her injuries, she was left with lots of bruises and abrasions. The assaults only occurred when he was drunk and almost always after he arrived home from the bar.

Dream—March 30, 1991

I'm walking down a hill near the house on Brooks Avenue with my ten-year-old son and our dog. I throw a ball across the street for the dog to fetch. Kurt grabs it and lofts it back over, but it smashes the windshield of an antique car. A well-to-do woman and her husband yell at Kurt. I try to calm them down. We exchange insurance information and end up laughing about the incident.

I take the couple to my parents' house and show them how the furnishings don't match; the rugs out of kilter.

My mother enters wearing a sweatband. Her black, shoulder-length hair is dirty, scraggily. She looks troubled. I introduce everyone. My father approaches the house in a police uniform. I tell myself that I can handle the situation. I turn to the couple and say, "Father is home. Now the fear begins." (cont'd to page 62)

> Dream—March 30, 1991 (cont'd from page 61)
>
> *I find myself in the basement laundry room, pulling clean clothes from the washer and putting another load in. I have the sense that I am "cleaning up what happens in the basement." Then I'm scraping grease and grime off a grill in the kitchen—an awful job.*

Dad's rages reached an alarming level before I entered high school. The police were never summoned through all of that madness, because incidents of domestic violence weren't reported in those days. We knew he'd seek revenge the next time he got drunk anyway. Police intervention might have led to change, but Mom wouldn't allow us to call. We had no choice, or so we thought. In that sense, we all enabled his abuse.

One of Dad's worst episodes occurred one evening when we were helping Mom paint the kitchen. He burst through the back door itching for a fight. An argument ignited. Normally, Mom would stand her ground, but this time she took care not to fuel his anger. She ignored his insults and continued brushing the woodwork. Furious at her lack of response, he shook her ladder, and she tumbled to the floor. A can of walnut stain came spilling down on top of her. We screamed for him to stop, and he shouted for us to shut up. I ran out the back door to listen from the safety of the yard. That night he retreated to the corner bar, refueled, and returned an hour later for round two.

> Dream—April 22, 1991
>
> *I'm sunbathing far from shore on Lake Ontario. I roll off my air mattress and into the lake to study the seaweed at the surface from below. I see a large paddlewheel from a riverboat churning up the weeds overhead, clouding the water. The turbulence is not frightening or threatening. It's interesting. I'm an observer.*

Mom and the three of us boys were forced to flee the house early one February morning when the outside temperature had dipped below zero. My sisters were on their own by then so I may have been twelve or thirteen years old. We were asleep when Dad arrived and began talking loudly to himself at the kitchen table—something we jokingly referred to as his "chewing." He normally griped about something Mom had said or done, or not done, his complaint *du jour*. When the stars were aligned, the rumpus stopped there. If he shuffled past our rooms to the end of the hall and shut his door, we could roll over and have a good sleep.

This night, though, his ranting didn't stop. Instead, his voice strengthened like the winds of a storm as he climbed the stairs to Mom's room where she'd been sleeping separately since Danny was born. Trouble was afoot. He leaned over the bed and verbally threatened her. She stayed quiet under the sheets. I was outside in the hall and heard his bullying words. "I'll kick yurass!" he shouted at the top of her covers. When Mom attempted to respond, he snapped at her. "Shaddup," he growled. He said it again, but softer . . . "Shaddup," his voice as calculating as a cat before the pounce. Whenever he uttered those two words slurred together, I knew the detonation point was near.

He roared into a rage and raised the foot of her bed to his shoulders with one hand. Her body slid down and crashed against the wall like a sack of potatoes. I had watched the whole scene from the hallway in horror and screamed at him to stop. When he turned on me, I quickly backed into my room. A free-for-all filled the hallway with screaming and shoving until we escaped down the stairs and out the front door. That could have been the night Lester put his fist through the plaster wall outside her room or the time he punched a hole through her door.

I remember that frigid walk with Mom and my two brothers under the cloudless sky to my sister Ann's house on Thurston Road. I was able to quickly throw a coat over my shirt and pajama bottoms, but I had no hat or gloves, and my feet were bare inside my moccasins. The sound of frozen slush crunching under my feet over the silent, twenty- block walk tracked deep in my memory. This journey had the feel of a death march. None of us talked. What was there to say?

The crackling of ice underfoot still invokes that memory.

> Dream—April 23, 1991
>
> *I'm in the kitchen of a house with others, but we don't have permission to be there. I want to get out. I'm worried someone is going to come home and find us. I pace around, trying to put things back the way they were supposed to be.*

A short-lived friend of mine was a nervous kid who lived in a rented house on Pioneer Street. Arnie's shirts were threadbare and faded, of even lesser quality than those purchased at the rummage sales down on Main Street. The two of us had something in common—violent behavior in our homes—but we had one difference between us. Arnie's torso was almost as tattered as his clothes. Scarred in three places around his head and with the surgical remnants of a badly broken arm, he had good reason to act as jittery as he did. At ten years of age, we both knew how it felt to live in fear, but we never discussed it. Call it a victim's code of silence.

While walking home together from school one day, a car screeched to the curb and stopped beside us on Brooks Avenue. A stranger jumped out. I guessed he might be Arnie's father, but I'd never met the man. He grabbed Arnie by the upper arm and twisted him around. "I'm gonna beat the shit out of your mother!" he said with perverted delight. Arnie whimpered and pleaded with the man not to hurt his mom. "You'll see," the man threatened. Then he laughed, jumped back in the car, and sped off. When I saw Arnie the next day, he refused to say what had happened. Similarly, I was unable to tell him that my dad pushed my mother around.

Arnie disappeared from our neighborhood in the middle of the semester. I still shiver whenever I think about that day. We might have developed a deeper kinship if we'd broken the silence. We might have been of comfort to each other, if only by cursing the darkness.

Mom was always at home when Dad was out drinking. When she did leave the house, she only went as far as the supermarket or downtown to shop for clothes. She might visit with her girlfriends in the neighborhood or talk to Mrs. Yorkey over the back fence, but she never discussed her personal life. As troubled as she must have been about Dad's thuggish behavior, she attempted to hide her disappointment. With six children in the house, however, how could she!

I developed a habit of assessing her mood each morning when I came down for breakfast. She was usually dressed in the housecoat we'd given her for Christmas. (No matter how often we resolved to buy her something different, she always ended up with a new robe from the bargain basement of E. W. Edwards & Sons every Christmas.) Most often, I found her sitting on the living room couch opposite the stairs with her head buried in the morning paper. Sometimes she was hunched over her coffee and toast at the kitchen table. She always clutched a balled wad of toilet paper in her left hand or pushed it up her loose sleeve. She sneezed and blew out her morning stuffiness, then feverishly picked at the top of her nose until it bled. After dabbing blood from the fresh wound, she tucked the tattered and stained tissue back up her sleeve. She could do all that without ever looking up. If she were sniffling, I could never tell whether she was just waking up or sadly mourning her life with Lester. The times I asked, I got no response.

> Journal Entry—June 10, 1991
>
> *Came out to my mother at my house last night, and it couldn't have gone worse. I'd been preparing what I would say for weeks. At forty-five, I thought it wouldn't be a big deal. Boy was I wrong. I asked her to sit on the edge of the bed, and I came right out with it. She groaned and leaned forward like she was in pain. Then she righted herself and demanded to know why I was telling her. I said I thought she would accept me no matter what, and I wanted to be honest with her. She burst into tears, ran whimpering down the hall, and slammed the bedroom door behind her. She left this morning without saying goodbye. This is what keeps us in the closet.*

Why do queers have to be in your face about being gay? Keep it to yourself. Who cares? That nagging critic inside my head had to add his two cents.

Conversation was sparse the mornings after Dad kept us all up. We saw Mom's face wrinkled with pain. We tiptoed around before school, not wanting to add to her burden. She deflected any attempt to give her comfort. She wanted only to shelter us from harm. Ironically, when she modeled how to stuff feelings inside, like stuffing toilet paper up a sleeve, she was teaching us how to fall on a sword. At least that's how I learned to lock my fears inside and suffer in silence—a strategy that never served me well.

A story from my grammar school reader portrayed a boy from ancient Sparta who stole a fox at the market. He shoved the animal under his robe as he ran off. In its attempts to escape, the fox clawed at his flesh, opening deep wounds in his abdomen. Rather than ask for help and be forced to admit his offense, the boy suffered in silence. He died in a ditch from his wounds.

Although I never understood why a fox would be for sale at a market, the story made sense from my mother's frame of reference. She kept her "foxes" well hidden in spite of the damage they inflicted. But no matter how hard she tried to hide them, I always knew the truth.

During those years, most of my mother's energy was spent protecting herself and shielding her children from harm. The potential for violence hung heavy in the air; we knew our father would come after us if we challenged him.

Letter from Mom—June 27, 1991

> *I believe homosexuality as well as male and female "shacking up" is immoral. I haven't been the same since you revealed your decision to pursue a course that is repugnant to me. How this all came about at age 45 is hard for me to comprehend. Your reliance on psychics and shrinks to chart your life is mind-boggling.*
>
> *You say when you told your kids that they were fine. How do you know what's in their minds? I'm sure the revelation alters your relationship with them as a father. I'm sure you would not have rejoiced at the fact that your father was "gay."*
>
> *I never expected anything of that nature. It hurt me down deep. I do not intend to discuss it with anyone. It's too painful, and I would hope that you keep this information to yourself down there in Maryland. After I'm gone you can shout it from the housetops.*
>
> *What happened to common sense, responsibility, good values and morals, self-control? In spite of what was lacking in the father department, I think you were blessed in that area.*
>
> *I never hated your father for his many shortcomings. I pitied him. We were all good to him in his last days. It wasn't easy, but I'm happy for what we did. We cared for him.*

> *I never thought I would be writing this letter to you. I have always been proud of your accomplishments in education. I wish I could say the same about your personal life.*
>
> *I've said all I wanted to say. I try my best to "grin and bear up" under all the problems. Take care. Especially take special care of your two children. May God bless.*
> Love
> Mother

Children who witness violence at home learn to be on guard for disaster. This heightened state of alertness, constantly scanning the environment for danger, is called "hyper-vigilance." Out of necessity, I became tense and uneasy. Fear of danger restricted my spontaneity and caused a "startle effect," a fearful reaction to loud noises and sudden movements. I became cautious and reserved. That may have been why another's touch caused me pain.

As a child, I learned to hide—under the dining room table, under a bed, or behind a piece of furniture. I knew when to disappear and how long to stay hidden. I never lingered in a place that had only one means of escape. I was so frightened one night that I curled into a fetal knot behind a living room couch. Breathing as shallowly as a holed rabbit after the chase, I eventually dozed off. I slept until I was awakened at daylight by the voices of my mother and siblings searching the house for me. I never made sense out of that night until decades later. Members of my family have said my nocturnal movements were frequent.

My Letter to Mom—July 15, 1991

You are missing so much in analyzing what you call "my situation." You reacted just as I feared by calling me immoral and using words like "repugnant." I was afraid of rejection. That's what I got. Can you wonder why it took me so long to tell you?

I'm angry with you. Your cruelty is unacceptable. You threw everything you could at me. To hurt me, I guess. Well, it won't work. I'm proud of what I've accomplished, and who I am. Whether you accept me or not, I will be fine.

I tried hard not to be gay, in part, to please you. This is not a choice. You are, or you are not. I suffered a lot trying to be someone I wasn't, and you don't seem to care.

You expected me to make you proud. So I did. It was not an easy path for me. I never told you about the panic attacks, the vomiting, and the depression.

What angers me most is how you questioned my decision to tell my children. Telling them was about honesty and one's ability to face difficult problems—something I had to learn on my own. I hope they will learn to be tolerant of others who are different. When I told Kurt, he said, "You're my dad and I love you." Your response was about yourself—how it hurt you.

You wrote that I would not have rejoiced if my father were gay. Frankly, I would have been relieved that someone (anyone) understood the feelings I had. I thought that your heart was gentle, and you would want me to confide in you, no matter what. I was wrong. I want to be a part of your life, but I will not let you shame me like you did in your letter. I hope we can reach an agreement.

Michael

Sweet Jesus! She's your mother for Christ's sake. How can you be so cruel?

5

DRAWN TO THE ACTION

When I was in high school, Dad started "running" bets for a local bookie. That was a good excuse for him to close the bars at two every morning. What he earned from bookmaking helped support the family, so some good did come of it. But the extra cash also meant he could afford to drink whiskey, and that was never good. His drunken disruptions accelerated at home. I wasn't foolish enough to cross him when he was potted. Joe had stepped between our parents once during a backyard argument and gotten his glasses knocked off in the scuffle.

I gained some distinction by participating in extracurricular activities. In freshman year, I played the role of Crown Prince Chulalongkorn in the school production of *The King and I*. My mother was excited, and Dad surprised everyone when he showed up unexpectedly at the final performance. He never said anything to me, but when a neighbor marveled at how talented his son was, Dad responded, "He didn't get it from me." I was never sure whether that was a compliment or a criticism.

Journal Entry—November 11, 1991

Distraught for days now. My sadness is rooted in anger at Dad that I've suppressed. I'm still shaking from having cried so hard in counseling. My spirit is raw and festering. Behind the pain is the anger, flipsides of the same coin.

Dad, you were such a pitiful mess. What were you thinking when I gave that sweet eulogy at your funeral?

Remarks at the Passing of Lester Allen Deninger
by Michael Deninger

>   A man's legacy rests with his family. Now we must try to put Dad's fears to rest and realize his dreams as we do what he would want us to do.
>   To Dad we would say:
>   You were taken away much too soon; long before we had the chance to say a proper goodbye. It was difficult to watch in your final hours, but we are relieved you have gone to your final resting place.
>   In the conduct of our lives we will help realize the dreams that always eluded you. You were a man whose blossoms never bloomed, who was never at ease.
>   In death Dad asks for understanding and for peace—the peace he never knew in life.

. . . My eulogy was a sham. You were a mess, a failure as a father and a husband. But I put you to rest with kind words. Shit! I burned your picture last night, a ritual to expel you from my thoughts. In the ashes, I saw an eye staring up at me from the grave. Then I was awakened at midnight when I heard you call my name. I'm still afraid, but I'm putting you on notice. Leave me alone. It's the least you can do.

A cruel classmate of mine—much bigger than I—tried to choke me from behind every day in freshman homeroom. I could tell from his demented look that inflicting pain gave him pleasure. He could have been deflecting anger at me from some abuse he himself was being subjected to at home. It would have been unwise to challenge him, although at times I thought I had no other course. I did learn one thing from that situation. I learned how to placate David or verbally draw his attention away from choking me. I'd seen my mother do this with my father. But when that failed, I took his abuse without protest, gritting my teeth each time, just the way my mother had taught me.

> Journal Entry—November 12, 1991
>
> *I can feel anger just below the surface, but I fear giving it expression. I want the memories to end. He doused his fears with booze, so selfish, so inconsiderate. I'm afraid even as I write this.*
>
> *I'm tired of his reign of terror. Until recently, I refused to think of him as evil. Now I'm facing how his addicted, maladjusted mind drove him to despicable acts. He must have known he was a menace, but he chose to do nothing about it.*

My second year in high school, Kathy Sweetland became my first serious girlfriend. We talked on the phone for hours. By that time, my family had come to expect nightly diatribes from Dad, but I managed to stay out of his way. When his car pulled into the driveway at night, I slid under the dining room table with the phone before he entered the kitchen to begin his "chewing." He never noticed me when his feet passed through on his way to bitch at Mom in the front room. Kathy and I suspended the conversation if he came near. She proved to be a source of strength through the two years we went steady. Kathy was just like her name—as sweet a person as one could meet. For the next two years, we became inseparable.

Kathy's Mom had passed away a few years before we met. She told me how life with her alcoholic father was as solemn as a funeral mass. Conversation was limited in the tomb of a house they shared. At only fifteen years of age, Kathy had full responsibility for managing the household. After dinner, her dad habitually passed out on the couch before she finished the dishes.

Clearly, she and I spoke the same language—like Siamese twins, joined at the hip by alcoholism, sharing a common organ pickled by our fathers' addictions. We met at a Catholic Youth Organization "tea" dance in the fall of our sophomore year. I bought her a cola afterwards at The Confectionary Shop on Clinton Avenue.

We stopped seeing each other in the fall of my senior year, but I'll always have fond memories of her. If we argued, the disagreements were trivial, and we quickly made amends. During our two years together, we did a lot of heavy petting, but we never went all the way. On occasion, I teased her by suggesting we go further. She always said no, and I respected her for that. Perhaps she never knew that I was the one afraid of crossing that line.

One month after Kathy and I met, I had my first full sexual experience—and my first orgasm—with a boy. Tom lived behind us on Terrace Park. Although we weren't close, we did share this prurient interest. The conversation that led up to our encounter was akin to the verbal foreplay in the Boy Scout tents.

Tom, decidedly more experienced than I, took matters in hand, masturbating me on the front porch of the house on Brooks Avenue. Unromantic first experience, but thrilling nevertheless. When the creamy stuff I had heard guys call "jizz" shot as high as my head and blotted the fabric of our summer cushions, I understood for the first time why homosexuality was forbidden. It had to be sinful. It felt too good.

That initial encounter set up confusion. I was excited about having met Kathy, but my attraction to men was provocative, compelling. I believed what I had done was a sin, but so was heavy petting. I didn't understand why I'd even *want* to mess around with a guy when I'd just met a nice girl. Clearly, I had to make a choice. Although the sex with Tom had been divine, it couldn't happen again, I resolved. So I committed to a relationship with Kathy and we started going steady within several weeks of our first meeting. With a girl in my life, I believed I could overcome my attraction to men.

This was my first attempt at a heterosexual "makeover." I continued to fantasize about guys when I masturbated, but I didn't have sex with a man again until a year after Kathy and I had parted ways. She was a wonderful part of my journey, easy to love, especially beautiful, kind, gentle, and passionate. If she had been a boy, my life would have taken an entirely different turn.

Dream—December 30, 1991

I'm driving to a therapy session. I find myself in the wrong lane heading into a tunnel. I meet a therapist I used to see. He says he'll meet me upstairs, but I go down a long flight of winding stairs leading to a bridge over a river. As I descend, an adult and a teenager are coming up. They're relieved to make it to the top.

The stairs are shaking back and forth, about to break away from the wall. I finally reach the bottom. I have to climb over several canoes frozen in the water to get to solid ground.

In my sophomore year of high school, the same year I met Kathy, I won first place at the New York State Optimist International Oratorical Contest in Jamestown. As state champion, I advanced to the northeast regional finals in Toronto. I placed third there with a speech titled "The Creative Force of Optimism."

Rising as high as I had in the competition was quite an accomplishment. My photo appeared with a brief story in the school newspaper and also in Rochester's *Democrat and Chronicle*. For weeks, the state trophy and my picture were displayed in the main lobby of my high school.

The same year, I played basketball with my brother Joe for St. Monica's. The parish team, undefeated in thirty-one games, captured the Catholic city championship. Things were going well. I had a nice girlfriend, so no one could question my virility. I was doing above-average work in school, nothing scholarly, just respectable, and I was receiving accolades for my achievements.

That was the year I had my first drink of alcohol.

After Sunday basketball games, the players and a few cheerleaders met at "pie rock" on the river with six-packs of beer. Yes, my boyhood fishing rock had become the team's drinking rock. After two beers that first night, I felt uncomfortably lightheaded and decided to stop. The feeling scared me. Unfortunately, it didn't make me stop experimenting. Because Kathy and I spent a lot of time together, I passed up many opportunities to drink with the team. She kept me out of loads of trouble.

Journal Entry—January 12, 1992

When I arrived at counseling yesterday, I was nervous and very sad.

Once relaxed and "hypnotized," I was on the verge of tears. I was thinking, "Hold it in. Don't let it out. Something awful will happen." I say, "My father is here" to Ned. I stave off the pain and feel it subside after expending a great deal of energy to keep it contained. Ned asks how I feel. I say, "Immobilized." He asks me to stay with it.

I have to face what's there, so I allow myself to open up. Tears are released. Ned asks what's going on. I think I'm holding my breath to stop crying, but I realize I'm not in control. I feel a sharp pain at my throat. I'm finding it hard to breathe. Someone is choking me. It's my father.

That thought triggers a release. I gasp for air and my head jerks up off the couch. I tell Ned my father is choking me and he says, "Stay with it." I'm afraid. I become immobilized again. Ned says my legs are trembling, but I can't feel them. Then the floodgates of rage burst open. I thrash about on the couch. I scream out with primitive, guttural sounds that echo off the walls. I clench the fabric of the couch and squeeze. My leg spasms and shoots straight up into the air from its crooked position. This continues for a long time.

I yell at Lester. "No! Leave me alone! No! God damn it! Fuck you. Fuck you!"

I don't want to believe that Lester is choking me, but I'm sure he is. I can't see where or when it happened. The anger is a raw regurgitation of stored emotions. My face is drenched with saline.

At home, things didn't change. One Sunday, Dad took Mom, my brother Dan, and me to dinner at an upscale restaurant on the outskirts of the city. Dad had "hit the ponies" that week and was feeling magnanimous. The *maître d'* seated us "on display" at the center of the crowded dining room. Dad was well oiled and ordered our young waiter to fish a live lobster from a glass tank and bring it over for inspection. When he gloated loudly about sending the crustacean off to its death, I began to sweat. Mom scolded him for behaving badly. We all tensed up, knowing the evening would end unpleasantly. The first time Dad raised his voice to her, Mom insisted we leave.

He was furious when he got behind the wheel and drove us recklessly into the country. When Mom screamed for him to stop, he gunned the engine, swerved to the left, and careened down a road between two cultivated fields. I went silent, fearing he'd take us to an early grave. I resented the control he had over us, but there was no arguing with him.

Acres of a yellow, flowering crop flanked both sides of the road down where he was speeding. Distracted by the vegetation, he pulled over and walked into the field. I remember thinking the man was nuts.

Back at the car, he proudly announced that the crop had to be "mustard." He sought opinions. No one responded. He talked to himself about whether it was mustard or not. He challenged us to debate the premise. Although he was angry at our silence, he reentered the car and drove to a farmhouse down the road. He staggered to the door and asked the woman of the house the name of the mystery crop. Because I was fifteen, I would soon be eligible to drive. I wanted to take the wheel and leave him behind, but Mom yelled at me to sit still. Dan and I slouched down in the back and shielded our faces with our hands. Neither one of us wanted to be seen with the drunken maniac. We got home safely that night, thanks to our silence.

Then Dad went back out to the bar.

> Journal Entry—January 13, 1992
>
> *I was listening to a classical radio station while idling at a red light today. I felt at peace. The music was soft, with airy strings and light brass in the background. I imagined a full moon rising over a tranquil sea. The light turned green just as the female radio announcer said (as if to me alone), "The light is green. You can go on your way now." I got a chill the way I do when something cosmic happens. I chuckled and drove off. It's time to move on, time to forget the past.*

During my junior year, our basketball team captured its second city championship and extended our winning streak to sixty-two consecutive games. Our team was reputed to be the best in the city, but we were also the most envied. Games against less experienced teams could be brutal, with opponents roughing us up on the court in retaliation for our dominance of the league. I became well known among my high school classmates as a member of that team. That same year, I won the junior class oratorical contest with a speech about the assassination of JFK. This put me in the running for class valedictorian the following year.

In my senior year, I moved through a period of rapid change. New friends I met through the drama club were racier than my neighborhood crowd. They came from upper class families with household incomes several times what my father earned. These friends exuded an air of privilege, even carried themselves like aristocrats. I witnessed their sophistication, as well as their pettiness, and I envied what they had. From them, I learned that I, too, could expect more, but I would have to play a role to pull it off.

That fall, I performed the lead in the comedy "Take Her She's Mine" at school. I was so enamored with my bleached-blonde leading lady who lived across town that I broke up with Kathy Sweetland. My attraction to my flamboyant, petulant co-star was based solely on status. On my only date with her, she bragged about being on the pill and hinted that we might go all the way. I got scared. In the spring I played the lead in the musical "Bye Bye Birdie," a stretch for me when it came to the dance numbers.

I got sloppy drunk twice that year. At the cast party for "Birdie" I downed several shots of peppermint schnapps with beer chasers. I donned a pair of pajamas I found in a bedroom and hid under the dining room table. On the way home, I puked out the passenger window of my friend Tom's car. Then, at a sleepover after graduation, I drank homemade Italian wine and threw up in the host's toilet in the middle of the night. Alcohol was not yet a chronic problem, but by the end of that summer, I was drinking like an alcoholic.

Because there was no steady girl friend to keep my attention, erotic thoughts of men streamed steadily through my mind. One handsome classmate became the object of my fantasies. I would have compromised my secrecy if Jim McDonald had suggested a liaison. Tall and slender, Jim was sensually arrogant with a flare for the dramatic, a gifted thespian who had never set foot on a stage. I enjoyed walking behind him, so I could admire his track-star lower torso. I had no evidence Jim was attracted to men, but that wasn't important.

I would never have disclosed my private desires . . . unless Jim had suggested a tryst.

> Journal Entry—January 14, 1992
>
> *My psychiatrist took me off antidepressants today. I'm confident this is the time to do that.*
>
> *"Messages" of a spiritual sort have been coming in the past few days. I had the urge to phone a friend and say, "I'm supposed to call you Lydia." She asked what I thought it meant. I thought of Winona Ryder's character named Lydia in the movie Betelgeuse—a morose, suicidal adolescent who was nothing like my friend. I was shocked when she said that character described her to a "T." We had our first talk about her bouts with depression.*

Our parish team was undefeated in league play again that year, but we lost the championship game at the Knights of Columbus Hall downtown. Amazingly, my father was in the stands that afternoon. He'd never attended even *one* of the ninety games in my career, but he had to show up for our first loss in three years.

In the second half of the hard-fought game, a teammate fed me the ball on a fast break. I was all alone down court without an opponent in sight. There was no way I could miss the easy lay-up . . . but I did. I was ashamed when I emerged from the locker room a loser. After years of ignoring all I'd achieved on and off the court, Dad teased me for blowing that lay-up. Although I was fuming, I held my disgust inside. He repeated that story at family gatherings for years until I finally told him never to mention it again.

Another disappointment came that year when I lost the election for class valedictorian to Greg Austen, the president of the debate society. I have no memory of my high school graduation, except a jealous thought that I would have given a much better valedictory address than the stodgy one Greg delivered. Fortunately, with my B average, I could enter the college of my choice—in Buffalo. I was poised for the next leg of my journey.

I remember being miserably alone the summer after graduation with no steady girl and no close friends. My drama buddies had scattered after the spring production and no longer included me in their plans, an important lesson in the workings of classism. Having been shunned by me for a time, my neighborhood friends had moved on as well. This proved the perfect time to start a serious relationship with alcohol. The urge took hold. Eighteen was the legal drinking age in New York, and I'd reached that milestone a month before school ended. After all, my brother Joe was a regular in the neighborhood beer joints, and my father was a senior member of those establishments. I assimilated into the bar scene with ease.

Every night that summer, I drank Genesee beer at Lou Izzo's Place until I was dizzy. I was unable to stop at one or two, so I was drinking habitually by the time I left for college. I blamed my lack of control on others. Someone would buy me a drink because I was Joe's brother or Lester's son. Couldn't say no. Protocol required that I buy a round back. Someone else would order a round for the bar, and soon four beers were lined up in front of me. One problem. If I had more than five beers, the room would spin, and I'd have to sing into the toilet before I could fall asleep. I hated throwing up, but my drive to drink was more compelling than anything. The cravings again.

Without a doubt, the most disgusting sight I ever saw took place at Kelly's across from Lou Izzo's on Genesee Street that Labor Day weekend. As I approached the bar near closing time, I could hear the patrons inside loudly chanting, "Go! Go! Go! Go!" I entered the smoke-filled room and saw a regular, Alvin Alger, at the far end of the bar chugging an entire mug of whiskey sours. When Alvin slammed down the empty stein, cheers of excitement rose up from the crowd huddled around him. But the cheers stopped just as quickly when Alvin began to sway back and forth, like he was about to go nose to the floor.

An uneasy silence descended on the room. People froze, mouths agape, watching soundlessly as Alvin steadied himself, inhaled haltingly, and then eased his backside down on the stool. Only after he had gently returned his head to its resting place on the bar did conversations return to their normal din. The bartender explained that Alvin was challenging his own record for number of whiskey sours consumed during a holiday weekend. The old record was thirty-one; he had just finished number thirty . . . and only twenty minutes remained until closing.

Alvin was tall and unattractive with Dumbo-like ears and soulful brown eyes. The poor man was often the victim of cruel barroom pranks. Bullies pulled his underwear up between his butt cheeks or snapped his ears as they passed his stool. He had known the regulars at Kelly's since grammar school and had been teased unmercifully by them for as long.

He drank in volume to override the hurt from those taunts, to deaden the pain. Alvin could hold amounts of alcohol that would have sent others to the detox center. The term "hard-core alcoholic" was coined for him. People remembered two things about Alvin: his knowledge of baseball statistics and how much he could drink. He was completely unathletic, and drinking became his only sport, whiskey sours his Olympic event.

That evening I fancied Alvin a gladiator facing a battle to the death in the Coliseum. The bartender mixed a fresh mug of sours and placed it before the warrior. Spectators rose from their seats in anticipation, calling for blood, pumping fists in the air. Shouts of "Come on Alvin!" and "You can do it!" and "Go Alvin!" echoed throughout the arena. As if in a trance, Alvin slowly raised his head from the bar, drew the mug up to his lips, and confronted his next opponent. His pupils were fixed and dilated. "Go! Go! Go! Go!" With two huge gulps, he downed half of number thirty-one. The crowd went into a frenzy. The collective roar grew louder, more intense. "Go! Go! Go!" But the event stopped abruptly when the gladiator ceased chugging and paused with his opponent halfway upended. A hush. The moment before a kill. Then, it happened.

Rooters close to the action could see the bubble move up his chest as his guts heaved in two distinct convulsions. A stream of vomit shot from the rear of his mouth with the force of a water cannon into the mug. The fluid bounced back from the bottom of the glass, ricocheted off the gladiator's cheeks, and splattered a few dumbfounded spectators. The fans staggered back until their shoulders were pinned to the wall. No one could believe what had happened. When they regained their senses, they wiped vomit chunks from their cheeks with forearms. While holding their noses in disgust, they raised cries of horror that could be heard up and down Genesee Street: "Oh my god!" and "Jesus Christ, Alvin!" and "Oh shit!"

What happened next was nothing short of spectacular. A fresh look of determination came over the warrior's face. His eyes bulged from their sockets, no longer fixed and dilated. It took the courage of all his forefathers to boldly re-lift that mug to his lips. Then, like a Popeye who had just downed his last can of spinach, he upended his opponent and swallowed the contents of the mug, puke and all. He was determined to leave no doubts about his prowess. He drained every drop of that mug before pounding the glass down on the bar.

The gladiator broadcasted a shaky grin across the room, and scanned the arena for a "thumbs up" from the emperor, strings of vomit bungee jumping from the corners of his mouth. The patrons screamed in terror, gripped their stomachs, and streamed out the front door like they were fleeing an inferno. Two spectators lunged to the curb where they blew their own lunch into the gutter.

This spectacle told the true story of the men at Kelly's—perverted, childish, and out of control. Hopelessness festered beneath their bravado, and recklessness ran amok. Alcoholism had ruined the lives of these men—my father one of the prime examples.

The neighborhood was rife with losers like Alvin, players who had succumbed to the ravages of distilled spirits, each drama with a slightly different twist, each tale as wretched as the next.

I understood their hopelessness. I was a worthless piece of shit in my own right, a pansy, a slave to my own carnal desires. What future could there be for me? A phrase from a Hemingway short story repeated in my head like a broken record: *"Nada, y pues nada, y pues nada."* In English—"Nothing, and then nothing, and then nothing."

That's what I would become, a big fat nothing.

> Journal Entry—January 16, 1992
>
> *Spoke to my mother after months of silence. I can call her "Mom" again. I hung up before it rang the first time I called, still afraid of rejection.*
>
> *The conversation went better than expected. No lies. No pretenses. I hope that someday she can accept her own culpability in letting the violence continue.*

The summer after my high school graduation, my brother-in-law finagled me a seasonal job as a groundskeeper in Genesee Valley Park. Working in the sun suited me, but I was unprepared for the men that zoomed into focus in the park environment. Like my work partner, a handsome college senior with a hairy chest, rock-hard biceps, and a sculpted body. It was a chore to keep my eyes off him while we wielded axes side by side.

I learned that parks were popular cruising spots where gay men came to meet. I knew nothing about homosexuals. I thought I was the only one with the curse. I watched how intensely they stared at each other, how they circled the parking lot in caravans of cars, how they loitered around the restrooms, and lingered inside. That summer I studied those behaviors that were yet un-chronicled by modern straight researchers. I became a scientist in the field, a budding anthropologist in pursuit of an aberrant species. I had no one with whom I could compare notes, no colleague with whom I could test my theories. With much more effort than I gave to studying for my final exams, I tried to decipher the code.

One afternoon, I had an experience that added to my confusion around religion and same-sex attractions. I was working near one of the restrooms when I had to use the facility. As I entered, I noticed a figure and some movement in a shadow at one of the urinals. A double take confirmed what I thought I had seen. Standing in a corner, playing with himself like the flasher by the river, was my high school librarian. The priest seemed as startled to see me as I was to catch him masturbating in his street clothes. He was in a panic to escape and zipped up so fast that he snagged his shirttail in his zipper as he scurried bowlegged out the door. Catching the portly librarian pulling his pud in that restroom certainly did level the playing field.

The normally jovial priest, must have been just as tortured by his attractions as I was about my own. I wish we could have talked man to man about our mutual malady. But that was out of the question once the cleric had pulled his member out and laid his sexual cards on the table. I wondered what advice he would have given me if I told him in confession that I was masturbating over sex with boys. Would he have insisted that I pray to be relieved of those sinful urges? Would he have advocated a closeted life in the priesthood with occasional forays into public restrooms to satisfy my wonton desires? Or would he have shamelessly drooled at me through the opaque screen like my parish priest had?

The struggle to reconcile my attractions with my religion would continue for years.

While falling off to sleep that evening (and still troubled by the incident with my high school librarian), I got an excruciating cramp in my left calf. I bounded out of bed and hobbled down the stairs in my underwear to ask my mother what to do about the cramp. She was watching the evening news. "There's nothing you can do but wait it out," she said. In a moment of courage (or stupidity), I explained I had seen my school's librarian playing with himself. It was a way of assessing how safe it would be to discuss my attraction to men with her.

That I was sitting beside her in my underwear was weird. Telling her about the priest jerking off in the park restroom was beyond bizarre. She had not seen me undressed since I was eleven, and we had never discussed sex. It occurred to me that I might be treading on the cusp of a disaster.

Mom showed no expression while I explained what happened. That worried me. I couldn't read her. Her upper body stiffened when she asked, "How can you be sure he was playing with himself?" She was pressing for details like the priest in the confessional. "What exactly did you see him doing?" No longer a conversation but an inquisition.

Feeling the finger being pointed at me, I answered sarcastically to deflect the inquiry. "It doesn't take a genius to figure out when someone's playing with himself." Inside I was panicking: "She must have seen men jerking off before, for Christ's sake! She has to know what it looks like! Shit! Why the third degree? And what if she asks me outright if I'm queer?"

If I got a question like that, I was prepared to lie. If she did learn about my interest in men, she was certain to disapprove. So I retreated from that conversation as fast as words could carry me. We never discussed that incident again. Following our brief but intense conversation, I concluded, right or wrong, that the topic was unsafe. My perceptions, perhaps a misinterpretation of her intent, made me lock and double bolt my closet door.

Maybe if I had been honest with her then about my struggle, she would have given me the support I needed. One can always hope for the best.

> Journal Entry—March 22, 1992
>
> *A striking series of events this week. I'm tearful, but relieved. A colleague and I were talking about the movie* Field of Dreams. *I explained how important it was to my son and me.*
>
> *That evening I hosted Renee and her boyfriend for dinner. I was uncomfortable drinking wine in their presence. The next day I had two drinks at a party. They didn't taste right. On the way home, I bought a bottle of wine and a fifth of vodka, as was my habit.*
>
> *When I entered the house, Kurt was watching* Field of Dreams. *I got a chill down my spine. He asked, "What's in the bag—booze?" He wasn't being critical. It's what he expected. I realized I've been a lousy role model for him—just like my father. But that didn't stop me from drinking that night.*
>
> *The next day I asked Kurt if he wanted to go to my counseling session with me rather than sit at home. I was certain he'd refuse, but he said, "Yes" right off—even suggested he could do his homework there. This was odd. He hates counseling.*
>
> *While driving to the session I had a panic attack. The closer we got, the more I feared going out of my mind. The muscles in my chest were trembling. I talked to Kurt to keep my mind off the fear. I had to get there. I had to.*
>
> (con'td to page 90)

> Journal Entry—March 22, 1992 (cont'd from page 89)
>
> *I left Kurt in the waiting room. I was still shaking all over. I zipped my jacket to the neck to contain my emotions. I told Ned about the series of events and the anxiety. I added that this was about my need to stop drinking. He agreed. He said Kurt was there for a reason. He encouraged me to have him join us. I resisted.*
>
> *I did go out and ask Kurt, but he said no. I assured him that it was about me, not him. He still refused. I knelt beside him. I told him about the panic attack, about being a bad role model, and about my need to stop drinking. I added how afraid I was to stop, but I had to. I asked for his support.*
>
> *Before leaving, I had admitted my powerlessness over alcohol. I had taken the first step in my recovery. I love my son and don't want to hurt him. The moment I voiced the decision, my upper torso stopped quivering. I hadn't noticed. Ned kindly brought it to my attention.*

Two other incidents of significance happened that summer in and around the same rest room where the Aquinas librarian had wiggled his wares.

"Are you nuts? People will think you're a sleazy, freakin' whore. You can't do this."

The nasty voice was never stronger than when I began writing about my encounters with strangers in the park. Sebastian cautioned me not to be too harsh with this voice. He counseled that the voice was part of me and had served a purpose in another era, adding that the protections provided by secrecy can sometimes be necessary.

I admit that I struggled with whether I should divulge certain events and in what detail. Most closeted homosexuals expend a lot of energy on keeping secrets. It's no surprise. I came to a difficult but liberating conclusion: Unless some of my private moments were revealed, readers would not understand my desolation as a young man, particularly the depths of my despair and what motivated me to act in certain ways.

All summer I watched the guys in the park, taking notes on the mating dance of my species. I learned the rituals like a straight boy studies his older brother's efforts at wooing females. The caravans in the parking lot were my first evidence that others like me even existed. At noon, I lunched under a tree and observed their mannerisms, their movements; how they stared at each other with impropriety; how they stretched and postured for effect; how they initiated conversations. I wished I could hear what they were saying. My observations were always conducted from remote vantage points. No one could know that I had any interest in those conventions. No one.

I was drawn closer to the action one day when I was mowing the lawn near an attractive sunbather. I could feel him watching me from the green army blanket on which he was outstretched. His tractor beams were locked on target as his eyes scanned me from head to toe without the least bit of shame. I could feel his energy. Once or twice he shifted his position and rubbed himself in a provocative manner, and then he watched to see my reaction. That was the first time I returned a gaze of interest from a man. I noticed the outline of an erection in his tight, nylon bathing suit. Aroused. His smirk gave me a thrill. I lost myself in that interaction. When I looked down, I saw I had mowed the turf around a tree down to the roots. I panicked and moved away.

Years later, I learned that what we had done was called

"cruising" in the language of the caravan men. And then there was the capstone experience from that summer.

"Hold on, Buster! You can't write about that. Please . . ."

During the last week of August, I stopped at the restroom every day on my way home from work, hoping to see real action. One afternoon an attractive older man was inside staring out into the parking lot. He looked at me the way the sunbather had weeks before. I decided to cross the line. I looked back at him, playing with fire.

His actions led me down a path I was ready to travel. Without much conversation, we moved closer to the touch. I explained that this was my first time, that I had never done what he had proposed. He told me not to worry.

The completely pleasurable experience was over in a matter of seconds. He departed the restroom without another word. I felt abandoned. Could we do it again sometime? I wanted to ask his name, where he lived, what he did for a living. I hadn't yet learned that personal questions were forbidden in the world of anonymous sex. The danger of being caught and the need for secrecy far outweighed the desire to chat once the business was over.

On my long walk home, my thoughts were tangled with conflicting emotions that would take a long time to reconcile. What I had done with a handsome man felt natural—easy, exciting, wonderful. Feeling a female's breast or rubbing a vagina couldn't compare. But I was also drowning in remorse for having crossed the line. The voice in my head kept preaching hellfire and brimstone, condemning me to an eternity with Satan.

"What you did was dirty, disgusting, unnatural, an abomination. You've got to change. What would your mother think?"

I had no one to turn to. My father was incapable of conversation. I would be crazy to tell my mother that I had done the librarian one better in the park restroom. Priests were no help. They jerked off at urinals or leered at you through confessional screens. The caravan men were no help either. They were all action and no talk, disappearing into the trees seconds after you caught your breath. Psychiatrists were for the rich and famous, and besides, I wasn't crazy.

I had only one way out. I would have to quash those desires by steering a heterosexual course. Without any source of support, I would turn to my most reliable companion—alcohol.

Call me an enthusiastic freshman at Canisius College in Buffalo in the fall of 1964. Although basically shy and unassuming, I had always been able to make close friends over time. After participating actively in my fraternity for three years, I was elected president of the residence hall association in senior year. I loved every part of college life except the studying. In fact, I had little confidence that I would ever graduate.

Five or more drinks every night allowed me to mask my insecurities.

I enjoyed living in a dorm with three hundred men, many with exquisite bodies. Watching them clad only in towels, shaving at the mirror beside me, or soaping themselves in the shower thrilled me. In that regard, my sexual appetite received constant stimulation. The campus was classically homophobic, however. Military training was mandatory and students had to minor in theology—two good reasons to conceal my homosexual stripes.

As conservative as Canisius was, one theology professor was shockingly liberal. During a lecture in my Contemporary Issues course, Father Courneen proposed that a homosexual act committed by a man with a very small penis might not be considered a sin. He argued that if one could not adequately perform with a woman, he might have a compelling moral reason to seek out men. Of course, I had to wonder whether Father Courneen was himself size-deprived.

I remained meticulously closeted in college. Two serious heterosexual relationships masked my identity, although I never had intercourse with either of the women. And I never had sex with any of my male classmates, although one dorm mate did attempt to seduce me. The guys on my floor would tease about man-to-man sex, even pile on each other and hump playfully. But for some of us, there was intent. During my four years in college, I had sex with men twice. Both times, I was drunk. Both times, the sex was with strangers. I continued to date women while masturbating over men, preening my heterosexual wings, hoping beyond hope that one day I would take flight and never look back at a man.

6

ANXIETY PERSONIFIED

All forward movement ceased one morning when I was thirty-eight years old. I was sitting frozen in my family room rocker like a mummy in snow. I couldn't stand without my head spinning. Outwardly, my life appeared as positive as it had always been. My wife of thirteen years was loving and supportive, my two children attractive and bright. We considered our four-bedroom colonial in the suburbs more than comfortable. My career as a leader in the education of deaf children had reached a pinnacle.

But no one could see the unbearable emptiness inside.

Although I felt my life slowly disintegrating, I refused to admit weakness or divulge my secrets. And it would have been heresy to complain, given all I had. In retrospect, Sebastian characterized my stubbornness as self-destructive, a character flaw that needed to be overcome. To my credit, I had made it to that point without a serious breakdown. Although I was taught that admitting mental illness was a personal failure, I would have welcomed a hospitalization that day, I was *that* scared.

I did call a psychiatrist—no other way out.

In a bit of sweet irony, though, this day would also mark the beginning of my recovery, my journey back.

> Journal Entry—March 31, 1992
>
> *Interesting day. Using a new meditation technique, I focused on the jitters I have in my hands and feet. I "heard" a thought that the nervousness is tied back to something that happened on the fishing trip with my dad. That was it. As I was disconnecting, I felt a cleansing rush, a kind of purging of negative emotions. A great experience!*

My first anxiety attack happened when I was a senior in high school.

I had spent a Saturday morning taking the College Board Examinations and was to star in a school musical that evening. When a friend drove me to the performance, I got strangely nervous in his car. The thought that I might vomit my steak dinner made my stomach churn. I could not stop salivating. Body sensations alternated between cold chills and hot flashes. A rush of fear zoomed across my scalp. I kept coughing and spitting gobs of saliva out the window. The terror passed after a few minutes, but I'll always remember my first panic attack.

Anxiety personified became my archenemy for the next two decades. I could speculate why the "imp" chose that night to begin his assault. Perhaps he understood how fraudulent I felt. My status as a queer, a homo, a fruitcake made me unworthy of recognition. My erotic fantasies of men were laughable, immoral. He might have known I feared being in the spotlight, where hecklers would see through my straight facade. Everyone knew actors were queer. I could be laughed off stage, my cover completely blown. The seeds of social phobia were germinating, saturated in low self-esteem and fed by obsessive thoughts.

I gave a stellar performance that evening, but my enemy had taken up residence as my ever-present stalker. That marked the beginning of years of stress. If I had known, I might have sought help sooner, or I might have ended it all before leaving high school.

Although I was stunned by the attack, I quickly dismissed the idea that it would ever recur. The loss of control had to be a result of opening night jitters, I reasoned. After eighteen months without a similar attack, I thought I had to be right. Of course, I did start drinking every day a few months after the attack.

Unfortunately, the curse returned in my sophomore year of college. On the first morning of an orientation program, a picnic was planned some distance from the campus. As I boarded the bus after breakfast for transit to the site, I suddenly felt trapped in the confines of the vehicle. I began to panic the way I had in my friend's car. I wasn't sick, not really. I tried to outpace the obsessive thoughts. Crazed fears were pitching and plunging inside my head.

Halfway down the aisle, a shock of terror dealt the final blow. Saliva pooled between my cheeks and gums. No holding back, my breakfast was on its way up. In full freakout, I pulled down a window and began spitting. I had to escape the bus. I hustled across the quadrangle to the student union without giving the impression that I was in distress. I barely made it to the men's room. Bursting into a stall, I flipped up the toilet seat with a whack. Abdominal spasms forced up enough breakfast to loosen the demon's chokehold.

> Dream—April 11, 1992
>
> *I'm in my office that's actually an overgrown jungle. A sleeping bag is open on the floor. There's danger. Alligators or caimans are lurking in a nearby swamp. I'm protecting two kittens. I grab one to rescue it from a caiman. When I turn, the second is gone, snatched by an alligator. I throw the one in my hand down hard on the gator to make him drop the other one. It doesn't work. The kitten bounces off the gator and is miraculously unharmed. I see a fox swallowing another kitten. I cautiously move out of the swamp. I tried to warn the kittens, but they couldn't understand.*

Reverse peristalsis is a coldly scientific term for this indignity, this horrid human malady. I re-boarded the bus with bloodshot eyes, putrid breath, and a cowering spirit, wondering if the panic would return later. Would there be a restroom at the picnic site? Woods where I could escape to lose more breakfast in private? I thought of nothing else until we arrived back at campus.

The probability that I would again puke in public without warning was then fixed in my awareness. My solution a few days later was simple but not sensible. I would skip breakfast. No input, no regurgitation. Food and anxiety had joined forces and hurtled me into a downward spiral from which I never thought I'd recover.

The no breakfast rule remained in force throughout four years of college. The more I worried, the more restrictive the self-imposed controls became. I sometimes skipped a lunch, or even a dinner, if a social situation arose in which I might be "on display." But I was also concerned that I wouldn't get enough to eat; would wither away like an indigent with a wasting disease. That caused me to develop alternate means and schedules for food consumption; enter alcohol as a remedy.

I could eat comfortably if I had two drinks before a meal. If an evening included a "tight spot," I'd forego dinner and eat something at the bar. Near closing time, I would load in calories of ghastly snacks like pork rinds, chips, pickled eggs, or grilled cheese sandwiches—the more carbs the better. This became a routine by the middle of my sophomore year. Because alcohol wasn't allowed in our dorms, I was out at the bar every night. The food and alcohol required money I didn't have, so I got a part-time job to pay for my eating habits. Beer was a staple for four years, until I discovered scotch was a more effective tranquilizer. Hard liquor worked faster on the neurological system. By the age of twenty-one, I was an alcoholic who consumed several drinks before my head hit the pillow at night.

Given the time and effort I expended to outfox the demon, I was amazed when I graduated with a degree in English in the spring of 1968. Good things should not have come to me. I didn't think I deserved them. Out of necessity, I'd become adept at predicting the events of a given day, where I'd be going, what I'd be doing, whether I'd find myself in an enclosed space, or a confining social situation. I became equally skilled at passing up food in risky settings.

I managed not to vomit again until I was on vacation with my close college friend Bill Robinson after graduation.

On our way to the beach, Bill and I stopped overnight

at his uncle's house in the southern tier of New York. The next morning his aunt served a hearty (but greasy) country breakfast. I forgot all that I had learned and ate most of the meal. While biting into my last slice of toast, anxiety swooped down and roosted in my throat. This called for quick thinking. I took stock. Could I hold it down until we left? Where in the house could I purge? The place was so small they would hear my heaving and retching. I lost the battle—no holding it back, no way out.

My scalp tightened over my cranium. My throat constricted. I thought I could feel the blood drain from my face. I dumped the flowing saliva into my juice glass, a temporary solution. The main event couldn't be postponed. In a matter of seconds, the demon seized control of my body.

I urged Bill to gather his things so we could leave. The panic was escalating. Hastily excusing myself from the table, I lurched up the stairs, bolted into the bathroom, and knelt before the toilet. Bill called up to say the car was packed and he was ready to go. I took a last breath and joined them on the front porch for good-byes. Small talk was always dangerous. I had to get away. It was coming.

I stumbled off the porch and onto the lawn where I repeatedly heaved until breakfast was broadcast over their manicured flowerbed. What does one say after tossing his cookies in the host's magenta petunias?

When it was over, I fabricated a story about not feeling well lately and asked Bill if we could be on our way. I apologized for ruining their garden and offered to hose it down. They wouldn't hear of it. All week at the beach, I ate less food than a jockey on the day of the Preakness. If I had any doubts about the persistence of this problem, they'd been decisively overruled. Bill and I are still close, and each time we get together, we laugh about how I fertilized his aunt's posies in the summer of '68.

> Journal Entry—April 13, 1992
>
> *As I was preparing to end my meditation today, I was asked to open my mind to a deeper level. I'm not sure by whom (and I'm not sure how I did this). A bright light flooded the screen in my mind's eye. I "heard" a thought: The pain in your upper back will lessen when you forgive your father's shortcomings.*

I saw my doctor back in Rochester, believing I must have a physical ailment. His exam revealed nothing. I wanted to believe I suffered from a rare disorder that would only respond to an exotic drug. The physician suggested I see a psychiatrist or begin taking a mild tranquilizer. I brushed off his suggestions, deciding I was nervous because of the start of graduate work. The anxiety was sure to diminish when I settled in at school. No, I didn't need a psychiatrist. Shrinks were for lunatics, the destitute, or the institutionalized. I continued to push through with selective abstinence from food and strategic consumption of alcohol.

Two weeks later, I was back in Buffalo beginning a masters program in deaf education at Canisius. Before attending a reception at the school for the deaf the first night, I ate pasta at home. The minute I walked into the gathering, a rush of fear prickled through me. When the thought that I might throw up gained momentum, I found the cake offered to me as repulsive as fish on Friday. The spaghetti I had eaten was on the move, defying gravity and plotting an invasion at the rear of my mouth.

My face sported a plastic smile as Sister Mary introduced me to my classmates and professors. Because I was stuck with no way out, brief conversations became excruciating challenges. When the noose tightened around my throat, saliva mass-produced by over-active glands gathered under my tongue. I had to escape. I eased out of the room and scurried down back corridors until I found an exit to the parking lot. Heaving the pasta outside would be better than tossing it in Mother Superior's punch bowl.

I lost just enough of my dinner to regain my composure. I slipped back into the reception and prayed no one had seen my display between two sedans out back. I learned how to feign interest in food that night. I grabbed a chocolate chip and brandished the disgusting morsel like an actor would a stage prop, being careful not to overplay the scene. When the charade was over, I crumbled the cookie in a napkin and dumped it into the trash, all to save face—an Oscar Award-winning performance.

The anxiety must have been worsened by my erotic fantasies involving men. Never before had Adam's quandary in the Garden of Eden been so clear to me: Either refuse the forbidden fruit, or indulge my appetites and be disenfranchised. In graduate school, I didn't date women, but I had a small circle of friends who socialized every weekend. On Friday nights, we were as raucous as sailors on shore leave, consuming pitchers of beer at Shakey's Pizza, screaming out songs and snake dancing the room until we were asked to leave. But each night, when the excitement was over, I hungered for physical companionship. A number of times, I ventured out in search of a man.

> Journal Entry—May 18, 1992
>
> *In a meditation, I asked for help in letting go of the past. A friendly presence responded with a tingling sensation in my middle back. I asked who it was. I "heard" a voice say, "Michael." I asked if he had the same name, but he said, "No, I am you." He said all the answers were within me, including the strength to clear my path. I believed I was talking to my higher power.*
>
> *He cautioned that every cigarette was a step away from my path. I was assured that I would find the insight to expand my consciousness.*

I met a handsome guy late one night while cruising downtown Buffalo. We sat and talked in my car for a long time. I was surprised how openly he lived as a gay man.

He invited me to his summer place on Lake Erie the following weekend. Although he was clearly interested in me, I wanted no entanglements. A brief sexual encounter was all I had in mind, because my attraction to men mirrored my fear of vomiting. They were both nuisances that had to be managed. I took directions and promised to meet him the following Friday, but I had no intention of doing so. I wasn't about to associate with a homo who lived that openly, regardless of my hankerings.

Near the end of graduate school, I was concerned that my family might suspect I was queer. I decided I'd have to find a girl friend. All of my siblings had married young. Questions about my own prospects had not yet surfaced, but they would, so I had to maintain my cover. Then, the night before I was to return to Rochester to begin teaching, something happened that would force a retreat even deeper into the closet.

"No, please don't do this. Have you lost your mind? This is a mistake."

The day I received my masters in education, several family members gathered in Buffalo to help me celebrate. No one had ever finished college! The fact that I had earned a graduate degree brought great honor to our side of the family. Even better, I announced I'd soon join the faculty of The National Technical Institute for the Deaf in Rochester. I had reason to be proud. However, when my mother and siblings left for home that evening, I felt alone with my discontent. I wanted to be in love and to have my love returned in that special way. I didn't want a woman in my life; I wanted to feel a man. I curled up on the dingy, green carpet in my apartment and cried. *Nada, y pues nada, y pues nada.*

Several cocktails later, I drove downtown in search of affection and ended up near the public library, circling a block where men went to meet. I knew of one gay bar in town, had almost entered the place once but was afraid I'd be recognized. This block was easier, safer—less of a chance I'd be seen.

When I first circled the block, a man standing curbside stared intensely as I passed. Encouraged by his interest and emboldened by the scotch, I parked and approached him. We made small talk until the man changed his tone from enticing to threatening. I don't remember what I said or did that warranted my arrest that night. The bastard was a police officer, operating undercover for the sole purpose of ensnaring naïve young men.

The cop was good at what he did, coyly playing the role of a queer in search of love then busting his victims. Entrapment is what they call it now. By any other name, it stinks just the same.

My subsequent incarceration could be called a nightmare times ten. I endured the humiliating arrest, transport in the paddy wagon with people of the night, and the booking at the jail. I declined my phone call, believing I had no one I could burden with my degeneracy. I chose to suffer in silence. This fox had to be stuffed deep under my cloak.

"That's what you get for letting your dick rule your life."

During my fingerprinting, the police photographer blabbered on like a narrow-minded, ultra-conservative, quack therapist. "Why do you think you're this way, son?" he asked. "You know it's a sin. Did your mother coddle you?"

"No," I answered, annoyed.

"Have you ever had sex with a woman?" I answered honestly that I hadn't. He nodded knowingly.

I was angry as hell, but answered each question respectfully. In the end, he must have decided I was worth saving. "All you need is a good screw with a talented hooker," he said, punching his index finger at my face. And I thought he was a Christian. When he led me off to the holding cell, his hand on my shoulder, he seemed proud to have saved another homosexual from a wayward life. I saw him beaming when he called in his next sinner for fingerprinting, mug shots, and conversion therapy.

I felt like a pariah, the lowest of the low; all because the institutions of my country—law, religion, and family—had branded me a criminal, a sinner, and an outcast. I had been jailed. I could be expelled from my church and thrown out of my house. In its simplest form, this systematic discrimination against a class of people was (and still is) oppression. It would be another four years before the American Psychiatric Association removed homosexuality as a mental illness from its manuals in 1973. Until that time, we were both criminals *and* crazy. It would take another thirty years to decriminalize private consensual sex among homosexuals as ordered by the U.S. Supreme Court's *Lawrence vs. Texas* decision.

On December 18, 2010, the same day I wrote this paragraph, the U.S. Senate voted 65-31 to repeal the military's discriminatory "Don't Ask, Don't Tell" policy, seventeen years after it had been enacted. The act, which forbade gays and lesbians from serving openly in the armed services, had resulted in the purging of over 13,000 qualified soldiers from military ranks, many of them "outed" in witch hunt fashion. Oppression is alive and well more than forty years after my incarceration in Buffalo, when all I was doing was looking for love.

I still harbor resentment for the close-mindedness of the "mug-shot man" the night of my arrest. If I could face him now, I would explain oppression to him. Each time I hear that a family has had a gay child of theirs abducted off the street and whisked away to a forced stint in an "ex-gay ministry," I'm angered. Those fraudulent programs purport to "cure" a person of same sex attractions through prayer. There is absolutely no objective evidence that they work, clouded in secrecy as they are. On the contrary, they lead to more self-hatred when participants blame themselves for lack of faith. And each time I hear that another youth has committed suicide due to harassment (like Tyler Clemente of Rutgers University whose video of a gay sexual encounter was broadcast by a roommate via the internet) those bitter feelings are reawakened in me.

Research has consistently shown that three times the number of gay adolescents attempt suicide compared to their straight peers. Why? It's about shame and lack of acceptance. Acceptance is *not* what I got from my jailhouse "counselor" as he locked the door behind me.

My cell's enameled metal shelf was suspended from the wall by heavy, gray chains. The stench of dried urine rose from a misshapen mattress, pockmarked with DNA from the hoards of convicts who had passed through. Overhead, a single incandescent bulb caged in heavy wire glared down at me.

The hours in jail before my arraignment were a restless eternity. By the grace of some compassionate overseer, an assistant to an attorney who specialized in entrapment cases attended court that morning. I later learned he came every Sunday to cherry pick cases from the crop of homosexuals snared from the streets the night before. He explained that his law firm could help if I needed representation. I accepted his offer. The charge was "solicitation for the purpose of committing a lewd or immoral act." After a court date was set, I was released under my own recognizance.

"You're lucky they didn't toss your ass back in the slammer where the inmates could teach you a lesson."

The attorney's assistant drove me to his boss's home where the elderly man greeted me in his foyer, his wife at his side. They offered me breakfast, but the vomit demon was eager to mess with me. When I broke down in tears at their table, the wife offered me comfort instead. The attorney excused himself, leaving me in her capable hands. She must have consoled many a gay man on Sunday mornings, not as work but as love. I had a good cry before her husband returned to do business. I needed that.

They both discouraged the self-loathing that frothed from my mouth, proving to be the perfect pair to give me assurance, to rekindle my self-respect. They asked about my family, my accomplishments, and my future. They promised that the problem would pass, and I could move on with my life. Although I wanted to believe them, I knew I was a long way from forgiving myself. I'd been shot down by the system for trying my gay wings the only way I knew how.

The next day I packed up my shame with my belongings and drove home to Rochester. When I returned for the trial two months later, I pled guilty to the charges. The sentence was suspended, but the punishment I meted out to myself was a lot worse. I resolved to eliminate the sordid desires that had lured me into the police sting. My homosexuality would have to be scuttled so deep that even space-age sonar wouldn't detect its presence. I had no other choice.

For years, each time I thought of that incarceration, a pain gripped my heart, undoubtedly psychosomatic, but real to me. To exorcise the guilt, I would groan sorrowfully, signifying my unworthiness, and condemn myself with the harsh Catholic prayer of penance: *"Mea culpa, mea culpa, mea maxima culpa."* (Through my fault, through my fault, through my most grievous fault.) But God was all but dead for me by then. My subtext for the prayer was more denigrating: "I'm a shit. I'm a shit. I'm a worthless piece of shit."

My arrest was almost a month to the day before the Stonewall Riots began in New York's Greenwich Village on June 28, 1969. When police raided a Mafia-controlled gay bar called the Stonewall Inn and roughed up its customers, their abuse sparked several evenings of protests. The riots, during which "girly" drag queens were the fiercest fighters confronting the police, are now recognized as the beginning of the gay civil rights movement. I don't recall hearing or reading about the uprising back then. In fact, when those gay pioneers were celebrating their true identities for the first time in New York, I was about to bury mine.

Back home in Rochester an invitation to my cousin's wedding was waiting for me. While at the church ceremony, I imagined myself at the altar pledging love to a cherished soul mate. The idea made sense. Sex with a woman was not as natural as my feelings for a man, but I *could* achieve arousal. Life doesn't always give you what you want. Although nothing was as exhilarating as a man's touch, perhaps I could actually have intercourse with a woman. And over time, my attraction to men might fade. I prayed, without really believing it could happen, to have my affinity for everything male removed, mindful that wishing for this was like flogging a dead horse.

I never got an answer. Nevertheless, I donned a heterosexual mask and came out as the most eligible bachelor in town. For the next twenty years, I worked hard to change my spots. Interestingly, within weeks I had met my future wife. One month into the relationship, we had intercourse and all my parts worked. We got engaged within two months.

> Journal Entry—July 20, 1992
>
> *Quit smoking five days ago. I was having brunch with a gorgeous man—nice body, great smile. While I gazed at him with love in my eyes, he said, "Are those cigarettes in your pocket?" "Yes," I answered, wondering what his point would be. "No one will kiss you if you taste like an ashtray," he said. Right between the eyes! Threw the pack out on the way home. Anyway, it didn't make any sense to be smoking when I'd stopped drinking four months ago.*

Begrudgingly, I wondered if the police photographer's advice about one good screw had been on target. Without a doubt, my sexual orientation was more complex than that, but I saw value in limiting my choices to black or white rather than allowing shades of grey. I should have known I'd never be able to turn off my attraction to men. However, even if I had known, I suspect my actions wouldn't have changed. My insistence on living as a straight man was a force that wouldn't be overridden.

On the other hand, ignoring natural instincts carries its consequences. In the years to come, movement against the tide of my tendencies would contribute to a slew of nondescript illnesses—low energy, dizziness, diarrhea, shortness of breath. I lost fifteen pounds during the year of our engagement. A chronic, low-grade depression soaked my mood in sourness. I drank to excess every night of our courtship; alcohol and marijuana became my prescription drugs. I was unsure of my direction, but I was going to the chapel come hell or high water.

At the same time, I was elated about the prospect of marriage. My fiancée and I joked that if we didn't marry soon, the drinking would cause permanent liver damage. My future wife was a beautiful, intelligent, sensitive woman. We had many interests in common, not the least of which was our connection to the deaf community. Her parents were deaf, we were both sign language interpreters, and I was teaching English to college-age deaf students at the National Technical Institute for the Deaf at Rochester Institute of Technology. I worked there for three years before being lured to an administrative position at Gallaudet University's newly established Model Secondary School for the Deaf when I was twenty-six years old.

We were sincerely in love. Family and friends believed that our union was predestined, planned in the heavens. No reason to think otherwise! Thus my attraction to men was forced underground. Love, marriage, career, and family came sharply into focus. However, that didn't stop the subliminal disharmony from nipping at my heels. It was intensified, not palliated, by alcohol. The attraction to men and my evil sidekick, the vomit-master, failed to be placated until I found my way.

I had nothing to eat the morning of our wedding. But just as the organ music announced my bride's arrival at the rear of the church, my social anxiety kicked in and I had to escape through the sacristy door to puke into the nearby shrubs. And during my first year of teaching, I had lunched with a friend one day at noon. While walking to my class afterward, I was bushwhacked by nausea and sidetracked into the nearest restroom where I lost enough salad to stop the obsession.

I threw up many other times or came very close. And even though I might not have an attack for sometimes years at a stretch, I was always cognizant of that possibility, always wary of new situations. These matters consumed my psychic energy, and years passed before I understood that, with help, there was a way out of the madness. It took me even longer to understand its underlying causes.

My daughter Renee Suzanne was born in May of 1973 and Kurt Michael arrived in February of 1978. What joy! Never a burden. Newborns, preschools, and science projects certainly do take one's mind off things. Blessed with remarkable hearts and talents, my children have always been a pleasure to parent.

Two stories come to mind that I am always tickled to tell.

Renee learned to communicate with us in sign language before she could talk. Because her maternal grandparents were deaf, her mom and I signed and talked simultaneously to Renee from the time she was an infant. She was "saying" words like milk, dog, tree, Daddy, and cookie with her hands months before the average child is ready to speak. This undoubtedly gave her an advantage in language development. I laugh when I recall a conversation with her one day when we came in from a snowstorm. She was almost three.

"Let's take off your coat. How do you say 'coat' with your hands?" I asked.

"I don't want to," she replied firmly.

"Why not, honey?"

"I don't do that anymore!" she said with finality.

In her way, she was telling me she had worked enough on sign language and was going to focus on her speech. Clear and to the point. At age thirty-seven, Renee still uses her American Sign Language skills as a doctoral level physical therapist and yoga teacher when she encounters a deaf person.

Kurt has always been the entertainer, whether in a casual conversation or on stage these days at West Hollywood's Whiskey A Go Go on drums and back-up vocals. Music makes him shine. At the repast at my sister Joan's house following my dad's funeral in 1984, six-year-old Kurt delighted his relatives with dance renditions of Michael Jackson songs.

He was the hit of the event as he Moonwalked across the grass beside the pool to boom-box music in his "Beat It" jacket and white spangled gloves. Kurt gets high marks for persistence. He's been playing drums since he was eleven, and now at thirty-two, he's living the music dream in L.A. with bands such as Cipes and the People, Static Pulse, and Faded Paper Figure. He's never been more comfortable.

The spring after Kurt was born I was promoted to a dean's position at the university. I was working full time and taking doctoral coursework at night. I also appeared as Christ in *Jesus Christ Superstar* that May in the first full production of a musical performed in American Sign Language. To deaden the stress, I was habitually drinking half a fifth of scotch before retiring. I remember telling a fellow student there wasn't enough booze in the world to make me sleep through the night. I was hung over each morning, queasy at noon, and then antsy until my first drink at night.

One morning when I reached for the soap in the shower, I lost my balance and had to grab the wall to steady myself. It was like the platform on which I was standing had been shaken. Vertigo. I envisioned myself collapsing at work. *What would I do if that happened?* I tried to push it out of my mind but couldn't. That was the first of many spells. I learned to wait out each attack, to pretend nothing was happening. No one knew but me. Another fox under my cloak.

I was a prisoner of my own devices, pushing through each day and keeping on the move to outpace the anxiety. Each night after dinner, I silenced my unruly emotions with liquor. Ironically, I managed to finish my doctorate on schedule and my dissertation was awarded with "distinction" for its excellence.

As the dean of Kendall Demonstration Elementary School, I also set in motion an administrative plan that brought significant improvements to the programs I was managing in my division of the university. In 1983, we developed a comprehensive Computer Managed Education System that networked early versions of Apple and IBM PCs sharing the same software—a project years ahead of its time. School accreditation was achieved from two national bodies, and comprehensive curricula were developed in the major subject areas.

But a greater irony permeated my success. In spite of all my achievements and recognition—especially given all the personal obstacles I faced—I gave myself no credit. These accomplishments did little to deter my self-loathing.

Dream—November 6, 1992

I'm in a smoke-filled room with my partner or, perhaps, an extension of me. We're there to seek approval from the "middle America types" in their fifties. I'm nervous about them discovering the guy is my lover, but I feel the need to let it be known.

My Uncle Vin enters wearing a priest's collar and eyeglasses like the ones I now wear. He doesn't speak, but I can read his thoughts. He asks the purpose of our request.

In the mid 1980s, my marriage began to falter. My wife and I had grown apart. Our separate struggles to achieve peace and independence as adults had been pulling us in opposite directions over a long time. In some ways, we took even better care of each other during our final years together, in spite of arguments over the future. We worked hard to give our children a good life in spite of our differences. We weren't perfect, but we did our best to support each other. I remain grateful for all the love and caring she gave me.

One summer, when she was out of town, I took Renee, then age eleven, and Kurt, who was six, on a short vacation to the Eastern Shore of Maryland. As I approached the four-mile Chesapeake Bay Bridge, a sense of dread rolled over me when I realized I couldn't turn back. I was consumed with thoughts that the bridge would collapse, or that I'd lose control behind the wheel and plummet into the bay far below. I yelled at the kids to be quiet. As sweat beaded on my brow and adrenaline pulsed through my arteries, I fixed my eyes on the roadway, white knuckling it across, nothing but sheer determination keeping my foot on the accelerator.

Two days later, we crossed the seventeen-mile Bay Bridge Tunnel that links the Eastern Shore of Virginia with the Hampton Roads area. When we entered the tunnel under the bay, another attack struck. I envisioned the ceramic walls caving in on us like in some disaster movie. Once again, I felt trapped with no way of escape, powerless to resist the irrational fears. When we emerged from the tunnel and drove off the last section of the bridge, I breathed an uncomfortable sigh of relief. I had to add bridges and tunnels to my list of phobias, creating more restrictions on my mobility, more fears to address, and yet another fox under the cloak.

A phobia of flying joined the list about the same time. Because my position required domestic and international travel, I added a new fix to my list of remedies. Before boarding, I'd down several drinks. Two more on the plane would deaden my nerves for the duration of a flight. I arrived late to the airport once and didn't have time to stop at the bar. As the plane lifted off, I was choking the armrests and digging my toes into the floor. I vowed never to board a plane sober again and began carrying a pint of vodka with me on my travels. I'd slip into a restroom stall before my flight was called and drink straight from the bottle. In my shirt pocket, I carried another few ounces in a cough syrup bottle that I could drink at my seat in an emergency. I have chugged vodka in the bathrooms of the most elegant airports of the world. Not a pleasant memory, but that's how I coped with my overwhelming fears.

"A paragon of depravity."

I was taught that people who drank from a bottle were disgusting, unshaven derelicts—men who slept on grates, psychotics who fed at the soup kitchens. Yet, there I was, just as debased. This is what I'd become.

Then came the Saturday when all forward movement ceased, my life in ruin. While at home alone with the children, I sat motionless in our orange, crushed-velvet rocker, a crippling despair descending over me. With cartoon voices barely audible, I was sinking lower.

I tried to rally. To resist the clutches of the terror, I went on the offensive. Even though I had no specific plan, I packed the kids in the car and drove toward Washington, D.C. Less than a mile down the road, I could go no farther. I was close to "losing it." Clearly, I didn't have the will to continue. And I had to protect my children.

I turned the car around and returned to my cage in the family room chair. I remained in there the rest of the day, on the edge of insanity. It was hard to imagine my life getting any worse, so I capitulated and called a doctor for an appointment.

7

ACHING TO LEARN

A psychiatrist in private practice became my first therapist. We discussed my marriage, depression, work, anxiety, and phobias, but not my attraction to men nor my drinking. He suspected sexuality as an issue. In one session, he talked about having had dinner at a gay restaurant in town. He described the setting as natural and comfortable for the clientele there. I knew what he was doing—fishing for information. But I wasn't biting. The topic threatened me. I chose denial as a safe harbor and stayed in port.

I knew if I admitted an attraction to men, he'd ask if I had told my wife. An outrageous scandal would ensue, and my name would be smeared to the west coast and back on the deaf "grapevine." Ultimately, I feared divorce. So I stared casually back at him as if his comment had no relevance to me at all. We moved on. The heat on my attraction to men was lowered once again and simmered before eventually coming to a boil. However, I did experience a number of dramatic changes as a result of our work together.

His diagnosis was dysthymia, a moderate but chronic depression. He prescribed medication as an adjunct to psychotherapy. The idea of a pill fixing my problem excited me. When I took 150 mg of Sinequan a day, I liked the immediate results. The drug alleviated the anxiety and stimulated my appetite. For the first time in fifteen years, I began eating at times and in places that used to be precarious. Within weeks, my fear of vomiting vanished, and eating restaurant meals without alcohol became routine. I no longer feared day trips as I had for years and stopped being reclusive. After being freed from the fear of vomiting, I felt a new burst of energy that launched the most creative period in my personal and professional life.

My wife and I discussed taking time apart. It had taken us five years to arrive at that point; it took several more to decide to split. Neither of us dared to mention the word "separation"; to speak it was to give it life, we believed. Because we cared about each other, we felt reluctant to end our marriage, but knew it was holding us both back.

Although my fear of vomiting had ceased, the panic attacks continued. Bridges, tunnels, elevators, tall buildings, and airplanes still threatened my well-being. I wrestled with panic in closed spaces: with a passenger in my car, in meetings with my boss, at special events. But one thing didn't change. I continued to drink, even while on medication. In fact, it allowed me to consume more alcohol and not be as affected by it.

After a therapeutic relationship that lasted three years, my psychiatrist took steps to reduce the size of his practice. This change came at an opportune time. I had gotten into a rut talking about the same things month after month while remaining in denial about my attraction to men and my drinking. My doctor was probably glad to turn me loose.

While driving to the first session with my next psychiatrist,

I practiced how I'd explain my desire for men—something I'd never discussed with another person in my 40 years. For most of the hour, I rambled about my failing marriage and the stress of my career, and I was sure to get a prescription for my medication. But I couldn't decide how to slip my bombshell into the dialogue. "I'm gay?" Not that simple. "I've got a thing for men?" He'd laugh at me. I'm sweating. And time's running out. Near the end of the hour, Dr. Hirschfield began to close out the session.

"Well, it's been a pleasure meeting you, and I look forward to our work together. Shall we get together at the same time next week?"

Now I'm petrified.

"Uh, sure, that's good and . . ."

He interrupted, took back the floor. "I'll send you an invoice for today." It was hovering in my throat. I had to get it out!

"There's one other . . . thing." Did that ever sound dumb!

"Yes, what's that?"

"I'M BISEXUAL!" Louder than thunder. Mortifying. Like Ellen DeGeneres coming out over the loudspeaker on TV.

"I see," he responded in a neutral tone.

"Sorry I saved this 'til the last minute. I've never said those words to anyone before." Now I'm totally embarrassed.

"I see. I'm not gay, but I have a cousin who is, and that doesn't seem to be a problem for him. We'll pick this up next time," he added.

Big sigh of relief for me. I left twenty pounds lighter.

Dream—February 1, 1993

I've discovered a narrow opening in a corner of our attic that leads to a dark cubbyhole with an unstable floor. The room is my place to hide, a secret apartment, reminiscent of The Diary of Anne Frank. I can't be seen entering.

Like other guys who have attempted to bury an attraction to men, I got lost in a "no man's land" between the gay and straight territories. On the one hand, living as a heterosexual hadn't worked because my desire for men was constant and powerful. I realized that forty years of suppressing what had always felt natural had been harmful, and I knew my attraction to men was fixed and unalterable. Even many conservative Christian leaders now agree that sexual attractions can't be changed. On the other hand, labeling myself gay was still inconceivable.

Bisexuality became a brief stop along the way for me, a holding pattern, or more precisely, a transition state.

Admittedly, it had always been a handsome guy on the street grabbing my attention, not a shapely female. Women would notice me and I'd see them checking me out, but I felt nothing. As a teenager, I noticed the size and shape of a girl's breasts ("Did you see the jugs on that babe?" as I was taught), but nothing moved behind my zipper. All my wet dreams centered on men. They provided my erotic fuel.

"Mike, boy. You're tripping yourself up here. If you can do one thing but you don't, you're making a choice. Why not do the right thing?"

In truth, I had to *work* at making love to a woman. That is the salient point. My erections had more to do with friction than fantasy. Two bodies rubbed together can produce arousal, even in the absence of desire or intent. One understands why a woman yields to a rapist—to stay alive. She's not being complicit; she's being pragmatic. Men attracted to other men sometimes choose to couple with women. This may not be what they desire or what feels natural, but it's what society expects.

It was that way for me, anyway.

And yet, I cared deeply for the women in my life, which allowed me to override my attraction to men for so many years. I learned how to love from these women—particularly my wife. We took care of each other during our seventeen years together. Our uncomfortable breakup was hard on everyone.

Following our marital separation, my therapist asked me to decide what I wanted for myself. I said I wanted to remarry, but my brainwashed head was talking. (I still had not made the connection.) So he helped me re-enter the dating scene after almost two decades on ice. My heart resisted, yet I still withheld information from my therapist about my ambivalence. Meanwhile, I had begun to seek out men. I started at a straight club on a Saturday evening, oiled my gears with a few cocktails, and ended up cruising for men across town.

Then I had an experience that resolved my forty-year identity struggle.

At last call, I met a tipsy young woman in a D.C. dance club. She called twice to set up a date for the following weekend. I accepted . . . with reservation. After dinner Sunday, we went to watch a Redskins football game at her place. She stared at me tenderly on the couch, an invitation to romance. My move. I felt obligated to give her what she wanted, which is what I always did. I leaned toward her, fully aware I was acting the role of the eligible bachelor. But at the moment our tongues touched, it finally registered.

I kissed her because I was *supposed* to, not because I *wanted to*.

Kissing generated no charge, not like the fire, the thrill, I felt from kissing a man. This kiss was forced. I pulled away. A thought followed: *Of course. Of course! This isn't me. This isn't what I want.*

I finally resolved the confusion I felt at age fifteen. At my next therapy session, I announced I wanted to find a man.

> Dream—May 10, 1993
>
> *Moving to a new house with my wife and kids. I'm padlocking the back of a U-Haul when three teenagers accost my son and me. A scuffle ensues. I subdue the leader.*
>
> *In a strange apartment. My children watch me rummage through a drawer. My wife is organizing clothes in a fold-up closet seven feet tall and just as wide. Inside is another closet with mirrors on the doors. I can't find what I need. She says the things I want are in the closet.*
>
> *The door to the room bursts open. Men rush in with weapons. They say they won't harm us, but I don't believe them. As proof, one of them puts down a knife he held at my throat. A gun goes off while I fight with one of them. Kurt and I escape with the men in pursuit. We jump over cars and dodge traffic with them at our heels. A flurry of bullets whizzes over our heads. Each time they have us cornered, we manage to escape.*
>
> *As I write this, I want to cry.*

Two weeks later, I was standing outside a D.C. gay club. I had approached the entrance several times, but retreated to the parking lot. Where was the courage to step out of the closet? Would I be recognized? Just then, a handsome man nodded toward me as he exited the club. My attraction meter crackled like a Geiger counter. I followed him up the street.

When he stopped to light a cigarette, I approached him for a conversation. I paused and thought about my night in the Buffalo jail. Deja vu. How could I avoid being hauled away in a paddy wagon?

I asked if he was a cop. He said no. I asked if he was gay and he chuckled. "New at this?" he asked. We both laughed. My status as "fresh meat" seemed to excite him. We exchanged phone numbers and the following week, he introduced me to gay nightlife. I spent the first rapturous night in bed beside him staring at the ceiling until dawn. Who could sleep?

I was afraid of being "outed" at work, so I insisted my new friend and I travel to gay bars in Baltimore. The first time I stepped onto the dance floor at the Club Hippo was as nerve-wracking as my doctoral defense. He uncapped a small glass vial, sucked amyl nitrate vapors up his nose, and flailed away to the music of Donna Summers. I had a lot to learn about gay culture—totally different than playing "doctor" in the Boy Scout tents. No (and I mean absolutely no) going back to talking about pussy the next day. At the age of forty-one, I was inching my way out of the closet.

I met my first live-in gay lover at a Washington club in the winter of 1988. Joe was standing under a spotlight on the edge of the dance floor, a tall, dark chap with a rugged Mediterranean look. He seduced me with his eyes, inviting me thither. I stared back; entrancing him like a cat does a sparrow through a window. Then I winked as I lowered my head, locked his eyes in my gaze, and moved toward him. He coyly turned away, self-conscious from the attention. When I asked him to dance, he waved me off with a laugh and a shake of the back of his hand. I kept up the pressure until he agreed to just one.

My dance moves impressed him. We laughed and traded drinks before ending up at my house for the night. I was taken by his looks, his youthfulness, and his sense of humor. We shared the same birthday, though he was twelve years my junior. We were infatuated from the start and began dating seriously three weeks later. By the end of the second month, I was in love, thinking I'd finally gotten it right. After several months, he moved in with my son and me, a mistake I later regretted. His charm and our mutual attraction blinded me to the problems we began to encounter, largely because I was drinking as much as ever, and he could match me drink for drink.

In fact, our relationship had already begun to unravel before he moved in. He was overly suspicious and obsessed that I was being unfaithful to him, even though he knew where I was at all times. He, on the other hand, often disappeared for days without explanation. I shouldn't have accepted that from him. Anger built and my anxiety intensified. Panic attacks were occurring everywhere—at home, in the car, at baseball games, and at the movies when the lights went down.

I took steps to end this relationship several times but kept relenting. My neighbors must have been amused to see him load his car each week, only to return with his belongings a few days later. I knew our relationship was unhealthy; my friend Elaine made that clear. But I was determined to make it work, because it had taken me so long to come out of the closet. I chose not to give up, no matter how mismatched we were, even if one of us got hurt. Besides, admitting failure would reflect negatively on my decision to live as a gay man . . . or so I thought.

That changed when we had a fierce argument while driving home from clubbing one night. We were exchanging verbal threats when he struck me on the right shoulder. I cuffed him with the back of my right hand. The works from the watch I'd won from the Optimists when I was fifteen flew out the window, leaving only the band and the crystal on my wrist. I was furious at him for goading me into the argument. He continued to press me as we entered the house. That's when I lost control. *He had destroyed my favorite possession.*

He shoved me across the room, and I lost awareness for several seconds. When my mind reconnected with my actions, I looked down to see my strong hands locked around his neck. *I was choking him on the kitchen floor.* Although he was taller and heavier, I was shaking him like a doll, squeezing the life out of him. His red cheeks and bulging childlike eyes screamed at me to stop. I was jolted out of my recklessness, released him from my grasp, and dropped his limp figure the few inches to the floor. Blood vessels in his temples were pulsing rapidly as I collapsed on the floor at his hips.

In that moment, when my primal self seized control, I broke all restraints and bared my yellow teeth. My nostrils flared as I panted like a quarter horse at the finish line. My eyes refocused on this trembling, twisted figure beside me. He sobbed spasmodically, trying to catch his breath. While glaring at me with the pouting eyes of a three year old, he whined, "Why did you hurted me so bad?" He had regressed to a previous and traumatic time and place.

To what end were we brought together to play out these vicious roles? Why was I cast as the abuser and he the victim? What were we to learn?

It all made me sick. I felt reprehensible and responsible for letting things get out of hand. In my whole life, I'd never intentionally caused physical harm to another person. The lesson I learned that evening would stay with me forever: the potential for violence lives in all of us. If we're not vigilant, it will have its expression.

Our relationship ended two months after that. It had been inflamed by alcohol, devoured by neediness, and destroyed by insecurities. Although he promised to settle the credit card debt he had amassed under my signature, he never did. I had to pay off several thousand dollars in charges I'd never incurred—a tough lesson.

I was miserable following the separation, desperate to find someone to replace the man I'd just lost. I placed personal ads in gay publications and, every weekend, met men for coffee or dinner. But I never found what I was looking for. I went to gay clubs every chance I got, always on the lookout for that one special person. Alone at home, I walked aimlessly from one room to another, looking for something but never knowing what. My friend Elaine said I was in search of myself.

A few weeks after our relationship ended, someone wrote an anonymous letter to my boss, Dr. Robert Davila, a vice president at Gallaudet University. At the time, I was dean of Curriculum and Instruction in the Pre-College Division.

Letter—August 31, 1987

Dr. Robert Davila
Vice President
Pre-College Programs
Gallaudet University

Dear Dr. Davila:

This letter is written out of grave concerns over management practices observed from the Pre-College Office. Of greatest concern is the influence and power you've given Dean Deninger and his misuse of that power. Facts have been grossly misrepresented in multitudes of situations. However, it is clear that you "buy into" whatever is fed your way from Mike without getting to the truth. This creates problems for those of us who believe that you can be fair and objective. We have no voice.

Now that Mike's homosexuality has surfaced openly, the problems are complicated further because of the powerful gay network on this campus. Mike cannot be trusted. He changes his story to favorably impress the power structure on his behalf. At some point, you will be one of his victims.

Wake up! The "real picture" is there, Dr. Davila, if you would only open your eyes to the truth. It is regrettable that we cannot talk with you without reprisal.

Best wishes for a good year.

cc: President Jerry C. Lee

My boss sent his assistant, Fran Parrotta, to personally deliver a copy of this letter to me. She poked her head into my office and said, "Mike, Dr. Davila will want to discuss this with you later." She handed it to me but stood watching at the door, her eyes trained on me for a reaction. On the outside I was unruffled, showing no visible reaction; inside I was crumbling. Dr. Davila often used Fran as his emissary, because she was astute in reading people and situations. Not only that, she was also an extension of him. What you said to her went directly back to him—word for word. This may have been a tactic on his part to gather more information, or he may have been allowing me time to prepare for a discussion with him later that day. As Fran and I talked about the letter, I chose my words cautiously, keeping my comments vague and indifferent. Shocked, I needed time to think.

It was illegal to discriminate against employees in the District of Columbia based on sexual orientation, but I had to be strategic. I was certain I had done nothing to discredit the university. On the contrary, I had an impressive record as an administrator who showed integrity and fairness. Nevertheless, my worst nightmare had come to pass. Because of the anonymous nature of the letter, I could never confront my accuser—not that I wanted to. I wasn't ready.

When we met, Dr. Davila knew not to ask if I was gay.

"What do you make of the letter?" he asked—a shrewd approach, non-probing, discreet, and casual. I tried to brush off the seriousness of the matter, though I knew the stakes were high.

"Since my wife and I separated, people have had me coupled with everyone under the sun. None of those stories are true," I said.

I didn't deny being gay; neither did I acknowledge it. We were both experienced enough to avoid the $64,000 question. I held my breath for his next query.

"Who do you think wrote it?" he asked. I didn't care to speculate about the creep's identity and said, "I have no idea. It could be a lot of people." Frankly, I was too busy with damage control to be playing a guessing game. He pressed me to guess, perhaps someone settling a grudge or a malcontent passed over for a promotion. He called names and studied my reactions. He got none.

Dr. Davila knew I was gay, and he knew any straight man would have vehemently denied the accusation. I had done nothing wrong, but I was not going to be hung like a politician for lying to the grand jury about a lesser crime. My defense was a weak offense. I was sure my tactics had tipped the hand I'd been playing so close to the chest. And I was okay with that.

He said it was university policy never to respond to anonymous letters and assured me he wouldn't pursue the matter. When our meeting concluded, he handed me his original copy of the letter. I saved it as an example of how homophobia can be wielded as a vicious weapon. One has to credit the university leaders with the sensitivity they showed me as a gay administrator. Dr. Davila must have discussed the matter with the president. Their response gave me a righteous vote of confidence, and this issue was never raised again.

Two years later, following a historic student uprising on the college campus in 1988, Dr. I. King Jordan was chosen president of Gallaudet. Several months later, Dr. Davila accepted a position as Assistant Secretary for Special Education and Rehabilitation Services with the U.S. Department of Education. I was promoted to chief of our division without having to compete for the position. As Dean of Pre-College Programs, I then held what many considered the most prestigious position in elementary and secondary education of the deaf, perhaps in the world.

Sure, foot-dragging to appoint me occurred on the part of the new president, but I had no indication his delay was related to my being gay. And if concerns had been expressed, they were trumped by my promotion. Still, I was unhappy.

8

MISSING PIECES

After living four and a half decades with what I thought was a complete set of memories, I had no reason to think anything was missing. But three weeks before my forty-sixth birthday, things began to shift. Events that had been foreshadowed in my dreams were dropping into place like lost pieces to a puzzle.

I began to remember times when I was sexually abused by my father.

"Hold on now. You're not even sure any of this really happened!"

My mordant friend was not about to let this one get by. He loved preying on my initial uncertainty about what I remembered. He went on to argue for less graphic descriptions of the events and against using terms such as "incest" or "pedophilia." My internal oppressor was pressuring me to soft-pedal the gravity of the maltreatment. I was naturally reluctant to believe that my father could have done what I recalled. *And* I was afraid people would not believe what I had to tell them. But using less offensive descriptors about the times I was raped would not alter reality.

The memories returned piecemeal over the next two years. Fragments reentered my consciousness—on their own schedule and in their own fashion.

During this period, I lost my balance, my integrity, my sanity, and my ability to confidently express who I was in the world. My voice was silenced. To get it back, I would have to speak the unspeakable—that is, talk frankly about events that would certainly make others uncomfortable. And I would have to confront whatever criticism I might get in return. I worried that my descriptions of the manner in which the memories actually returned would be ridiculed by doubting readers or judged inadequate by literary critics. Rejection from family and friends would be even more devastating.

An artist friend gave me helpful advice about my writing. Jon, who had AIDS, had been close to death the previous winter before starting a three-drug cocktail that greatly improved his chances of survival. After a strong recovery, he was looking at life very differently. He was wiser, and I liked what he'd become. He could speak the truth with greater clarity and self-assurance. He told me his illness had helped him "cut through a lot of crap."

Jon compared *his* need to face the reality of his disease with my need to face the abuse in my past. He said, "That shit has you by the balls anyway, so you might as well just take the phone off the hook, turn on some music, and begin writing." And that's what I did.

While I was writing about the first memory, several tears dropped to the keyboard, marking the opening of the floodgates. I felt no pleasure in calling up these events for reexamination, just a realization that this was work I had to do.

When I attempted to write about the incest, the depression worsened. Sleeplessness returned, and hopelessness descended like a pall over my apartment. I was at a standstill. The gains I'd made in the four years since I had recalled the memory of being choked by my father were pushed aside. In a real sense, I was back at the beginning. For weeks I dreaded rising from my bed. I was crying without warning and for no apparent reason.

That pushed me to go back into therapy where I talked with ease about all facets of my life—except that one. As soon as I told Ned I was putting off writing about the abuse, I immediately began to cry. Not hard to figure out what was troubling me. I had resisted the truth about my father from the time the first memory materialized. I doubted the accuracy of each memory in turn until I was forced to capitulate in the face of overwhelming evidence.

I'd been in therapy on and off for three years before the first memory surfaced. During that time, I was never led to believe that I might have been sexually abused by my dad or anyone else. Neither had I ever read anything about recovered memories before the first one appeared. I was soon to learn a lot about the effects of trauma and the mind's ability to shelter us from overwhelming tragedies.

In March of 1993, I celebrated one year of sobriety at my AA home group. The first year had been good. After resigning my stressful position as Dean of Pre-College Programs in June, 1992, I was reassigned to a research and teaching position much more compatible with my temperament. Before the reassignment, I had come out of the closet at work and experienced no serious ill effects from that decision.

My most embarrassing secrets—alcoholism and my sexual orientation—had been disclosed to co-workers, family, and friends. I had begun work on a graduate degree in Mental Health Counseling and was anticipating a new career in that field. Although at times I was still unhappy, the anxiety that had crippled me for years had quieted to a murmur. It had subsided several weeks after I got sober, evidence that my problems had, to some extent, been alcohol induced. After giving up booze, I also stopped smoking cigarettes four months later, and I was no longer taking antidepressant medication.

Right after my first AA anniversary, I noticed a significant change. Anxiety returned—not the same fear of vomiting like before, but I did lose my appetite and start to skip meals. I lost weight and had to take corrective measures to put it back on. I had no full-blown panic attacks, but I sometimes got "the jitters" in my hands and feet. I ceased writing in my journals and lost interest in the things that normally gave me pleasure, like going to the gym. When I began having a hard time sleeping, my positive outlook faltered.

Even when exhausted, I frequently woke up at two in the morning and was up the rest of the night. I moved from bed to couch and back again, searching for a place I could doze off. I was crying without reason at work, in the car, or while watching TV, particularly if I saw a parent showing affection to a child. In therapy, I was distraught week after week and discussed taking antidepressant medication again.

A few close friends gave me great support, especially Carlene Thumann-Prezioso. She listened to me express my hopelessness and reassured me while I cried at work. *It was discouraging to be that upset after having made so many positive changes in my life.* Week after week, I talked about how bad I felt in therapy, not knowing why, begging my therapist for a solution. He didn't have one to give me.

Journal Entry—April 13, 1993

No sleep. Appetite is gone. Can't concentrate. Now I know the reason. My father sexually abused me on a fishing trip to The Thousand Islands when I was about eight. I'm a mess. Thank God for Carlene. She sits with me while I cry at my desk. This all fell into place this week.

Dad has been haunting me for months. I arrived at therapy a bundle of nerves after crying all the way to the appointment. I told Ned I was afraid; that I didn't want to be there. He suggested we work in the relaxed state, something I've done before.

I reclined on the couch, closed my eyes, and deepened my breathing. Right away, I felt something shift inside. I started to squirm with pain as a visual memory played like an eight-millimeter movie in my mind's eye.

It was familiar but new at the same time. I saw something that happened forty years ago at Humphrey's Harbor. I was looking down from the ceiling of the whitewashed cottage.

My adult body convulsed when it saw my father's hand pull my small head toward his erect penis. The little guy resisted. He was terrified. Ned asked what was going on.

Then the oddest thing happened. I had a sensation of disconnecting. When I responded, I had the voice of a dispassionate observer. My tears stopped. I became a witness instead of a participant and said: "His dad's hand is behind his neck, but his thumb is pressing on his windpipe. He can't breathe. He's forcing him to do what he wants. His dad is speaking softly, but he's mean; words I can't understand. Now it's over. He can see his dad through the curtains at the kitchen table with a beer and a cigarette. He won't sleep tonight."

Suddenly, my awarenes shifted back to the office. I could feel my legs on the couch like I'd been beamed back to the present. No longer the dispassionate observer, I became a participant again.

> *Agony rose inside me. It triggered an overpowering rush of pain, followed by a flood of tears. Sobbing heavily, I asked why my father did that to me. Ned didn't know. No one ever will.*
>
> *When the anguish subsided, Ned asked me to take a breath and return to the room. My tear-swollen eyes fluttered open. While I stared at the ceiling, he asked if I knew what just happened. Of course I did.*

After the session, I wandered aimlessly through a Hallmark shop across the street. I felt like a freak stuck in a parallel universe. Bizarro on steroids, that was me. I felt empty, raw, my emotions purged from the inside out. I had no thoughts, only images of what I had just seen. Eerie white noise buzzed in my head. What I had seen was horrible, devastating. Did I dare believe it?

I had so many questions. My older brother was in an adjacent sleeping area that night. Could the same thing have happened to him? Should I ask him? Could anything like that have happened to my younger gay brother? Where was I to go from there?

That week I sought help by locating a men's group of Survivors of Incest Anonymous (SIA) that met weekly just minutes from my home. Before attending my first meeting, I called my older brother Joe to talk about what I had recalled. I described the session and how upset I was about the discovery. I asked if he could tell me anything about the trip that might shed light on what I had remembered. He didn't answer the question, but chose instead to go on the offensive.

"Are you sure this really happened?" I was revolted by his

question. He didn't believe me. When I protested his insensitivity, he fired back, using language designed to put me in my place.

"I'm not going to buy into this," he said. "It's all in your head." He asked a pointed question with dour authority. "What are you trying to do?" How strange. Was he insinuating that I was masterminding a plot to overthrow the existing family order? I answered simply, "I just want to understand what happened, so I can put this behind me. I thought you might remember something."

"Like I said, I don't think it ever happened."

He was threatened. Did he know something? Were there other secrets that could account for his overreaction? If there were, he was unwilling to tell me.

When I explained the conversation to my younger brother, he told me something I'd never known. When Dan was about the same age I was when I'd been abused at Humphrey's, my father wanted to take him up there, too. Reluctant to give her permission, Mom asked Joe's opinion. His reaction was severe. He was strongly opposed to Dan going away alone with Dad. If he had been that concerned then, he must have had his reasons. Why had he not told me about that?

"Come on. He probably forgot. It doesn't mean he's hiding something."

Joe's rebuke was a slap in the face, but I shouldn't have been surprised. When I came out to him years before, he'd rebuffed me just as harshly. "I don't understand the gay thing, and I don't understand you anymore." Perhaps I shouldn't have expected the fifty-year-old leopard to change his spots. Regrettably, only he could corroborate what happened at Humphrey's, and he'd just slammed the door shut on that discussion.

❧ ❧ ❧

I'd never heard the phrase "blaming the victim" until I went to my first SIA meeting. That concept actually helped me understand reactions from family members when I sought their support.

I also learned that perpetrators are clever. They use manipulation and threats to keep victims under control, or to confuse them into thinking they did something to cause the molestation. They might tell a child that the abuse is punishment for something they'd done wrong, or threaten to harm a family member if anyone is told. These maneuvers tie a sense of guilt to the acts, a shrewd way of preventing a child from reporting an incident.

But often, the first condemnation a survivor hears comes from a family member who doubts the story. Abuse victims may even be accused of having acted seductively. Or sometimes they're blamed for not having done enough to stop the perpetrator. A victim can be peppered with questions: Why were you alone with him? Why didn't you tell him to stop? Why didn't you report it sooner? Why didn't you see it coming?

Most often, they're told they must have been mistaken, that it never really happened the way they thought. They might even be told that the perpetrator would never do such a terrible thing.

Consequently, victims blame themselves unnecessarily for abuse, even though they could have done little to prevent the assault. When family members discount the reports, children then conclude that *they* are somehow at fault, that *they* caused it. Therefore they must be flawed, unworthy, or undeserving. These powerful messages follow them through life.

I saw my brother's rejection as an act of blaming. By

dismissing what I had remembered, he was finding fault with me. I already had doubts. His response could have shaken me, but it made me angry instead. At the same time, I could understand his reluctance to believe what I'd told him. If he did, he would have to accept that his father had molested children—his own children. Denying that possibility, labeling it a fabrication of his brother's imagination, may have been easier than facing that reality.

I found the men at the SIA meeting loving and supportive. They listened without interruption as I told my story, no questions asked. When I cried, they shed parallel tears of their own. They knew exactly what I was going through and all shared some version of my story. Responding with words of encouragement, they loved me the way the attorney and his wife had loved me following my arrest in Buffalo. That's all I wanted from my own family.

I called my mother in April to wish her a happy birthday. We limited our conversation to safe topics—the grandchildren, the weather, my house, my career. Even two years after I'd come out to her, we were still unable to talk comfortably about my life as a gay man. She didn't ask, so I didn't tell. I said nothing about the incest, although I wanted to tell her. I yearned for the mother who could comfort me, who could help me through a difficult time, but our peace was fragile. What if she snubbed me the way my brother had? I wanted to know whether she believed me, but I also wanted to avoid another rejection.

Before ending the call, she said, "I love you now more than ever." She was reaching out, mending fences, trying to rebuild our relationship. That gesture prompted me to invite her to visit her grandchildren in the spring of 1993. Two years had passed since we'd seen each other, and she had to be as uneasy about the visit as I was.

> Letter to Mom—May 12, 1993
>
> *Dear Mom:*
>
> *As I recover, I'm finding that being honest is important. I'm more alive now than I've ever been. I have many friends, but not a special male friend at this time. When it is time, I think I will know.*
>
> *I've been busy lately working on healing the past. I struggle with certain issues, but nothing is so terrible that I can't handle it. The panic attacks I used to have stopped after I quit drinking.*
>
> *These things are difficult for me to say to you. I know you are trying to accept and to understand. I heard you when you told me you loved me now more than ever. It just takes time to heal. I'm a bit fearful of how you might judge me, but I'm looking forward to your visit. Hope all is well with you and the clan up north. See you soon enough.*
>
> *Love,*
> *Michael*

SIA meetings became the main course in my recovery diet that spring. The group helped me deal with the fallout after recovery of the memories. I listened to their stories of incest. Some were complex; all were potent. They discussed the problems they faced—anger, self-loathing, sex addiction, substance abuse, and distrust of anyone who got too close. I learned something important from them—that eloquence is assured when you speak from the heart.

These men became my lifeline back to sanity. Several of them had had active memories of incest inflicted on them by family members or friends. A few had recalled blocked memories the way I had. When they spoke, I listened intently, searching for meaning. I'd have to rekindle my belief in myself and rebuild my self-respect.

My AA sponsor—another model of unconditional love—encouraged me to talk about the memories as often as necessary and for as long as needed until they had run their course. At his urging, I talked about the incest at my home group meeting. Although it was tough getting started, once I did speak out, I received support from my AA friends as well. From them, I learned that newcomers to recovery sometimes re-experience feelings associated with traumatic events after a period of sobriety. It's because emotions that had been deadened for years by alcohol or drugs resurface for resolution.

After I spoke with difficulty at one meeting, my sponsor asked if he could walk me to my car. As we stood under the lights in the tree-lined parking lot, he asked whether my father had hurt me. When I explained about the choking, he gently placed his hand to my cheek and said, "Oh Mike, he could have killed you!" The fact that he understood how I feared for my life moved me. Tears rolled down my cheeks as he let me weep on his shoulder, a safe harbor. By listening to me put my fears into words, he had also given me permission to grieve. Because of him, I learned that giving a survivor of incest permission to talk while one listens is one of the most helpful things a friend or family member can do. We need to hear that we are believed without equivocation. And then we need to be held while we cry.

> Dream—May 24, 1993
>
> *Standing in a San Francisco street with Mom, Dad and my brother Joe. My parents have been arguing and the atmosphere is heavy. Two trams hanging from overhead cables are descending a steep hill toward us. I'm about to get into one with my father and ride up. He's obese and will have a hard time climbing into the car. My brother and my mother offer no assistance, and expect me to do it. I realize it's actually an open coal car, not a tram. Before I step in, I realize something inappropriate or indecent is about to happen in there. I feel unsafe.*

I sobbed when I recorded the dream that morning. All day at work I felt dull, non-communicative, morose, and I hid in my closed-door office. Only Carlene was able to push into my inner circle. I told her the dream up to the point when I was about to step into the coal car with my father. I couldn't go on. I broke down. At my regular therapy appointment that evening, I was nervous and tense.

> Journal Entry—May 27, 1993
>
> *At therapy, I explained the S.F. dream. Ned asked me to recline and breathe deeply. As soon as I relaxed, a new memory was dislodged like a menacing iceberg from the cold and distant past. No question about this one. It lurked right below the surface.*
>
> *In a flash, I "saw" a scene reenacted. Looking down on the action from above and to the side, I witnessed myself as a young boy standing in the dark basement of the house on Brooks Avenue. My back was against the*
>
> (cont'd to page 144)

> Journal Entry—May 27, 1993 (cont'd from page 143)
>
> *left wall of the coal bin. My father was pulling my head in on him, forcing oral sodomy. With my eyes the height of his zipper, I may have been seven or eight years old. I gagged. My mouth was too small for the task.*
>
> *My back arched up off the couch in the therapy room. My chest muscles contracted. I could feel a grimace reconfigure my face as my head jerked to the side. I said nothing about the pain. Ned asked what was going on. An internal switch disabled my emotions. The objective observer emerged again. I calmly described the event in the third person as I had the last time.*
>
> *When I drifted back to the present, I felt sad and defeated, my energy spent—nothing left. I had to pull myself together and go on my way. Where I would go, what I would do?*

This memory was hard to discount, having been foreshadowed by the coal car dream the night before. I still ripple with chills when I recall how the information had been preserved in my mind. The visual images of the day we moved the coal, obviously related to what my father did to me in the coal bin, were cleverly linked to the repressed event. Now I understood why my memories from that day—coal, the basement, my cousin's cut, the blood, and our naked upper bodies—were important. They served as a kind of bookmark or link to the incest.

There, in the sea of my unconscious, a vessel had been waiting for decades to be salvaged, held until conditions were favorable. As I see it, the coal car dream was the charge that blasted the memory loose from its mooring on the seabed.

The relaxation technique calmed the sea and allowed the vessel to rise to consciousness. What an incredible experience, but painful and obscene. For 40 years that part of my history had been submerged, the memories held underwater in suspended animation.

How could I deny what had happened to me after that? Yet, I would continue to have doubts.

Two years later, I read Lenore Terr's *Unchained Memories: True Stories of Traumatic Memories, Lost and Found,* published in 1994. In her book she describes how Sigmund Freud postulated at the turn of the century that some childhood memories can hide emotionally significant events behind what seem to be trivialities. Called "screen memories," they are laid down at about the time of a tragedy and hold prominence in the conscious memory as a connection back to a traumatic experience. It made sense. What happened in the coal bin had been preserved for a later time in that manner. The memory of abuse at Humphrey's Harbor was also aligned with strong, persistent conscious images I had retained about that trip. Hunting for earthworms, an eyeless sea tortoise, minnows in tanks and stale candy were all connected to the incident.

Couple this evidence with my emotional turmoil leading up to the recollection—the sleeplessness, the nausea, the sadness, the irritability—and I had compelling evidence to support the validity of these memories. I wanted this one to be the last. I asked Ned when the memories would stop. His response annoyed me. "When it's time," he said. For several weeks, I continued to deteriorate emotionally, sinking into what would be my second bout with major depression. I didn't want to start antidepressant medication again, but I was losing balance, spinning out of control, and feeling either sad or angry most of the time.

At Safeway one evening, I was standing behind a woman in a "nine items or less" checkout line. I was incensed when I counted twelve items in her cart. A minor transgression, but one that outraged me. *She was not going to take advantage of me.* I considered ways to punish her. I imagined tackling her at the knees outdoors, snickering as she tumbled to the sidewalk. Then I'd plow over her with my shopping cart before callously turning and walking away. I was pleased with that thought. When I jarred myself back from this brutal fantasy, I couldn't believe where I'd been. At home, I was short-tempered. There must have been days when I was unrecognizable to my son—days he must have thought his father was possessed.

I knew from all my training, my instincts, and my experience that taking positive action could help me recover. An accomplished administrator doesn't let problems fester. I couldn't suffer in silence any longer. Secrets were for clandestine societies with something to hide, not someone in recovery.

I decided to be proactive and inform my family of the memories, but the question was *how*. Telephoning everyone was out of the question, because I was unwilling to repeat what happened with my brother. *I needed to be in control this time.* So to prevent miscommunication, I wrote a lengthy letter explaining everything in detail. I thought of calling my mother in advance but decided against it.

Letter to My Family—June 1, 1993

Dear Family:

My stomach is doing flip-flops as I compose this letter. You'll see why. I'm writing to let you know that I was sexually abuse by Dad and the impact of that on my life. I'm sending copies to everyone. I hope you can understand that this was difficult for me.

I was afraid you wouldn't believe me, or that you might criticize me for "doing this to Mom." Victims of incest are sometimes blamed for breaking the silence about abuse in a family. I have a great deal of pain inside, and I've shed many tears as I've recalled these events.

I was unhappy for years, but I kept pushing through. I had anxiety that I blamed on stress and problems with my marriage. I was an alcoholic for twenty-five years but hid that well. Booze was my escape, my anesthetic. I drank to help me sleep. After a while, that didn't work.

In my twenties, I took Valium because I had a fear of vomiting in public. This was one of several phobias that eventually became serious. I couldn't drive over bridges or through tunnels, couldn't fly in planes, and couldn't use glass elevators. Sometimes I had panic attacks just sitting in my boss's office. I started taking antidepressant medication twelve years ago. The medication did bring my appetite back and I was able to eat without the fear of vomiting. I was in my thirties then.

After my divorce, I began to deal with the fact that I was different. Two years later, I told my wife and the kids that I was gay. I thought if I came out of the closet, the anxiety would subside. But the panic attacks continued.

I was drinking, smoking, and taking antidepressants when Dad died. You expect to mourn the death of your father, but my grief was out of proportion to the facts. We were never close. He was cold, unemotional, and unavailable. His next drink was more important to him than his family. He was angry, explosive, and unpredictable. I should have been glad he was gone.

When I saw a movie called When Pigeons Come Home to Die *starring Art Carney, I cried uncontrollably at the father-son connections in the story. That sadness was always with me, just below the surface.*

I stopped drinking and smoking last year. The intense sadness over Dad continued. It didn't make sense. People in recovery sometimes experience feelings that were deadened by the alcohol for years. Then I began to remember unpleasant things.

Now I understand. Dad sexually abused me while we were fishing at Humphrey's Harbor. I was between seven and ten years old. Joe and I were there alone with him. I've always remembered a number of details about the trip, but didn't remember the abuse until now. Late one night, he came into the curtained area where I was sleeping. He stroked my head and urged me to perform oral sodomy on him. I resisted. With his thumb on my windpipe, he stopped my breathing. I stayed awake worrying that he might come back.

I've known for over a year that Dad choked me once, but I couldn't remember when or where. I've remembered one other incident. It happened in the coal bin on Brooks Ave. He forced oral sodomy on me then as well.

You can imagine what this has done to me. I've been unable to think of anything else, and I'm outraged at the son-of-a-bitch. What I already knew he had done was abominable. This was sickening and unconscionable.

I hid from him at night. He would seek me out when he arrived home late. I would "sleep" in strange places to avoid him. One night I hid behind a couch in the living room under the window. I've always had a clear memory of that night. I could hear the floor creaking as he roamed from room to room in search of me, breathing heavily. I'm told I might remember more.

The first memory came back six weeks ago. I talked with Dan and Joe to seek their support. I asked if anything similar had happened to them. Neither one remembered anything. Dan was very supportive. My conversation with Joe did not go well. He said he wasn't going to "buy into this" because he didn't know what happened. He asked if I was imagining it.

The anger and hurt I felt when he wouldn't even talk made me decide to write this as a family letter. That way, the same information will exist in one place. I won't contribute to the silence about Dad anymore—especially when my well-being is at stake. Indeed, that was the major illness in the family. We all sat by while he caused us all a lot of pain, whether it was physical, emotional, or sexual.

The eulogy I gave at his funeral was a crock of shit. I talked about how he was so misunderstood and all that crap. It wasn't a complete lie, but it did honor our silent conspiracy. I understood that was my role. No one had to tell me. Mom asked me to send her the eulogy. I carried it in my briefcase for FIVE YEARS. I didn't know why. I do now. I'm including a copy of those remarks for you.

I'm not asking anyone to respond. You can call, and we can talk if you want. I know some people think these things are better left undisturbed. My experience tells me differently. People go out and drink again or stay in self-destructive patterns because of things like this. I'm not willing to do that.

Sorry for the nature of this news, but I hope this finds you and your families well.

Love,
Michael

I phoned my mother a few days after I sent the letter. When I asked if she had received it, she simply answered "Yes." That was it. I waited for her to say more, but she said nothing. I froze like road kill in her high beams, not sure if she would run me down or swerve and avoid the discussion. Her silence felt like a fresh pile of dog shit steaming somewhere between us. Uncomfortable with the pause and quite embarrassed, I tried again by mentioning how difficult it had been for me to write the letter.

She cut me off with a surprising comment. "He was a beast!" she said. Nothing more. Short. Staccato. I knew that, but I wanted to hear what she thought.

"Do you believe me?" I asked timidly.

"What?" she asked. Short. Staccato.

"Do you believe me?" I repeated, now painfully exposed. If what she said next had been spoken with conviction, I would have felt exonerated. But her tone was disturbingly blasé.

"It could have happened. If that's what you say happened, then I believe you."

What the hell did that mean? I deserved more than that. I didn't want any ifs, ands, or buts! No damn qualifiers—not now. I wanted a definite yes. I wanted comfort. I wanted to hear she was sorry it happened to me. I wanted her to say she would have killed the bastard if she'd known. But she didn't. I guess that's the way it goes in the world of sports and incest. *Shit! She doesn't believe me. What do I say now? What do I do?*

Stunned, I had to strain to hear what she said next. She complained about her life, how Lester had been a disappointment to her, and how she had decided to focus instead on her children. She even said she had stopped having sex with him after Dan was born. Too much information. Now I had to wonder if that had anything to do with his interest in me, age seven at the time. I wasn't about to explore the topic of her sex life with her.

I had called to talk about *me*. Instead, we were discussing how difficult her marriage had been. The strength I had garnered for my heart-to-heart talk disappeared, siphoned off by her disinterest. I can't recall how the conversation ended; I just know that was the only time we talked about the molestations.

Two of my siblings contacted me after receiving the letter. Ann left a message on my answering machine and invited me to call if I wanted to talk. I phoned her from work that afternoon. She and her two daughters talked with me for a long time. My niece Marilyn said flat out she believed everything, no hesitancy, no equivocation. She thought it was an insult to question my word, given my father's reputation as a louse.

Her blunt statement stopped me cold. Unable to speak, I broke down, the phone cradled on my shoulder. *They had given me permission to cry.* The three of them were believers who sent their love and promised their support. They understood the road to recovery.

My letter was slow to reach Dan in San Francisco. We finally connected by phone two weeks later. He listened quietly while I explained the memories and how they had returned. He told me how sorry he was, adding that he was unsure how to help. I told him he already had, simply by believing what I had written. It was then that he told me about the fuss Joe had made when Dad wanted to take my younger brother to The Thousand Islands. He did go on that trip with Dad, but he didn't recall anything unusual. Dad was drunk most of the time, and that certainly wasn't extraordinary. Neither did he remember ever having been sexually abused by our father. But he did have plenty of scars from the physical and emotional abuse inflicted on him.

As the youngest, Dan suffered the most and for the longest. When I left for college, he was only eleven years old. I worried about how he would fare in the house by himself with our parents. Dan and my mother had been close since he was a baby, and that was all Dad needed to dream up a conspiracy. And Mom was going to protect Dan at all costs. My father hinted that their relationship was *unnatural* and blamed my mother for coddling her youngest child. Violence and the threat of it ran more rampant than when I lived at home.

Dan recalled one night when Dad repeatedly punched the wall beside Mom's head in the living room, coming ever closer as she sat unflinching, trying to ignore him. He also remembered a time when he and Mom ran shoeless across Brooks Avenue lawns and hid from him in a neighbor's bushes. Once my father accidentally set his Ford Fairlane on fire in the driveway, and another time he lost all his teeth on the steering wheel when he passed out and drove into a snow bank. He remained toothless the rest of his life.

Dan literally feared for his life. He routinely stayed up until midnight, school notwithstanding, to make sure he could sleep without danger. The worst of the terror lasted until my father's heart attack in 1971 when Dan was nineteen. It's surprising that he stayed home until his mid-twenties when he escaped to the West Coast.

> Dream—June 2, 1993
>
> *I wake up in my bedroom, but it's actually the kitchen on Brooks Avenue. In the backyard, my old stereo speakers are face down on the lawn. Something is wrong. The house has been broken into. I walk to the front room where Kurt is waking up with two friends who stayed the night. Out the front door, three pairs of men are talking about the "botched robbery" as they casually walk away from the house. I try to yell, "Help!" or "Stop!" but the words won't come out. A squad car pulls up. Two police officers confront the men and start questioning them.*

In June of that year, I took my counselor's suggestion and went to a massage therapist for some bodywork. When I drove to the appointment that afternoon, my disposition was as hot and muggy as the ninety-degree day. While the therapist was working on the lower region of my back, this relaxing experience took an unexpected turn. Without warning, another memory played back in my head. When I began to sob, the therapist stopped and asked twice if I was all right. I reluctantly told him I had just recalled another memory. He knew from our initial interview that I was a survivor of sexual victimization, so he was prepared.

In this flashback, I saw myself as a boy of no more than five years because the event happened at the house on Cottage Street. My father was coaxing me out from underneath our dining room table, assuring me I would come to no harm. Still, I was fearful, so I stayed where I was. He slowly pulled me from under the table and lifted me under the armpits from behind. Like dead weight, I was carried with my feet dangling into the living room where he sat on the couch. He undressed me from the waist down, then bounced me naked up and down around his erect penis. I was facing away from him.

The therapist never asked, but I volunteered enough information so he could understand what I had just seen. He explained that early trauma, especially of a sexual nature, is sometimes stored as a body memory in the region of the back where he had been working. He asked my permission to use a healing technique called Reiki. I readily agreed. His hands felt hot, like a heating pad moving across my skin. I left the office in a haze, flabbergasted by the experience. When I told my SIA friends how I'd gotten more than a massage that day, five of the six men shared their own stories about body memories.

9

COSMIC CONNECTION

To take my mind off what I was going through, I placed a personal ad in the local gay newspaper. It netted four responses from hopeful suitors. I returned a call from a guy with a deep baritone voice who said he was in great shape. He sounded nice on the phone, so we made plans to meet for dinner. I arrived early and decided to kill time in the greeting card section of a nearby CVS. It was Friday night in Washington's Dupont Circle, our haven in town, our natural habitat, a place where you can be openly queer without worrying about who's watching.

Gay men were cruising the store for either a soul mate or for "Mr. Right for the Night." Pushing out the front door, I noticed a boyishly handsome, perfectly sculpted guy with a closely cropped beard in the checkout line. I allowed my eyes to linger long enough to express interest and caught him raising his eyebrows in a return acknowledgement. Nodding, I smiled and left for the restaurant. I thought of ditching my date and following this hot number, but I had better manners than that.

Strolling up 17th Street, I watched gay America coming alive for the weekend. Same-sex couples were walking arm in arm, carrying flowers or bottles of wine and Brie. Just being in Dupont made me feel alive, energetic. When I climbed the metal stairs to the restaurant, the hunk I saw at CVS was waiting outside. *He* was my blind date! His handsome face and rock-solid physique sparked an aortic meltdown (while also giving rise to a certain appendage of mine).

Our dinner over julienne salads at The Front Page Restaurant was spent gazing into each other's eyes and blushing. We could have been Lady and The Tramp, dining romantically over pasta at Luigi's, our snouts touching in a moment of bliss as we ate to the center of the same strand of spaghetti. Love at first bite.

This man with the sweetest smile and a deep, dreamy voice was named Bob Tyler. I sensed something special about him. Before parting, we agreed to spend the next day together. I awkwardly asked if I could steal a kiss. "There's no need for that. I'll gladly give you one free of charge," he said coyly. He cupped his right hand behind my neck, pulled me gently toward him, and planted a French kiss that caused my hooter to snake up my leg.

We made love from noon until sundown the next day. I was never more alive. Our lovemaking was seamless, instinctive, and original. It was only interrupted twice for brief forays downstairs for food and drink. We knew how to take care of each other in bed, something I had always struggled to achieve with sexual partners. Individual desires were blended into a symphony of affection. Startled by the strength of our attraction to each other, we vowed to take things slowly. But the gods had willed this union and, over the next several weeks, we fell in love. Bob was handsome and virile, but the fact that he was also a gentleman—a kind, tender, considerate person, a *mensch* in every sense of the word—reinforced my physical attraction to him.

> Dream—June 3, 1993
>
> *I'm in an old D.C. row house, narrow, deep, and cluttered with items that might be considered treasures. A young man is with me. I'm very attracted to him. He rubs my arm in an affectionate way. Sexual feelings stir inside. We're working side by side, scraping old putty and grit from between the cracks in the hardwood floor. We accumulate a lot of dirt and grime. I'm aware that I must keep the boundaries between us clear.*
>
> *My mother warns that one of my sisters might take the chandelier if I'm not careful. I realize many items in the house can be recovered and restored—drawers full of treasures yet to be discovered.*

Bob and I enjoyed working out, but I was a neophyte compared to what he knew about nutrition and bodybuilding. Both of us were in recovery—me from alcohol and him from speed and tranquilizers. When we met on June 18, 1993, Bob had three years of sobriety, and I had just celebrated my first anniversary. Acknowledging our blemished histories, we each entered the relationship with other baggage as well: I was recalling sexual abuse and Bob was seeking peace after the AIDS death of his long-term lover in 1990.

I wasn't sure when I should tell him my story, fearing I'd scare him away. Men who've been sexually abused can be insecure when relationships are forming. We tend to have difficulty trusting others, particularly the love interests in our lives. I had no guarantee that Bob would even believe what I told him. When I did explain the assaults, I saw a flinch of vicarious pain register on his face. "I'm sorry that happened to you," he said with sincerity. "Let me know if there's anything I can do to help." *He believed me.* I could add him to my list of safe friends. He knew how to comfort me, even when all I could do was wallow in the past.

No shame clouded my desire for this man who was unabashedly gay, who wore three earrings in his left lobe, and who kissed me full on the mouth on a city street. It was a thrill to stand beside him, to run my hands over his tight torso, and to think of him when we were apart.

Poem—June 22, 1993

Who Is This Man?

Who is this man who came bouncing into my life
All loving, handsome, kind, gentle and serene?
Why did he appear at this moment in time?
Just to bring me to and set me free?

Who is this man who sends shivers down my spine
And appears unsummoned in my thoughts from
    moment to moment?
A guardian angel? A spirit guide from the heavens?
A local savior whose job it is to fuel recovering souls?

Who is this man who seems remarkably unblemished?
Who reads my mind and says the things I most need to hear?
Is he the best memory from my most fabulous dream,
Or simply part of the grand plan for my fulfillment?

Should I even care who he is or from whence he comes?
His timing is near perfect and he feels so delicious.
With him, my guard is down, my shoulders relaxed.
With him, I am whole for the first time in a millennium.

The first few weeks felt intoxicating, giving and receiving physical pleasure, talking tenderly on the phone, dancing a wondrous waltz in the world. At the same time, I experienced doubts, skulking in my shadow, warning me not to lean into this man, or any man, no matter how perfect he might appear to be.

Lawless ghosts mumbled from the past. From an insular corner of my mind, echoes of old fears demanded attention, eroding the confidence that Bob would be different from the others—my first lover . . . my father. That was the real problem—my father. His actions had diminished my confidence and dampened my capacity for intimacy. The closer Bob got, the more uncomfortable I became. I began to self-destruct, undermining our relationship without intending to do so.

"Come on. This isn't about your father."

My mother arrived in town the week after Bob and I met. We made small talk at home the first night, the usual gossip about who was doing what to whom in the family. I'd hoped she would initiate a discussion of the abuse or ask how I was doing. But it didn't happen. I wanted her to affirm that she believed what I'd told her. That never happened either. After breakfast the next morning, we chatted at the kitchen table. Her mood was carefree and relaxed. Encouraged by her disposition, I mentioned I'd recently met someone special, just testing the waters. If boyfriend talk was *verboten,* there was no sense bringing up the darker topic of incest.

She shot an angry look at me, registering her disapproval. Breaking eye contact, she turned away. "We don't need to talk about that," she said, declaring the topic off limits.

When her disapproval registered, my temper began to flare. Angry thoughts were coalescing: Don't let her do this to you. She has no right. Don't be silenced again. Silence equals death!

I countered her attempt to end the discussion by saying, "Don't you understand that when you do this, you're pushing me away?" She studied the back of her left hand, rotating her mother's ring between a thumb and middle finger. "I don't mean to push you away," she said, oozing passive-aggressiveness.

By now my pot had reached a running boil. Disgust began a frenzied spin inside me when I saw a bogus look of innocence on her face. "Well you are. This is who I am, and when you won't talk to me, I feel like . . ." She cut me off mid-sentence by slamming both palms on the table and rising from her seat.

Bolting into the family room, she cupped her hands over her ears and screamed, "Oh, shut up, Michael! Just shut up!" I couldn't believe what I was hearing and seeing. An avalanche of rejection from the person I wanted most to please crushed me under its weight. Resisting the urge to explode, I suppressed my anger, holding it down like the lid on a pressure cooker. Although I was shaking inside, an unstable calm came over my exterior. With my desire to challenge her gone, I turned and quietly left the room—bruised, battered, and defeated.

We were unable to talk about the incest, or anything else important, for the rest of her visit. I chose to ignore her outburst, to act as if she'd never screamed like a banshee. If she wanted me to shut up, that's exactly what I'd do.

"How can you be so dumb? Stop throwing that gay shit in your poor mother's face!"

We spent the final two days of her visit talking about safe subjects—Congress, health care—anything to steer our course away from the hot topics. She pretended to be nice as compensation for screaming at me. I was minimally cordial, but otherwise as cold as mackerel on fish market ice. We had an opportunity to talk that night, but I turned on the TV instead. A movie was being broadcast on the channel that came up about a mother who ignores the signs of incest in her family—a choice that was unintentional but provocative!

Tension pumped into the room like a cloud of gas. Her eyes were glued to the screen. My head was throbbing with anticipation. I waited for her to speak. Silence. I refused to be the target for her arrows of disapproval again. My exterior was as docile as a lamb, but inside, I felt as angry as a viper.

Neither of us flinched. I couldn't tolerate the stalemate, so I turned my back on her and left the room without a good night. I retreated grimly upstairs and locked my bedroom door behind me. I was self-blaming, slicing away at my gut like a *samurai* intent on *seppuku*. I was alone in the dark again, just like Thumper after he stomped up the stairs in a rage at the age of four. No difference. At four or forty-four, I was still alone, but this time in my own house.

Why did I keep letting her immobilize me? She was in control. A prisoner of prejudice, I stood hip deep in a grave I had dug and was woefully pulling in mounds of self-pity on top of myself.

> Dream—June 10, 1993
>
> *I'm on a subway platform with a deaf friend. We're teaching two groups of high school boys a lesson. One group boards a train while the other must stay behind. My job is to convince the latter group not to feel left out or angry.*
>
> *Three of my boys are upset. They smash their shoulders into an overhead door at the back of the platform. I tell them it's senseless to act out when you're left behind, but they ignore me.*

> Dream—June 10, 1993
>
> *In exasperation I yell, "Fuck you!" and walk down an enclosed concrete staircase carrying a beach ball. The three boys follow. I motion them away, but they stay close. On the other side of a wrought-iron fence at the bottom of the stairs is a platform with a director's chair in its middle.*
>
> *Beyond that is a river. We're on this property without permission! A woman in an equestrian outfit passes us. She asks if we're there for the ride. I say no and ask whether she's the trainer. She unlocks the gate on the platform.*

I escaped the standoff with my mother the next evening by telling her I was going to an AA meeting. Instead, I met Bob in town for dinner. At the restaurant, I was sullen and withdrawn, nausea breeding future generations in my belly. Seeing me downtrodden, he suggested we stroll over to a "pocket-park" at St. Thomas Episcopal Church. The property had seen a better day, with landscape timbers that had buckled and split from years of neglect. But it was Bob's place to find peace whenever he was troubled. He invited me to sit by patting his palm on the timber beside him. He pulled me close, and my head came to rest on his shoulder. We were impervious to the Yuppies rushing to happy hour and the stylish dowagers being pulled along by their pedigreed poodles. We sat quietly until it was time for me to return home.

The next day, just after Mom disappeared down the airport runway, I called Bob from the departure lounge. "The bitch is gone," I intoned in the grave voice of a funeral director. We laughed hard. The humor was a moment's relief but only a small band aid on a spurting artery. To think seriously about the conflict was too painful.

Two weeks passed before the anger prompted me to act. I was furious about the way she treated me. After much thought, I decided to prevent her from ever hurting me that way again.

Letter to Mom—July 14, 1993

Dear Mom:

I tried to ignore how you talked to me while you were here, but it won't work. In order to move on, I've decided to say goodbye. It's clear you will never change. I'm tired of feeling unacceptable in your eyes. There's nothing wrong with me. The emptiness is in you.

I'm angry. When you yelled, I knew what was behind your words, "Oh, shut up, Michael. Just shut up!" You want me to shut up about being gay and about the sexual abuse. On the phone, when I asked you about what Dad did, you said, "It could have happened." I thought, "Oh shit, she doesn't believe me!" All I wanted was your love and support.

I was vulnerable and begging for help. I wanted you to say that you loved me and you would help in any way you could. Instead, you said, "If you say it happened, then I believe you." Then you told me how you dealt with Dad in the past, how you did this and you did that. Will you get it through your head? This is not about you. It's about ME! What he did to ME! I felt let down. What little support I got, I had to pry out of you.

I thought I could ignore your outburst. Now I'm angry as a result. This is sick. I need to talk about what happened in that house. I had my clothes and my vitality stripped away by that degenerate man, but you couldn't even say you were sorry that it happened.

I won't accept your disapproval anymore. Because our relationship is so unhealthy, I think it best we not communicate with each other for as long as I feel necessary. Do not expect to hear from me and please do not call or write me. I decided this after attempts to work things out with you. I know this to be in my best interest. Trying to find sustenance in the devastation and shallowness that was once my family is not what I need. I want healthy people around me who don't cower from the pain of the past.

I hope you will find the peace you deserve. In spite of how you feel about me, I will hold a place for you in my heart and wish you only the best.
Michael

More than a year would pass before we communicated, and then only after a tragic event.

10

ON THE BRINK OF INSANITY

Sleeplessness was a dreadful problem for me as 1993's spring jumped into summer. Bob was concerned. Whenever he caught me roaming the house at night, he would coax me back to our bed. I was too anxious to relax. None of the natural cures for insomnia worked. Warm milk wouldn't stay down, herbal teas made me piss like a racehorse, and over-the-counter sleep aids made me anxious. To satisfy him, I returned to bed until he dozed off, and then slipped out again.

It hurt him to see me in distress. He absorbed my pain as his own, suffering along with me. Bob was too fragile to thrive in a ruthless world.

Journal Entry—July 16, 1993

It's 2:30 AM Lack of sleep does me in. It's been several months now. I wander through the house, trying to shake it off. I'd do anything to stop the restless hours in my uneasy bed. I get strung out. I'm grouchy. I want to scream, "This is unfair! Take it away from me." Today the floodgates burst open, and I sobbed uncontrollably in Bob's arms.

It's like clockwork. I can't sleep more than two hours at a stretch. I know how it feels to be afraid to close your eyes. That's when I relive what it was like as a frightened child in an unsafe house. I don't like to talk about it. It hurts too much. But they tell me I must if I want to heal.

During my worst nights, my body was infested with the heebie-jeebies, like I had legions of prickly ants streaming in and out of my toes and fingers. I had to throw off the covers and jump out of bed. I shuffled brain dead from one room to another, eluding the vile memories, stranded somewhere between the past and the present. Relief came when dawn edged over the horizon, and songbirds heralded the approaching day. The curse of the undead would recede until the next darkness. Dracula was never more in a pucker to return to his musty coffin than I was to slip into bed before Bob noticed my absence.

A few times, I stayed on the couch until Bob woke and joined me downstairs. He was adroit at assessing my mood with a glance. If I felt miserable, he saw it in my eyes. I had a love-hate relationship with that talent of his. I could admire the ability, but I felt exposed. I had no place to hide, to isolate myself. But I also found comfort in knowing that someone understood.

Each morning a gang of gremlins nested in my belly and plotted the overthrow of my intestinal tract. If I ate half a bagel or drank a spot of juice to placate Bob, I'd worry about keeping it down. The uncertainty could escalate into one or more loud, unsettling coughs. Bob knew what that meant. On the worst days, the gremlins staged a coup and completely disabled my appetite center. Bob cringed at the sound of my retching, once even begging me not to cough. I snapped at him that day. "Don't you think I'd stop if I could?" I was quick to apologize. The problem was not between us—it was the frigging stomach monsters goaded on by the memories of incest. Getting enough to eat and maintaining my weight threatened a replay of the nasty struggle with eating that had been a problem for years.

We did spend two great nights at the ocean that July. I'd rented a room for ten days in a house full of guys at Dewey Beach, Delaware, before we'd met. Bob drove out for the first weekend. One evening we strolled on the beach just before midnight. A clear moonless sky crowded with stars hung overhead. As I relaxed between Bob's legs on the wet sand, the back of my head nestled against his chest, he whispered in my ear:

"I'm waiting for a sign from Leo." Leo was Bob's lover who died of AIDS.

"A sign?" I asked. "About what?"

"That you're the one."

"Don't be silly."

"Really! I've been praying for a man. Leo will show me a sign when it's right."

"What kind of sign?"

"A shooting star. We'll see one tonight."

"I've never seen one."

"Never?"

"Nope."

Staring straight up at the worlds above, the only sounds were the rhythm of the waves and the beat of Bob's heart at my ear. A veil of peacefulness blanketed the two of us. I studied the sky for the slightest movement. We held each other as motionless as statues, praying for the miracle. My awareness was split by two senses. My eyes were searching for the sign, but I was also lost in Bob's manly scent. Then, to my surprise, the heavens stirred. There was no mistaking the dot that streaked across the sky dead above us, a sparkling white tail blazing behind.

A goddamn shooting star!

Goosebumps erupted over every inch of flesh, my body all a tingle. Bob broke the silence.

"Did you see that?"

"Yeah. I can't believe it. That was Leo, huh?"

"Yes, that was Leo. I told you he'd give me a sign."

"I'll be damned. Thanks Leo."

"We can go now."

He was right. No need to linger. We had been to the source and were given the word. We rose, brushed off the sacred sand, and quietly departed, two mystics granted permission to consummate their love.

August of that year had me teetering on the brink of insanity, holding back a wall of tears, and barely one step ahead of a memory. I joked that those who knew me well would say I was a couple of bubbles off plumb. I thirsted for rest like a straight-jacketed alcoholic craves a drink, my body screaming for a fix. If Satan had offered me eight hours of deep slumber in exchange for my first born, it would have been a tough call. Counseling felt useless. It was boring, repetitive, a broken record. I wanted it all to stop: the memories, the sleeplessness, the anxiety, the depression, and especially the nausea.

Unless I was able to sleep through the night, I was at risk for a self-destructive response—suicide, a drink, a drug, or some other method of escape from the wreck that was my life. At the frayed end of a very short rope, something had to give. I convinced my AA sponsor and my counselor I needed medication to break the entrenched pattern of sleeplessness.

They knew me well enough to take me at my word.

My physician prescribed a nine-day cycle of Lorazepam, a tranquilizer similar to Valium, but warned me about its addictiveness. We all hoped a week on the drug would be enough to establish a sleep pattern. The first night I slept eight hours and woke so refreshed, I was off the charts with energy. The reaction I got from Bob was un-customarily cool. His addiction to Valium made him the undisputed expert on the matter. When the medication was gone, the sleeplessness returned immediately. The addict in me went right back for a refill. The physician called to issue a warning. "You're an alcoholic," he said. "This drug is addictive. You're playing with fire."

The gig was up. But I didn't stop there. I made an appointment with a doctor I hadn't seen in several years and got another prescription. I never hid what I had done, but I knew my behavior was slippery.

Fortunately, my twelve-step meetings kept me honest. The decision to continue taking an addictive drug wasn't in keeping with a life in recovery. I decided to consult a psychiatrist. The first appointment I could schedule was for three weeks later, the middle of September.

Bob spoke highly of the newer class of antidepressant drugs. He had been taking Prozac for more than three years.

> Dream—August 27, 1993
>
> *I'm on the porch of a house at the foot of a lake. A party is going on and the guests are familiar. A seven-year-old blond boy is watching me from the corner of his eye. He sneaks into the crowd in front of the house. I hear the roar of a motorcycle, a screech, and then a crash. I run to the railing and look down to the road below. The boy is sprawled in a heap. He appears to have been killed. I dial 911 for help.*
>
> *A man answers. I describe the accident and request an ambulance. He says he can't do that—something about the rules preventing it. I tell him he must, but he still says no. There's a group watching me. I scream into the phone. The response is still no. I fall to my knees sobbing and begging for help, but the man on the phone and the people at the house refuse.*

After Labor Day, Bob and I left for a few days at The Outer Banks—his first vacation since getting sober. He was as giddy as a schoolboy as we drove down the coast. My spirits hung heavily at the other end of the spectrum, but I lectured myself about not ruining our nice stay at the remote resort town. The beaches were deserted, the forecast was perfect, and we had no thoughts of work to interfere with our time together. Unfortunately, my three days at Nags Head were filled with anxiety.

When the lights went out in our motel room, I felt like a prisoner in the arms of the man I loved. If I told Bob how anxious I was, he was sure to be upset. My nervousness had nothing to do with him. No one could have made me comfortable. I resolved to be calm (the Spartan kid) and to remain as still as I could under the covers. After Bob drifted off to sleep, I slowly squiggled out of bed. I sat or reclined in every nook and corner of that room in search of rest. A long night's journey into day. After a light breakfast the next morning, I had to rush from the restaurant when I began to cough up the little I had eaten.

Back at the motel, the wigglies in my stomach settled enough for us to sunbathe beside the pool. Because I was dozing off at poolside, I returned to the room to see if I could nap. After listening to a meditation tape, I was wide awake again. Feeling alone, I left the room to rejoin Bob at the pool. He was gone. I was shaken and worried. He never told me he was leaving. Where was he? I had to find him. With no trace of him on the road, I ran to the beach and looked up and down the shoreline. Making my way south toward the pier and the only cluster of people in sight, tears dropped from my cheeks and were swallowed by the sand. Why had he left? I imagined him in the arms of some other man just before I saw him in the distance, smiling and bouncing toward me. The closer he got, the more furious I became.

I waited near the water's edge, tapping my left foot in the waves. I could have been dressed in an apron, with curlers in my hair, fuzzy slippers on my feet, and a rolling pin clutched at my side. That man was going to get a piece of this housewife's mind.

"Where were you?" I shouted at him.

"I went for a walk," he said innocently, a smirk on his face. The third degree continued.

"Why didn't you tell me where you were going?"

In a calm voice Bob asked, "What's going on? Come here. Tell me what's wrong." He took me by the hand, and sat me down near the surf.

My resolve to stay angry melted with his expression of

concern. My rage was not about him, not even about the present. It was about what had happened forty years earlier. I stretched out on the sand and sobbed, ashamed of my behavior and unaware that vacationers were beginning to take notice. What a sight: two middle-aged men huddled shamelessly on the (heterosexual) beach, he consoling me with his hand on my shoulder whispering assurances in my ear.

"Just relax," he said.

"I'm so sorry," I groaned. "This is not about you. It's me."

"I understand."

"I thought you left me."

"I didn't *leave* you. I just went for a walk."

"I know. I'm sorry."

A father with his young son in tow turned and noticed our moment in the sand. Disgusted, he shouted over his shoulder. "God damn queers!" That was enough to rouse us from our intimate conversation. The guy may have feared we would go at it in the surf, having been told by his preacher that homosexuals were oversexed and insatiable. If the father had known the circumstance, it might have changed his opinion. Bob pulled me to my feet. We strolled back down the beach, me with my tail tucked snugly between my legs. Back at the room, Bob held me in his arms. We stayed quiet a long time. That was exactly what I wanted at that moment.

While huddled on a secluded part of the beach the next day, I admitted how depressed I felt, how I wanted to give up, and how tired I was of feeling that way. I explained how unsafe I felt, and, as crazy as it sounded, how I feared Bob would hurt me like my father had. "Are you safe, or will you hurt me some day?" I asked. The pause that followed did not instill confidence. "I think I'm safe," he said. "I don't think I'd ever hurt you intentionally. You'll just have to trust me." That wasn't what I wanted to hear. It felt too much like, "If you say it happened, then I believe you." Why couldn't a person promise never to hurt you, no matter what? Why couldn't it be absolute?

Poem—September 15, 1993

Cocoon of Pain

Another day cocooned in pain
Is there no escape?

Barrage of nasty memories
Brutal childhood rape.

This obscene hurt, it pummels me
Wrenches at my soul.

Exhausted by the remedies
I give up all control.

A poltergeist must come for me
Each morning just at two.

Like Scrooge I'm forced to walk the past
And restless all night through.

The sleepless nights they take their toll
I muddle through each day.

Then fall in bed again at night
Peace is far away.

11

SHOWDOWN AT THE CEMETERY

The diagnoses came as no surprise. The sleeplessness, the flashbacks, the irritability, the hopelessness, the loss of appetite, and the anxiety all added up on the psychiatrist's ten-point scales to two maladies: Major Depression and Post Traumatic Stress Disorder. We talked about medication options and agreed to go with Prozac. He also prescribed something to help me sleep. Because it wasn't addictive, Trazodone was given to patients in recovery who suffer from sleep disturbance—quite a *good* solution for me, if it worked.

I began sleeping six or seven hours each night. To someone who had not slept in months, that was heaven, simply heaven. I was more alert during the day, but I continued to feel anxious and sad. During this in-between period while waiting for the Prozac to take effect, something strange was brewing below the surface. I was suddenly inundated with violent thoughts, images of blood and of someone violating me.

Dream—September 23, 1993

I'm in a large house where a celebration is taking place. It could be a family gathering after a wedding or graduation. From my room in the basement, I can hear a racket upstairs—snide laughter, raucousness, clinking of glasses.

My narrow room is cluttered with clothes, fabric remnants, and stale food. At one end, a sliding glass door is slightly ajar. A three-foot drift of snow outside blocks that entrance. I can hear my father shoveling snow and calling to me from outside. I don't want him to come in.

On the floor across the room is a sheet cake in the shape of a sleeping, black jaguar. When I look closer, it's actually two jaguars, not one, and they're alive and breathing. I escape into the hallway, only to find my father blocking my way. His hands are hanging limply at his sides and his face is sullen and angry. Unshaven and drooling from a corner of his mouth, he's been waiting for me. He's drunk and thin as a vagrant. We're locked into a stare until the tension is broken by noise from the upstairs party. Distracted, he turns and shuffles down the corridor in that direction. I'm spared for the moment.

I leave the house and walk out to a summer scene by an adjacent pond. As the only sober person there, I have an obligation to prevent a tragedy. Partygoers are carelessly splashing about in the water, pushing and falling on one another. Four women are walking swiftly abreast, and in lock-step, toward the water. The woman in the center is carrying a huge rock that causes her to fall on her face. I know she must be hurt.

The people in the water are out of control. A young couple enters the pond with their blonde seven-year-old son. The boy swims past me with his dad wading behind. The boy's doing the face-float, kicking away with his hands at his sides. He's in danger and going to be hurt.

Across the pond, I see two snakes writhing in a mound of sand near the shore. They look like boa constrictors. One is enormous, thick, long and powerful. I walk around the pond to do something about them. The snakes disappear into holes in the sand, but I can still see the big one's head peering out at me. My cat Bud Man is sniffing and poking at the holes. I yell at him to move before he gets snatched by the snake. I ask someone to get me an ax so I can cut off the fucker's head. I know if I don't, something tragic will happen.

The sight of my father blocking my way looking like a cannibal was gruesome. I was still frightened the next morning. I called in sick and scheduled a therapy appointment for that afternoon.

Journal Entry – September 24, 1993

Emergency session with Ned today. The twenty-mile drive to his office was a blur. I don't remember being this upset; all based on a dream last night about my father. I was blubbering like a fountain all day.

I explained the dream to Ned, crying throughout. All he had to do was suggest I take a breath. Another memory returned. I was thinking of the snakes writhing in the sand when that image was replaced by one of me as a young boy struggling to resist my father.

I was in the bedroom I shared with Joe on Brooks Avenue. He must have been asleep in his bed in the other corner. The room was dark. The only light was filtering through the blinds from a corner street lamp. My bed was against the wall to the right of the closet. My father was restraining me by the wrists. The flailing of my arms matched the movements of the snakes in the mound. He was talking tenderly to me like he would to the dog, saying he wasn't going to hurt me. I fought him. I wanted to scream but knew he might hurt me if I did.

The odor of tobacco and alcohol, distinctively my father's, was on his clothes. With his big, grubby hand covering my mouth and nose, my air supply was cut off. I was fighting him all over again on the couch in Ned's office. He asked me what was going on, but I was unable to answer, distracted by the pain of the rape.

Then I detached—just as I must have years ago during the assault. The boy let him have his way. He might have died if he hadn't. He turned his head to the wall and went somewhere else to be safe. The objective observer again, I explained the events to Ned, dispassionately describing

> *what had happened to "the kid in the bed." Without emotion, I told Ned how his father had pulled down his underwear, played with the boy's penis, fingered his anus, and hovered over him while masturbating. I described how his father shot sperm all over his lifeless body and turned his back on him, leaving him in a pool of disgust with a smell that he would never forget.*
>
> *I reconnected to the present. I may have been prompted back by Ned. I was in pain from what I'd just witnessed. I was unable to speak. I cried . . . and cried . . . and cried.*

What I had remembered was incredible—the rape itself, the violence used in its execution, and my father's callous disregard for me.

The recollection of the event was astounding—particularly the surrogate images that channeled the information back to the present. The image of my father in the dream as a loathsome night stalker was foreboding and predictive. But the visual of the snakes writhing in the mound was the access code, the bridge back to the memory. Was that a connection to the recurring dream of snakes under my bed when I was young?

I can't adequately put into words what it was like to see the snakes undulating in the sand one second and then have them seamlessly transformed into my flailing arms during the rape the next. The snakes didn't merely represent my arms; they became my arms. Computerized cinematography can transform one visual image to another with relative ease on the screen. But, in this case, even greater wonders were at work; a blocked memory was mysteriously called back from the past, and its reappearance was perfectly orchestrated by the neurological gatekeepers of the conscious and unconscious minds.

The entire cluster of memories had unfolded serendipitously, one snippet at a time, without any apparent logic or sequence. This last episode proved that the process was entirely out of my control. I learned to lean into it rather than resist.

My dreams had been instructive. They could portend the recall of historical events and elucidate their relationship to the experiences in my life. The emotions preceding and following each dream, each memory, were also germane to the subject matter. For me, pain and distress were side effects of the recovery process, not a separate pathology. I hoped they would eventually fade with the memories.

Early one Sunday I awoke feeling downcast and nauseous. I had been up for hours when Bob found me at the kitchen table unable to focus, unwilling to talk, and self-conscious about being so distant.

"What's the matter?" he asked. I shook my head, eyes on the floor.

"Nothing," I answered. He wasn't going to accept my response.

"Don't even try that, mister man!" he teased. "I've got your number."

His words nudged me off the ledge to which I was barely clinging. The dread I'd been holding back broke through its boundaries, throwing off my delicate balance. Resting my right temple on the table, I sobbed quietly until Bob intervened.

"Come here." He guided me to the family room couch where he cradled me between his legs.

"Tell me what's going on. . . . Is it your father?"

I nodded. "I don't want to remember anymore."

"You don't have a choice. Looks like your storm has arrived."

I knew that to be true, but I was refusing to yield.

Journal Entry—October 3, 1993

Hounded by dual memories for two weeks now. In one, I'm bent forward at the waist, my palms against the wall of the upstairs hallway on Brooks Avenue. I'm in the position one would assume to be entered from behind. Looking back over my shoulder, I see my father walking naked down the hall, his penis flopping up and down.

This all resurfaced last Sunday when Bob coaxed me to talk. Nestled in his arms on the couch, I thought of a wet dream I've had several times as an adult. A man is on top of me. It's pleasurable. Suddenly, I cry out—wail really—as another memory comes back.

My father is on me in the same bed from the dream two weeks ago. This time he's fully clothed and "dry humping" me. His pants are brown, his shirt dark. Having "detached" from the situation, I could feel only pressure. I tell Bob what I remembered. He asks a question. "Do you feel the same now? Pressure and nothing else?" I answer, "Yes." He asks, "Do you know where you are now?" I answer, "Yes." One more question. "Can you feel me holding you now?" I say yes. Then a final question: "Do you know I love you?" I say, "Yes," and continue to cry.

Then it was over. I wanted to make passionate love to Bob for his support, excitedly stroking and kissing him around the face. But Bob lobbied to go to the gym instead. For him, there was something vulgar about having sex in close proximity to the memory. I could easily separate the memory from the moment and was slightly offended to be rebuffed.

Later, Bob told me he couldn't understand how a father could use his child that way, how he could cross that boundary "just to get his rocks off." I wondered if something similar could have happened to my father that may have fostered a warped desire to victimize his own son.

My younger brother called with an interesting story about Dad. Mom had told him she'd once broken up a friendship between her husband and a man who an undisclosed source told her was a "homo." Apparently, Lester and the guy were spending too much time together on the Cottage Street porch. The next time the man came by, my mother asked him if he was queer. The gent got flustered, quickly departed, and was never seen again. She also confronted Lester with the rumor, but he insisted there was nothing to it. Even if Dad were gay, though, that wouldn't explain why he preyed on children.

I was studying for a graduate degree in counseling when these memories were unfolding. I wrote a research paper on pedophilia, obviously interested in the topic. I found that the vast majority of pedophiles are heterosexual men who are more likely to prey on young girls than boys. Some pedophiles are fixated only on girls or only on boys, but others abuse children without regard to their victim's gender. One consistent factor stood out in the research about pedophiles: a very high percentage of them were themselves molested as children. Could that have been the case with my father?

> Journal Entry—October 6, 1993
>
> *Feeling ill for the last three nights. Remembering how I hid from my father behind the couch.*
>
> *Last Sunday I woke up nauseous at Bob's place. He heard me cough and asked what was wrong. I explained that, as a child, I had felt disgusting in the morning, just how I was then feeling.*
>
> *What else do I remember? His hands . . . His hands . . . His hands . . . Pulling me . . . too strong . . . Pulling the back of my head toward him. I turn my head from side to side to avoid the inevitable.*

The Prozac took effect three weeks after I took the first pill. I felt no dramatic shift, but a gradual return of a sense of well being and energy I hadn't had for months. The memories remained troublesome, but I was stronger. From somewhere came the thought that I could face anything, if necessary. I couldn't imagine things getting much worse. The Prozac did suppress my libido, and I lost my ability to orgasm, a common side effect of the medication. Aside from that setback, I was pleased to have near normal feelings again. Because I was sleeping at night and more in control during the day, my focus in therapy shifted once again to actions I could take to rekindle my confidence, to affirm my integrity, to reclaim my life.

The idea formed easily when the therapist asked me what I would do if my father were still alive. I decided to confront him at his grave in Rochester—a showdown at the not-so-OK Corral. Bob agreed to accompany me and provide moral support. I decided not to tell family members of my plans. In preparation, I wrote a letter that I would read to my dad at the cemetery.

Letter to Dad—October 29, 1993

Mr. Lester Deninger
Holy Ghost Cemetery
Rochester, New York

Dear Lester:

I'm sure you didn't expect to hear from me, but we need to settle a score. I'm outraged that you destroyed my life just to satisfy your own wanton desires. I want you to know the pain you caused me.

When I was young, you threatened us with drunken violence every day. But that was nothing compared to what you did to me. If you were here now, I'd punch your lights out. I want revenge for all the pain you caused me. If I had it in me to kill someone, that's what I would want to do. You shattered my life. I want retribution.

I feel like a sucker. I nursed you on your deathbed, kept a vigil after others had abandoned you. I kissed your forehead. I told you I loved you. I grieved over you—even gave you a glowing eulogy. All lies.

I had a bright future until you stripped me of my clothes and my vitality. I have no idea what your problem was and I don't give a shit. Even if someone fucked with you, that gave you no right to do the same thing to me.

And don't blame it on the alcohol. That's cowardly. Today, you would be jailed a long time for what you did. You bastard!

I want you out of my thoughts and my life for good. I'm not your victim any longer, so get out of my way. I'm here at your grave to deliver this letter. I want you to lie with this filth the way I did, alone in my bed with your sperm years ago. You see how it feels and let it be an eternal reminder of all the pain you caused me.

Now leave me alone so I can get on with my life in peace. I deserve that.

Your son,
Michael

As the DC-9 pushed its nose up through the clouds above Baltimore, I was listening to a relaxation tape for fear of flying that Ned had made for me. I was also nervously fingering a crystal Carlene had given me in lieu of her presence at my father's gravesite.

It was the first Friday in November, 1993. I didn't know which was more troubling: boarding the plane with my heart in my throat, or the thought of the cemetery the next morning. Bob laid his hand gently on my knee and encouraged me to relax. That was impossible, but I smiled in return for the gesture. When I looked into his eyes, I noticed something wasn't right with him. He complained of a headache after our arrival in Rochester, confirming my suspicion. We tried to relax in the room that evening, but I was preparing for battle, and Bob was nursing his headache.

I had decided to make the trip to the cemetery alone. Bob was uncomfortable with that but respected my decision. He hardly stirred when I rose and showered at seven in the morning. I felt shaky but otherwise determined to accomplish what I had set out to do. The weather was overcast, an ill-omened autumn morning ideally suited for the macabre. En route to the graveyard, a slow drizzle swelled to a light rain, but it was well above freezing, and no wind was blowing to deter my work.

My father was waiting in the cemetery, a level tract of land directly opposite Holy Ghost Church on Coldwater Road. I hadn't been there since he was buried ten years before. When I cut the rental car's engine in the parking lot, I briefly questioned my plan. Would I be overcome with sadness and cry? Would I find the rage and scream bloody murder, or would I freeze, unable to invoke the tangle of emotions that had tormented me for months? Negative chatter buzzed through my head:

"This is such a lame-brained idea! You really think it will make a bit of difference? You're going to look like an idiot. What if somebody hears you? Jesus!

Sebastian urged patience and resolve. I breathed in a slow, cleansing breath and calmed the vortex of internal voices by saying the Serenity Prayer, my solace when tempests rage around me: "God grant me the serenity to accept the things I cannot change, courage to change the things I can, and the wisdom to know the difference."

This time I asked for courage and clear-headedness—the courage to settle all accounts with my father, to remove his chronic curse from my awareness, and a clear head to guide me through the morning. I reached across the front seat and grabbed an envelope containing two items: the letter and a pack of Ramada Inn matches.

The church across the street drew my attention, a four-story, gray, stone edifice with massive, brown, wooden doors. A dark steeple encasing a small, black bell had beckoned parishioners to mass each Sunday for decades. Passing through the arch to the graveyard, I called up the memory of Lester's burial day to help me locate the plot. Twenty minutes later, I was still searching for the dolt, unnerved that he wasn't making himself available. I imagined him laughing at me the way he had after I blew that easy lay-up in the championship basketball game.

I thought of chucking the whole idea, but I had come too far to give up that easily. So how the hell would I find him? The light rain escalated to a heavier shower. Rather than squelch my determination, the drumming of the rain on the tombstones emboldened my resolve. When faced with elusive problems, I have always favored an organized approach. I started at the foot of the cemetery and walked row-by-row, reading every blooming gravestone until I located the creep. An angry voice inside was coming of age.

A third of the way to the back, I found the schmuck. The polished, rose-colored, granite gravestone seemed much too nice for this creep. I noticed one small consolation. A single withered geranium, left untended on his plot, was about to expire. His neglect had caused similar stress to my system. I wondered if the plant had also been choked and defiled as a seedling. The lifeless vegetation seemed a more fitting commemoration of his life than the flowery eulogy I had delivered at his funeral.

I scowled at the grave and imagined what Lester would look like after ten years, how decayed and rotten his remains must be, how ridiculous. But then, as implausible as it seemed, I imagined him busting out of his coffin six feet below. What if he exploded through the turf like Freddie Krueger and seized me by the throat with those unyielding hands? A cold, hard chill left a lump in my throat. I dissolved the image with a twitch of my head and quickly raised the envelope I had been holding at my side. Time for our talk. I glanced around to see if anyone was within earshot. No. I unfolded the letter and began to read, feeling moderately silly.

The recitation was meek and awkward, my enunciation garbled, my voice a few decibels above a whisper, until something clicked inside. Testimony was about to be given, embarrassment replaced with self-assurance. Adrenaline pulsed through my arteries, energy shimmied across my chest. The more I read and the more I relived the indignities, the more tenacious I became. Three times, I slapped the letter to my side in anger, digressed from the script, and cursed him like a trooper.

"YOU FUCKING ASSHOLE. I HATE YOUR FUCKING GUTS FOR WHAT YOU DID. YOU STUPID SON OF A BITCH."

After each digression, my voice rose in volume and deepened in resonance until it had sportscaster quality. No stopping me.

"YOU STUPID JERK! YOU GET THE FUCK OUT OF MY WAY!"

Who gave a shit if anyone was listening?

In a classic role reversal, I was now the one calling the shots. I slowed the pace and began to savor what I had come so far to say, speaking each phrase with precision, imagining I was staring my father straight in the eye. In death, I had his full attention. I shouted the last two lines of the letter with more strength and conviction than I knew I could summon.

"NOW LEAVE ME ALONE SO I CAN GET ON WITH MY LIFE IN PEACE! I DESERVE THAT!"

Rock-solid fortitude backed up every word. I was prize-fighter strong, ready to go twelve rounds with the contender if that would end the nightmare. What followed was a spontaneous outburst spawned by my heightened emotions. With my teeth tightly clenched and rage oozing from every pore, I dropped to my knees on the soft grave.

I was oblivious to the heavy downpour. The muscles of my upper torso contracted as I raised my right fist high above my head and repeatedly hammered the grave with forty years of retaliation.

"You MUther FUCKing, COCK-SUCKing SON of a BITCH!"

I screamed at him in his casket, punctuating syllables with thumps of my closed fist into the wet sod. I kept up the attack.

"You LEAVE me aLONE you GOD-DAMN SON of a BITCH! You HEAR ME? LEAVE ME aLONE!"

A sharp pain shot through my wrist, warning me that I might do serious harm. But I continued the rhythmic beating even after the words stopped coming, pulverizing my father's mistreatment until I could pound no longer. At the end of the tirade, I saw I had hollowed a hole in the turf deep enough to bury a small bird. Winded and exhausted, I leaned forward, rested my forehead on the back of my muddied fist, and breathed a heavy sigh. The splattering of raindrops on the gravestones matched the echo-rhythm of the pummeling that was abating in my ears.

But the song was not over. The bell in the steeple at my back picked up the beat and rang the hour, shattering the stillness. The chiming was perfectly timed to the exact cadence of my fist hammering the earth just seconds before. An arctic chill surged up my spine.

One (You MUther) . . . two (FUCKing) . . . three (COCK-) . . . four (SUCKing) . . . five (SON of a) . . . six (BITCH) . . . seven . . . eight.

"Holy shit! Eight o'clock and all is well," I mumbled. The message was clear: that part of my work was done.

When I rose to my feet, my right hand was throbbing. I felt powerful despite the pain. Rain trickled from my forehead into my eyes, and my jeans were soaked through at the knees. I removed the letter from my back pocket where I'd stuffed it before my assault on the grave. I rummaged through my pockets for the hotel matches, then dropped to my knees again and began clawing with both hands at the hole I had punched in the dirt. Exhilarated, full of life. There was something electrifying about scratching out a mini-grave with my bare hands. About six inches down I stopped. Holding the letter above the hole, I struck a match and set the epistle afire.

As each page flashed yellow with flames and then dropped black ashes into the hole, I imagined letting go of all that had held me back: the pain, the abuse, the nausea, the depression, the anger, the tears, the sleeplessness, the memories, the anxiety, and my father—the whole shooting match. As painstakingly as any Fido worth his biscuits would bury his favorite bone, I brushed the ashes into the hole, raked the loose dirt over the heap, and ceremoniously tamped it firmly into place with an open palm.

NOW my work was done—or so I thought.

For a reason I didn't understand, I drifted away from my father's plot toward a bank of mammoth evergreens beside the road. An internal voice—Sebastian's voice—softly suggested that my work was incomplete. This communication was more experienced than heard, more telepathic than sensory, more ethereal than of this world, but real nonetheless.

I approached the stately evergreens, a variety of Norway Spruce. I admired them from trunk to treetop, tall and dense, their branches lush and dark as shamrocks, their tips pushing out new, pea-green growth like puffs of hopefulness. The trees had recently peppered the earth with a crop of large, healthy cones, each an agent of new life, of regeneration, each a promise for the future. I selected two cones to take with me as a remembrance. As I turned to leave, Sebastian whispered, "No, not two. Take three." Without hesitation, I selected a third and departed.

Back at the hotel, I found Bob in a deep sleep with the curtains drawn. While staring at the ceiling, I reviewed the events of the morning. One by one, I thought about the people in my life—Bob, my friends, my family, especially my mother, knowing she lived less than fifteen minutes from the hotel. I had no interest in seeing her, although Bob believed I should. As I relaxed with the thought that the worst was over, I fell into a light sleep.

When we woke an hour later, Bob wanted to hear the details of the cemetery visit. He pulled me in close and listened fervently while I described the expedition from start to finish. Time would tell whether the dreams, the anxiety, and the memories would fade. Regardless of the outcome, I felt remarkably confident after my harangue at Lester's grave.

That afternoon, we visited places of significance in my childhood. When Bob opened the door to the rental car, he saw the three pinecones on the passenger seat.

"What are they for?" he asked.

"Oh, I forgot to tell you. After acting crazy at the grave, I was 'told' to take something with me." I explained the inner voice and what it said. "When I looked around I saw all these pinecones, so I brought three back with me."

"Why three?"

"I don't know. I picked up two at first, but I was told it had to be three."

"You're not going to believe this."

"Believe what?"

When Bob had moved back to Virginia from Florida, he brought three pinecones with him as a gift to his mother.

The separate events could have been unrelated, but there was some evidence to the contrary.

Bob and I drove by the Cottage Street and Brooks Avenue houses and, from the car, I pointed out the rooms where my father had molested me. Then we drove north to the shore of Lake Ontario and walked on the beach where I had played the make-out king around bonfires. While there, Bob told me his headache had become a migraine. He had done a good job of hiding his pain, so I could do my work. He'd never mentioned migraines before, so I was naturally concerned. We purchased pain medication at a drugstore and returned to the hotel. Because the pain had upset his appetite, we ate dinner in the room and retired early.

Feeling much better the next morning, Bob suggested we go for a swim in the hotel pool. Afterwards, we made love in the room, showered together, and relaxed until it was time to leave for the airport. As we drove away from the hotel, Bob reminded me that my mother was close by. When I didn't respond, he became more insistent.

"Just drive by. You don't have to stop." I still didn't answer. "If you want to go in, I'll stay in the car. Come on. I'd like to see the house."

"All right. I'll drive by, but I'm not going in. It's not a good idea. Believe me."

As the car slowly idled past her place, we were both startled to see my mother appear at the front window. She was looking in our direction over a brightly lit table lamp, her tortured face as grotesque as a camper grimacing above a chinned flashlight. In the brief glimpse of her, I saw a harried woman. Then, just as quickly as she had materialized at the window, she turned off the lamp and disappeared back into the room. Bob felt the scene she had just played had been staged for my benefit, perfectly timed and executed to prey on my sympathies.

The thought was too much for me. I made a U-turn and drove to the airport.

12

DESCENT INTO MADNESS

Back in Washington a presence came between us, a force that would forever alter our future. The rhythm of our life together transitioned from an upbeat tempo to the blues. Bob was less carefree, gentle, and thoughtful. His eating habits changed as well. He spurned his normal diet of whole grains, fat-free milk products, fruits, salads, and egg whites and began experimenting with frozen yogurts, peanut butter, and foods higher in fat. He foraged nightly in the kitchen for snacks. The frequency of his headaches increased, as did his visits to the doctor for progressively stronger pain medications. Although I cautioned him about his preoccupation with a chemical fix for his discomfort, my advice was all but ignored.

His primary care physician finally refused to write prescriptions for a reason Bob was unwilling to discuss. I encouraged him to return to twelve-step meetings. His attendance had always been sporadic, and when he did go, it pained him to speak. Getting honest was hard, because he hated the embarrassment he felt discussing his shortcomings. He was steadily withdrawing, disengaging from the world. I was concerned that my recovery had overwhelmed him, but he insisted that wasn't the case. He talked about returning to therapy but wasn't enthusiastic about opening old wounds. When I suggested couples counseling, he agreed to go with me.

In our first session, we discussed his preoccupation with pain medications and my fear that his sobriety was in jeopardy.

I raised concerns the day I found a new copy of the *Physician's Desk Reference*—a handbook of medications—in his apartment. This was a dangerous text in his hands. The tables had turned. I was warning *him* about behaviors that could cause him to slip. When asked by Ned what I thought was happening, I lied and said I wasn't sure. Bob admitted his behaviors were symptomatic of someone on the brink of a relapse, but he insisted everything was under control. Until I had evidence to the contrary, I felt I had to accept what he was telling me.

Then Bob called me at the office one Friday and said he wanted to cancel our plans for the evening because of a headache. He had scheduled an appointment with a new doctor for that afternoon. He didn't want to be a burden, adding that he would return to his place by himself after the appointment. What he said made no sense. His primary care physician hadn't given him the required referral to see another doctor.

I convinced him to stay at my house where he could rest for the weekend. When we met after work, he was holding a prescription for Percodan, a notoriously addictive pain reliever. While in traffic, he took one pill and then another fifteen minutes later. The way he popped and swallowed both without fluids was unsettling. When I warned him about the drug, he said he was aware of the risk. I didn't want him to suffer. How could I, after all he had done for me?

The house was dark. When I unlocked the front door Bud Man the cat trotted up to greet us in the foyer. I went directly up to the bedroom to check for phone messages. When I came back down, I saw no sign of Bob in the living room and no lights in the kitchen at the back of the house. "Bob, where are you?" He didn't answer.

Sheet metal ducts crackled to life as the heating system tripped on. Something was very wrong. Afraid of what I'd find, I walked slowly into the kitchen and turned on the overhead light. Bob was sprawled on the linoleum floor, all akimbo, writhing senselessly in a state of delirium, by that time in much more pleasure than pain.

"What are you doing?" I asked.

"I feel . . . soooo weird, man," he said, trying to push himself up into a sitting position. "Jeez, that stuff is powerful shit," he added, sounding like a seventies' hippie on acid. He lost his balance and rolled onto his back. Like a feline rollicking in catnip, he was stretching and recoiling rapturously, rocking and swaying in his euphoria, not caring who was watching. When he planted the back of his head on the linoleum and arched his torso up off the floor, his level of intoxication was abundantly clear. Concerned that he had overdosed on the medication, I was furious with him for being so reckless. I couldn't decide whether to kick or comfort him.

"Stop that. You're scaring me!" I commanded. Making eye contact with me, he propped himself up on one elbow.

"Don't worry, I'll be fine. It's just that this shit has KNOCKED ME OUT!"

"Then why did you take a double dose?" I asked sternly.

"I didn't know it was such powerful shit."

"How many are left?"

"Stop worrying. I'LL BE FINE!" He was louder and aggressive, signaling a mounting irritation. I wanted to avoid a confrontation.

"If you give me the medication, we can both relax."

"What are you going to do with it?"

"I'll put it away."

Bob pulled the vial from his pocket and handed it to me. I stuffed it in the back of a drawer. My urge to flush the pills was overridden only by my resolve not to betray his confidence.

For the rest of the evening, we watched TV in separate worlds. He was in the outer reaches of *The Twilight Zone* while I was fretting over our future like a soap opera diva from *A Darker Day*.

The climate was understandably cool when we encountered each other in the kitchen late the next morning. Bob had slept the clock around but didn't appear rested. Nothing was said until I spoke softly. "You scared me last night."

"There's nothing to worry about," Bob said pleadingly.

"You didn't see yourself."

"I know, but I've got bad headaches. . . ."

"There must be a better way. What does the doctor think is causing them?"

"He doesn't know."

"Has he ordered x-rays or an MRI?"

"No."

"Why not?"

"I don't know."

After a protracted silence, Bob asked for the Percodan. I retrieved the bottle from the drawer and handed it him. Inviting me to watch, he dumped the remaining tablets in the toilet and flushed.

We both felt uncomfortable all week. The more questions I asked, the less he would talk. The less we talked, the more frustrated I became. When I confided in close friends, they all gave me the same assessment: Bob was "using" but not admitting to it. I resented hearing that, even though I knew they were right.

When I tried to reach him at his apartment the next week, I couldn't get through. Bob always screened his calls, but we'd worked out a special signal so he'd know I was calling. Either he was not at home, or he simply wasn't answering my calls. When I finally got through after two days, Bob was angered when I told him he sounded incoherent. By Friday, we had agreed to spend the weekend together, but the situation felt tense.

When I picked him up from work, I wanted to say something cheerful or supportive, but nothing came to mind. We were two islands in the front seat of my small Nissan, physically close, but separated by cold, shark-infested waters. His silence also fueled my suspicions. I thought of dropping him back at his apartment but continued.

Dream—November 20, 1993

Bob and I are at the beach in Rochester where we strolled a few weeks ago. Several gay men are watching us, and Bob is checking them out. I'm annoyed that he would do that. As we're leaving, Bob takes off down a trail that is littered with dog shit. When I warn him, he nods like he understands but continues plodding along. He steps on a mound of shit and tries to scrape it off the soles of his gym shoes by scuffing his feet in the grass.

We watched a movie and went to bed early, turning out the lights without any display of affection, a serious departure from our routine. Rolling over with my disappointment, I whispered The Serenity Prayer to soothe myself to sleep. I would be no good if I were not rested in the morning.

I slept soundly and woke at seven, surprised to find Bud Man, and not Bob, slumbering beside me. Outside, the first snowstorm of the year was dropping a blanket of snow on the back lawn. While descending the stairs with the cat matching me step for step, my thoughts were of the night a week before when Bob was squirming on the kitchen floor. "Please let me find him well," I prayed to any god who would listen. I was relieved to find him quietly doing a crossword puzzle in the family room.

He greeted me warmly, his voice more firm and positive than it had been in weeks.

"Good morning!"

"Well, good morning." My surprise at his cheerfulness must have been evident in my voice.

"I can't think of a six-letter word that begins with 'a,' and the description is, 'English gentlemen don them at the races.'"

"That's simple—ascots."

"Jeez, that's right! Why didn't I think of that?"

I peered over his shoulder to see a mass of scribbles across the puzzle and three places where the force of his erasure had perforated the paper. Bob's face was eight inches from the puzzle. I had never seen him focus so intently on a task.

"What time did you get up?" I asked.

"I had trouble sleeping, so I got up early."

"What time?"

"I don't know, six maybe."

That was odd. He always stayed in bed until the last possible moment. How could he have been so lethargic the night before but so energetic this morning? A question was forming in my mind that I dared not entertain.

Fearing the worst, I retreated into the safety of my world upstairs, straightened my room, and watered and groomed the plants. Ninety minutes later my resolve to ignore him was gone. Back downstairs, I felt my intestines churn when I found him hunched over the puzzle, exactly as I had left him. I had to know.

"I'm worried. You haven't taken your eyes off that puzzle in three hours," I said.

"Relax. There's nothing wrong!"

Bob was lying, and I refused to let the bastard have his way. I posed the question I had been afraid to ask. "Are you using? I figure you must be."

"WOULD YOU STOP? I'm not using."

I softened my tone. "Are you sure?"

"Yes, I'm sure."

"All right. I'll take your word for it. I'm going to wash up." In the shower, I held the crown of my head under the spray. I asked to be free of the thoughts dueling in my consciousness, but they refused to fade.

While tying my shoes on the edge of the bed, I thought of going through Bob's belongings in search of contraband, but that would be a betrayal. Lowering my foot to the floor, I noticed a blue capsule on the white carpet where Bob had dressed that morning. It could not have been more conspicuous if it had been planted there. I picked it up. Even without my glasses, when I rotated the capsule between a thumb and forefinger I could see the word "Pfizer" printed on its side.

Descending the stairs for the third time that morning, my thoughts were of the upcoming confrontation. My little boy was demanding retribution after having been raped by another man. Holding the capsule in the air as I entered the family room, I paused before I spoke. "What's this?" I asked in a stern voice. He answered without hesitation.

"A hit of speed."

Speed. Of course. When Bob was himself, he was incapable of staying with a task for more than twenty minutes.

"Thank you for being so honest!" I responded sarcastically. I got a blank stare in return. My temper flared, and I yelled at him. "HOW COULD YOU DO THIS?"

Startled by my anger, he rose and hustled to the front of the house. I followed closely behind, shouting at the back of his head. "ANSWER ME! HOW COULD YOU DO THIS?"

Bob ascended the stairs and sat on the fourth step. "It's not bad. I'm not using a lot. It's under control."

His comment triggered the outrage that had been building, and I charged into a tirade. From where I stood at the foot of the stairs, I began to rave, banging my closed fist on the top of the banister.

"HOW COULD YOU DO THIS TO ME?" Bob sat emotionless, saying nothing. I darted into the living room and vented from a distance. Pounding my right fist on my thigh, I screeched at him. "YOU KNOW HOW HARD IT IS FOR ME TO TRUST, AND YOU DO THIS! HOW COULD YOU LIE TO ME LIKE THAT?"

He stood and climbed the stairs and returned in a few minutes with his overnight bag.

Outside, three inches of snow had fallen; not a time for pedestrians to be trekking the highways in the suburbs. My house was three miles from the nearest subway and more than twenty miles from Bob's apartment. I struggled to regain my composure, not wanting Bob to leave in the middle of a storm.

"Where are you going?" I asked calmly.

"Home."

"You can't go out in the middle of a storm. I'll give you a ride."

"I don't want a ride." He disappeared into the snow.

"Bob? . . . Come back here! . . . Bob!"

"Just what you were afraid of, right chum? Don't say I didn't warn you. Sooner or later they all leave."

A mix of emotions smothered me—anger, sadness, rejection, and a desire for retribution. I wanted to tackle him from behind, pin him to the ground and shake sense into him, but that would be a dead end. I'd learned that from the scuffle with my first lover. A quotation I had heard years before snarled my thoughts: "A man convinced against his will is of the same opinion still."

I needed to find a way to calm the rancorous feelings gurgling in my chest. Staring through the glass storm door, mesmerized by the penny-sized snowflakes floating windless to the ground, I thought I should let go.

December 10, 1993

I'm surrounded by evergreens and boulders. In the distance, I can see Kurt at ten years old, his mother, and a friend of mine from college. All three are laughing at me and ducking behind trees when I look in their

> *direction. My college friend goads me into a fight. We grapple but no punches are thrown. He's drunk and has difficulty speaking. My ex-wife sits in our Dodge Voyager, sobbing.*
>
> *When I turn back, Bob is there and not my friend. His lower lip is swollen with a cut that runs its length. I kiss him on the cheek and tell him I hope I wasn't the one who hurt him. He says, "No, I got it from flappin' my mouth." Any ill feelings are resolved.*

I closed the door and returned to the warmth of my living room. Lying flat on the plush carpet, I studied the textured ceiling for an answer until I decided to call the local drug and alcohol help line for advice. After the second ring, I found myself explaining the situation to a woman who sounded African American. I was afraid she would give me a hard time because I was gay. My stereotyping was decimated when this throaty-voiced southern belle named Gladys gave me her straight, but tender advice:

"You love him, don't you, hon?" she asked. Startled but encouraged, I responded slowly.

"Yes . . . I do."

"And I know he must love you, too."

"He says he does."

"I'm sure he does. But he's using, right darlin'?"

"Yes . . . speed."

"It don't matter what he's using, hon. If he's gone out, you got no business bein' roun' him. You wanna stay sober, right?"

"Yes, of course."

"Then you leave him be. He'll let you know when he's had enough."

"You mean don't call him?"

"That's up to you, hon. Jes' be sure you don't get yer own self in trouble. You know about Alanon, right?"

"Yes. That's good advice. Thank you."

"You're welcome darlin'. Good luck!"

Bob partied for two weeks before he surfaced for air. Although we were in touch, our conversations were stilted and vitriolic. He revealed little about the drugs he was using. I kept to my schedule of twelve-step meetings where I could vent and keep myself sane.

At the end of the second week, Bob phoned and requested a meeting to "come clean." We spent the weekend together, and I told him what I wanted. He would have to stop using, go to meetings, and attend couples sessions. For the first time, he explained his patterns of drug use. "Cross-addicted" was the term he used to describe counter-dependence on speed and Valium. Diet pills had been his drug of choice since adolescence, his response to feelings of sadness or inadequacy whenever he was threatened. He almost always began with prescription amphetamines. One small hit would lead to increasingly higher doses. It could continue for several weeks before he would use Valium or some other tranquilizer to bring him down from his ride with the "Mad Hatter."

By the time we met for the weekend, Bob had stopped using speed and was "weaning" himself off the tranquilizers. He warned that stopping would not be easy. He had been through withdrawal from the deadly combo many times before. Twice his stomach had to be pumped after he overdosed. But it was withdrawal from Valium that was the bigger problem. So it came to pass that, several days before Christmas, Bob sought shelter with me for the weekend. My house became the rehab ward where he "checked in" to begin the withdrawal process.

> Letter from Bob—December 18, 1993
>
> *I don't even know what I want to tell you or where to start.*
> *I do know the last few weeks have been hell. For that, I apologize. I also know that upon reentry into the earth's atmosphere, the love I have for you is very, very strong. I know it's stronger than my addiction, and I feel it reciprocally from you.*
> *I thank God for bringing us together. You are a wonderful man, and your presence in my life is a total bonus. Just know that after these past six months, I have grown more connected to you and hope to keep doing so. I love you.*
> Happy 6th month,
> Bob

Bob saw a psychiatrist who reduced his Valium by five milligrams per day. Withdrawing too rapidly could cause seizures, severe headaches, tremors, nausea, or even coronary arrest. The seriousness of the matter was clear, and watching Bob suffer was difficult. He never left the bedroom that weekend, except to accompany me to a counseling session. He admitted using both drugs before the trip to Rochester, but he couldn't give a reason why. His withdrawal from Valium caused the migraines; pain that he felt obligated to endure, because I needed his support. His condition dampened the holiday season. When he wasn't at work, he lay in bed with the lights off, day and night.

He began an outpatient drug rehab program after the holidays, but he was unhappy from the start. I hoped he would bounce back quickly from his slip and had every reason to expect a rapid and sustained recovery. Bob had a good track record. It was January of 1994, seven months after we met. Planning our future went on hold until he could stabilize from the relapse.

My life was on the upswing. The vexing symptoms that had plagued me during the gestation and birth of the memories had quieted to a murmur. I was happier and more settled than I had been in years. What remained were mere remnants of those symptoms, faint blips on the screen, lesser disturbances that I could tolerate—mild nausea, occasional sleeplessness, and manageable variations in mood. I also had a distinct change in my dreams after Rochester. All but one featured Bob as a character, someone named Bob, or topics relating to Bob, including the use of drugs.

The spotlight on incest was dimmed for a time, and shifted from my past to Bob's present. It seemed as if my rise from the abyss was right on schedule, promoted by some force overseeing our interconnected lives. Had we been coupled by the heavens to fulfill an earthly contract requiring mutual support in distressing times?

Bob's commitment to recovery was lukewarm. He skipped group meetings and cancelled appointments with his psychiatrist. His languid disposition and disregard for recovery whittled away at my expectations for an end to his relapse. I had little idea what was going on inside him, try as I did to pull it out of him. Occasionally, and for brief periods, dormant craters would burst open on his unstable surface, exposing angry feelings festering inside, smoldering like molten lava.

Nightmares disrupted his sleep. His body would rear up in bed, his eyes shut, but twitching with pain. It began with him grumbling. Then he might shout incoherently as he sprang up from his sleep to challenge the enemy. I listened to his complaints, straining to understand the nature of his turmoil or its players. A few times, I shook him awake and asked what the dreams were about. Only twice did he recall the content. In one, he was yelling at his former partner for cheating on him, and in the other, he was arguing with his father.

Bob's disinclination to commit to recovery was prompting me to express concerns as persuasively as I could without destroying his confidence. In spite of my intention not to push too hard, on a few occasions, he accused me of preaching. He wanted encouragement, not criticism. Like others with addicted loved ones, it was difficult to strike a balance between praise and castigation. The advice from Gladys from the hotline served me well through that winter. In all situations save one, I turned away and focused on my own recovery.

As the last days of the month faded unceremoniously into the next, so did Bob's efforts at staying clean. He withdrew from his rehab group, claiming it was filled with brash newcomers who knew far less than he about recovery. He was about to be thrown out for poor attendance anyway. His promises to attend other twelve-step meetings went unfulfilled. Our life, once a lively brook cascading with excitement, had become a stagnant pool.

Finally, in the dead of February, in that cold, desolate void before winter begins a shift to spring, I lost all touch with him for a week.

He didn't return my phone calls. When I called his office

on Thursday, and Friday, I was told he was out sick. Alone at home on Sunday, my determination began to falter. It was a bitterly cold and windy night. An afternoon storm had dowsed the area with two inches of wet snow that quickly melted to slush. Everything froze solid when the temperature plummeted into the teens after sundown. Standing next to my kitchen wall phone, staring at its curled and tangled ivory cord stretching to the floor, I faced the fact that our relationship was just as gnarled. Sebastian urged me to accept that reality, to leave it alone, but that was more than I could abide. I dialed and listened to his voicemail greeting.

"What a mistake, my friend. When the hell will you learn?"

"Hi, this is Bob. I'm not here, so leave a message and I'll call you back."

"Bob, it's me. We can't go on like this. You've got to call me so we can straighten this out. I love you. Bye." The phone rang back right away.

"Hello?"

"What did you want to talk about?" Not a word of greeting; rather an arrogance that revealed his state of intoxication.

"You're using again," I said.

"No I'm not," he countered.

"Do I have to come over there?"

"DON'T COME OVER HERE!" It was an order.

"All right. This conversation is going nowhere. When you've had enough, give me a call."

I hung up without waiting for a response, pissed as hell. There was nothing I could do, no way I could get him to stop . . . or was there? Sebastian was elbowed aside by an angry youngster. I drove over to his place, even though I was unclear about the purpose of my visit. Maybe I'd tell him off, let him know what a jerk he was, what a worthless, spineless junkie ... or something like that. I ... I ... would DO something about it! I refused to think about *why* I was going because the reasons would be exposed as unhealthy or unwise. Responding out of anger, that depraved and destructive human emotion, I would seize control of the situation, even wrestle Bob to the floor if I had to.

As I walked to Bob's high-rise from my car, galling thoughts, defiant and unruly, were surging over Sebastian's soothing voice of reason like a hurricane demolishing a bulkhead. I must have been a dreadful sight, trudging through the frost, my brutish mug jutting out of my parka into the biting winds. Going up in the elevator, I wondered what I would find in his apartment, praying only that it not be another man. We had agreed to be monogamous but addicts lose their morals when they're high. Unlocking the door with my key, I moved silently through the narrow foyer, as quiet as a cat on carpet. The efficiency was dark as sin, dimly lit by candles and the cold light of street lamps shining through the window and reflecting off the ceiling—a setting for devil worship. A white candle, three inches up and across, flickered beside Bob where he sat lotus style on the oak parquet floor.

He was thumbing through the Yellow Pages. Across the room, a votive was fluttering inside a small ceramic holiday house atop his china cabinet. Flames danced seductively in its tiny windows. Bob's head swiveled unnaturally in my direction, like Linda Blair's in *The Exorcist,* a grisly sight if I'd ever seen one. The creature that glowered brazen-faced back at me wasn't Bob, but a deathly angel of darkness. Malice gleamed in his eyes, circled in black and bloodshot from days without sleep. I was looking at a shadow of my lover, a disembodied spirit, one of the walking dead.

"I told you not to come here."

"What are you doing?" I glanced over his shoulder to see he was reading the "Physicians" section of the Yellow Pages.

"Looking for a doctor."

"For speed or Valium?" I asked sarcastically. I was begging for trouble.

"That's none of your business!"

"I didn't come here to argue. I wanted to make sure you were all right."

"I'm fine. I want you to leave."

"How much have you been using?"

"I said, none of your business."

"I think I'll hang out for a while." I plopped down on the futon. Bob approached and glared down at me from a position of authority.

"I want you to leave . . . NOW!" His tone was gruff and imperious. He had never spoken like that before.

"I'm going to stay. I'm worried about you."

"GET OUT, I TOLD YOU!" His attitude pissed me off. The fiend took up residence in my head.

"OK! FINE! I'LL LEAVE YOU ALONE. GO AHEAD AND KILL YOURSELF, YOU LOUSY JUNKIE!" I was ashamed as soon as I spoke. I had promised never to use that word, but I'd gone and done it.

"I'M NOT GOING TO KILL MYSELF," he countered. "NOW LEAVE!"

"FINE! DO IT YOUR WAY!"

I grabbed my coat and left, my departure made final when the steel door slammed shut behind me. The elevator trip to the ground floor lasted much longer than the ride up. I was frantic about leaving him in that condition.

A procession of nihilistic thoughts, each more negative than the one before, paraded through my mind when I punched the panic bar on the lobby door and put my shoulder to metal like I was shoving a heckler out of my way.

"It was only a matter of time. You knew that. Cut your losses. He'll be in the arms of another man before you know it. Run!"

Outside, glacial winds aggravated the subfreezing temperature. I zipped my parka and fastened it at the neck before pulling on my gloves and angrily retracing my steps to the car. It was no surprise when the noise of frozen sidewalk ice crunching underfoot summoned a racking memory from decades before. I recalled with clarity the morning when my mother, my brothers, and I, dressed in the clothes we had time to throw on, were forced to flee our house on Brooks Avenue. With each crackling step, my thoughts shuttled back and forth between the two nightmares, one past and one present.

In both situations, I was running from anger, addiction, and lives skyrocketing out of control. As a child I had no choice but to flee with my family. But this was different. I was not a child, powerless over the rages of an intoxicated father. Everything inside me began to shift, to soften. Halfway to the car I turned around and trekked at a slow pace back to the building. The anger I harbored for Bob, for his insults and his behavior, began to dissolve. I couldn't leave him at a time when he might do harm to himself. It was not my father up in that apartment. It was the man I loved.

The dying flame of my anger was extinguished like a match

in a gust of wind the moment the elevator's "ding, ding" announced my arrival on his floor for the second time. Even more peculiar was the sensation I felt as I moved down the wide, carpeted hall toward his apartment. From somewhere up above, a peaceful, tender cloak descended, wrapping me in tranquility, and affirming the return of Sebastian, the one who traveled with the sainted. He was whispering in my ear and standing by my side. A fearful heart transformed into a vessel of love introduces all kinds of new possibilities.

Bob's reaction when I reappeared was not what I predicted.

"I thought you were leaving." He wasn't angry. I could even detect relief in his voice.

"I changed my mind."

"You don't need to stay."

"I know, but I want to." I stroked his cheek with the back of my knuckles in a show of affection. Bob brushed his flattop briskly with an open palm, indicating his frustration with the situation, but he said nothing to challenge my return. Over the next few hours, he became progressively more bizarre.

I didn't initiate conversations. If he spoke, I responded simply and with kindness. The strategy worked. Before long, he was confiding in me, revealing the kind of freakish suspicions that brew inside a mind frazzled by amphetamines. I became an observer of his madness, a witness to his crash dive into pandemonium. He insisted the CIA was spying on him via a surveillance device hidden in his cable jack. He studied the box for thirty minutes before splitting the cable with a jackknife and pulling it apart. When two "hot" wires crossed and the box exploded, an electrical fire scorched his white wall black and filled the room with smoke. Losing interest, he dropped the pocketknife to the floor with the frayed wires and backed slowly away from the fire that had put itself out. For safety reasons, I casually kicked the knife from view behind a bookcase.

Bob lumbered awkwardly to the rear of the room like a wounded predator stalking prey in his natural habitat. His attention was drawn to the tea light burning in the miniature ceramic house on his china cabinet. His face was a foot from the flickering candle, his arms folded at the chest. He peered through its tiny windows for fifteen minutes, like a voyeur lurking in the bushes. Afraid to be seen, he would duck from view whenever he imagined a resident was peering through a drawn curtain. In *sotto voce,* he whispered the intentions of the saboteurs he had under surveillance and the threat they posed to his safety.

He swore me to secrecy and insisted that the front door to the apartment remain locked. I was no longer distrusted. I had joined him as a fellow freedom fighter in league against the nefarious forces plotting his downfall.

An hour later, as I was dozing on the futon, he tapped me excitedly on the shoulder and motioned me over to the foyer.

"What?" I asked.

"Come here. You won't believe this." Pulling me over to the closet, he pointed to a dried can of paint on the shelf. "Look," he said. "Do you see it?"

"See what?"

"Code."

"Code?"

"On the side of the can!"

"I see instructions."

"It's binary code. A warning. It says this is the night."

"For what?"

"The abduction."

"Why don't you lie down and rest?"

"I'm not tired."

He had taken enough speed to keep Manhattan up for a week. I returned to the futon. I needed to disengage from my lunatic lover. All indications were his descent into madness was far from over. My last image before closing my eyes and drifting into a fitful slumber was of Bob, standing stiffly before the hall closet, his arms planted defiantly on his hips, his face contorted and anguished.

I was vaguely aware of his movements until the front door slammed and startled me awake at four in the morning. I called out to him. No response. A dark intuition rumbled through me. A quick search confirmed he was gone. At the door, I put an eye to the peephole, hoping he might be visible in the hallway. Nothing. I peered out the door in time to catch Bob disappearing down the stairs at the end of the hall.

I pulled on my jeans, rushed barefooted to the stairwell, and cautiously opened the door. I saw no trace of him up or down from the landing. I skipped down the stairs, two at a time, thinking I might catch him before he exited the building on the main level. There was no need for haste. He was sitting sullenly on the top step of the lower landing, his elbow propped on his knee and his chin on his fist, Rodin's *The Thinker* on speed.

"Hey," I said softly. "Where are you going?"

"Did you call them?" He was worried.

"Call who?"

"The men in the white suits! You heard the sirens!" He was serious.

"No, I didn't call them. Why would I?"

"They're coming for me!"

"Relax. No one's coming."

Another siren moaned in the distance. Bob jumped to his feet and paced back and forth. "They're getting closer!" I placed a hand on his shoulder, which he immediately shrugged off. "Relax," I said without conviction. I had run out of things to say.

Then, from a far corner of the universe, an inspiration reached me. I could call his parents. At first consideration, the idea was every bit as loony as Bob was acting in the stairwell. I'd never met his parents, and it was unlikely they'd appreciate a phone call from a stranger in the middle of the night. Bob had resisted introducing me to them. But the situation was more than I could handle alone, and maybe they could help. He was too far gone, a danger to himself—and to others if he got behind the wheel. What if he overdosed and didn't make it through this time? I decided a call to his parents was the best option under the circumstances. I needed to act fast. Bob could leave, and I couldn't force him to stay.

Moving quickly, I told Bob I had to go to the bathroom and asked him not to leave until I returned. He seemed content to hide in the stairwell. Back in the apartment, I dialed information and called his parents. A man answered after one ring, his voice sounding ill humored.

"Hello?"

"Is this Mr. Tyler?"

"Yes. Who is this?"

"Mr. Tyler, do you have a son named Bob?" After a brief pause, he answered.

"Yes, I do. Why? What's the matter?" An agitated woman in the background demanded information. "Who is it? What's wrong?" Mr. Tyler spoke to her. "It's about Timmy" (Bob's nickname).

"Timmy? What's the matter with Timmy?" He told her to be calm.

"My name is Mike Deninger," I said to Bob's dad. "Bob and I have been seeing each other for about eight months now."

"Well this is the first I've heard about it!" He wasn't pleased to be learning of our relationship in the middle of the night.

"I understand. I'm calling to let you know that Bob is using drugs again. I'm worried about him."

"Hold on." He muffled the phone again. "Timmy's using drugs again. It's some friend of his." Bob's mother got on the line.

"Hello? Who is this?" She was concerned but polite.

"Hi. My name is Mike Deninger. Bob and I have been seeing each other for eight months now."

"Timmy mentioned he was seeing someone, but he didn't tell me your name. Where is he? Is he all right?"

"We're at his apartment. He's out in the stairwell now. I'm afraid he's going to take off. He's been hallucinating all night, and now he's paranoid someone's going to take him away. I thought you'd want to know."

"Do you think we should come over there?"

"It might help."

"Will he leave if he knows we're coming?"

"I'm not sure. We'll have to see."

"What time should we come?"

"As soon as you can. I'll try to keep him here until you arrive."

"All right. We'll call you when we're ready to leave."

"Thanks."

While walking back down the hall, I composed what I would say. He was seated on the same stair, in the same position. Off in the distance, another siren began to wail, setting him off again. He jumped up.

"They're coming. What should I do?"

"They're not coming. . . . Anyway, I have something to tell you. I called your parents."

"YOU WHAT?"

"I called your parents."

"No, you didn't. You don't know their number."

"I got it from directory assistance. They're coming over."

"How could you do that?"

"I didn't know what else to do. Come back to your apartment, and let's get ready for them."

"DAMN IT! YOU SHOULDN'T HAVE DONE THAT."

Gripping the banister and hoisting himself up, he snatched his gym bag from the step in a show of disgust. After stomping angrily up to his floor and storming back down the hallway, he pushed his way into the apartment and headed straight for the shower. His parents called to say they were leaving Virginia at six in the morning. Bob took the call. He was no longer the anxious, paranoid mess he'd been on the stairwell, fretting over men in white jackets. Much more clear-headed and subdued, the prospects for guiding him back to sanity had improved considerably. The decision to call his parents had changed things for the moment.

For four hours, the three of us sat with Bob in a close circle, slowly and patiently wearing away at his stubbornness with logic and love, like water chiseling through rock over a millennium. We used every conceivable argument to convince him to stop his dance with death. Several times during the marathon, Bob lashed out at me. One accusation in particular caught me off guard. When his mother asked if he was healthy, he threw mud in my face.

"I think so, unless he's been keeping something from me," he said, looking me square in the eye.

"That's designed to discredit me," I said. "We were tested recently. We're both HIV negative."

Those barbs were a price I was willing to pay to get him back. At the end of the talk, Bob agreed to stop using and gave his father the few hits of speed he had left. We were all exhausted. His mother thanked me for calling them, then turned and stared him down, locking in his attention. "He saved your life," she said with grave emphasis. "I think you should thank him." The tears of relief forming in my eyes belied my collected appearance. "I do thank him," Bob replied, his tone bleeding sarcasm.

We attended couples counseling over the next few months, my conditions for continuing the relationship the same as they had been after Bob's first slip. He did regain his physical equilibrium after a month, but his sense of self and his capacity for joy were seriously damaged as a result of his last skirmish with drugs.

Although we never discussed it, we both knew Bob would have to be stronger before we could rebuild what we once had. He apologized several times. I had no doubt about his sincerity, making his indiscretions easy to forgive, but I did wonder whether we'd seen his last relapse.

13

SPOILED

On the second leg of his recovery, Bob committed to a more honest approach to sobriety. We talked about staying clean, family problems, and achieving equilibrium in our lives. Our conversations became highly intimate, continuing for hours at deeper levels than ever before. Discussions about his early years and his relationship with Leo, his deceased lover, helped shed light on the combustible emotions he had trapped inside. He spoke about a rift that occurred between him and his father when he was an adolescent. They were able to repair the breach to some extent, but their bond remained fragile throughout his adult life. However, that disturbance didn't compare to the indignation he expressed about Leo's unfaithfulness. Although he had no desire to keep the memories alive, he was haunted by the anger they caused.

"Leo's dead! Why lose sleep over his philandering ways?" he'd ask rhetorically.

Letter to Mom—April 28, 1994

Dear Mom:

I sent you flowers this morning. I hope you have a nice birthday. I'm doing well. In March, I celebrated two years of sobriety and I've been in a relationship with a nice man for almost a year now. I am relaxed and happy.

When I wrote to you last year, I was protecting myself as best I could. I can't explain the agony I was in, crying every day and unable to sleep more than a few hours at a time.

Once all the memories subsided and I understood the links between what Dad had done to me and my problems as an adult, things got better. I was understandably angry with everyone.

I visited Dad's grave last November to have a "chat" with him. I read a letter I'd written and cursed him out. That visit and all the counseling I've had helped me turn a corner on the pain. Nobody should have to live that way.

And now . . . what about us? If you feel guilty for what happened to me or believe you didn't do enough to stop him, let it go. I forgive you. I can't blame you for something he did. He would have found some way to abuse me, whether you were around or not. And it's possible the same thing happened to him when he was young. The past is not standing in my way when it comes to our relationship.

The present is another matter. I am who I am. People have told me you are too old to change, that you won't ever accept me. I choose to think of you more positively, as a woman who has greater capacity for love than for hatred or intolerance. But that's up to you. I would like to have you in my life, but I can't unless you accept me. For me to expect any less would be like retreating back down the hill when I'm destined for much higher ground.

I've had dreams about you recently. In one, you seemed troubled or worried. That was my sign that it was time to write to you again. I do think about you and hope you are well. If you want to talk, we can and see where to go from there.

Love,
Mike

For his part, Bob was there to support me when residuals from the past threatened my composure. During the final week of May, I regressed slowly back into a place somewhere between "depressed" and "normal." Actually, I felt too lethargic to be normal but not down enough to call myself depressed. This was my disposition the night I had an unusual dream.

> Dream—May 25, 1994
>
> *Driving down a highway, I see a large billboard with a word in dark, capital letters on a white background. It begins with an "S," but the other letters are blurred and indecipherable.*

After a sluggish morning, when it was hard to follow simple conversations, Bob and I departed for a couples' session. Tightly gripping the wheel as I sped down the expressway, I was nervous but comforted to have Bob's left palm resting softly on my right thigh. Minutes from our destination, my attention was drawn to a car flying past in the outside lane. My heart flipped when I thought I saw my father alive and behind the wheel. I was so startled that I clutched my breast and pulled off the road.

The events of the morning took an even more outlandish turn at our session.

I explained the "billboard" dream to Ned and the mysterious encounter with my dead father on the highway. Ned asked me to stretch out on the couch and begin breathing deeply. He asked Bob to pull his chair close and to hold my outside hand, never letting go, no matter what happened. Ned spoke softly, telling me to be open to whatever needed expression. I could feel Bob tenderly stroking my forearm, coaching me from the sidelines.

Feeling more at ease after several rounds of deep breaths, the tension in my chest began to dissolve. I could feel my consciousness melting away like spring snow off an old mountain. The water of my awareness was flowing down, rounding turns, trickling down through cracks and crevices, deeper and deeper, until it arrived at a clear, placid pool at my center. A message was waiting there to make a run upstream.

I could feel my spirit slipping out of my body, escaping the room, zooming off to another time and place. Every part of me was whisked away, except for the forearm connected to Bob in the therapy room. Completely severed from my emotions, I became the objective observer once again, a detached navigator on autopilot about to calmly explain what I saw.

The sounds and smells of the office receded into the background and were replaced by a menacing image that rushed forward into my mind's eye. Like a flash of lightning, the indecipherable word from the dream was projected in Panavision across the wide screen of my mind, its hidden meaning catapulted into my awareness. No longer blurry, the letters were black as tar and frighteningly clear against a blinding white background. Popping into sharp focus like the letters of an eye chart when the optometrist's perfect lens clicks into place, they spelled out "S-P-O-I-L-E-D!" This was the message being teleported up from my unconscious mind. I had been "spoiled" by my father, deflated by his neglect, but sadistically debauched by the abuse. Bob and Ned sat in silence as I impassively reported what I was seeing.

"I can see it now."

"See what," Ned asked.

"The word from the dream. I can see it . . ."

"What does it say?"

"Spoiled. It says SPOILED in huge black letters."

Suddenly, my observer status was revoked. A film clip of each assault I had recalled was telecast over my closed-circuit network. Each of the rapes was excavated from the past and reenacted in the sequence in which I had remembered them—from the fishing cottage to the bedroom. Each was given a split-second viewing. Intense pain surged through my body, an electrical charge short-circuiting every neuron, invading every cell. I doubled over but was prevented from curling into a full fetal position by the firm grip Bob had on my forearm. With each memory, I could feel my life force diminish in mass, like Alice in her Wonderland, down to thimble size, until, in all respects, I became a little boy again.

I began to whimper uncontrollably until my six-year-old sobs were interrupted by a question from Ned. "What's going on now, Mike?" Little Mike refused to answer. He didn't want to say. He was curled up behind his couch.

"What's going on, Mike?" He was speaking as softly as he could. The little guy finally responded.

"I'm spoiled," he whined in the pouting voice of a first grader. "I'm no good no more."

"You're no good no more?"

"No, I'm no good no more. My daddy hurt me and made me no good." Tears and tremors halted the discussion for a long time.

"He *did* hurt you, didn't he?" Ned was affirming the seriousness of what had happened.

"Uh huh."

"He did terrible things to you." He was reinforcing what they knew, but my adult self was still having a hard time accepting.

"Yeah!" There was resignation and a hint of acceptance in his young voice.

"And do you know where you are now?" The unanticipated question was summoning me back from the past. I felt a shift in perception. My adult self was slow to respond; it was a long journey back to that office from where the little guy was.

Relegated to observer status again, the adult responded with caution.

"Yes . . . I'm in your office."

"And do you know who's here with you?"

"Yes, Bob is here."

"And he's holding your hand now."

"Yes. I can feel him." My awareness shifted to the arm Bob had been cradling. Only after my little boy had been called forward to the present did I realize that my entire body was numb, except for the arm nestled in my lover's hands. I was stretched across two dimensions, forty years apart. The arm connected to Bob was awake in the present while the rest of me was "asleep," adrift in an ancient time warp into which Little Mike had escaped to avoid the wretchedness of the sexual assaults.

Ned invited me back to the room, gently guiding me to open my eyes slowly. He asked if I could remember what happened. I stared at the ceiling, focused my vision, and turned my head to the side. I smiled faintly at Bob.

"Are you all right?" Bob asked, concerned.

"Yes. Washed out, but I'm okay. I saw a reenactment of each time I was abused, one scene after another, like a low-budget x-rated movie. The dream makes sense now. That's how I was spoiled. He made me damaged goods, ruined me forever."

"I wish you could have seen yourself," Bob said animatedly. "It's like you actually became Little Mike!"

"I'm not sure I'd want to."

"I didn't know what to do. You were in so much pain."

"Your hand was my only link to the present. My arm was here with you, but the rest of me was back in my childhood."

In this moment of clarity, I understood the relationship between the abuse and the protective mechanisms employed by my young mind to shield me from the trauma. Called "dissociation," it's the capacity to dislodge experiences too horrible to endure from the conscious plane and then occlude them from active memory. Scientists speculate that memories are effectively blocked when special enzymes are secreted, temporarily altering the brain's chemistry. Others believe that shifts occur in short- and long-term memory patterns to help mask the recollections. I was willing to leave the science to the researchers. But I had come to know exactly how it felt to have dormant memories reappear.

That was the last time I recalled a traumatic event for a full year.

14

THE UNTHINKABLE

Weeks after that day in Ned's office, Bob began to lose his balance again. He informed me he was no longer seeing the psychiatrist, citing their incompatibility as the reason. He saw a gay psychologist for two sessions, but then dropped him as well. For the next several months, Bob was unable to stop using.

We planned a week-long vacation at the beach, but he couldn't get time off because of excessive absences. He did join me there for the first weekend, but when I called him on Monday, he wasn't at work. He told me everything was fine, but I knew otherwise. One look into his bloodshot eyes as he walked up the driveway to the beach house the next Friday night confirmed his dishonesty.

Nothing went well that weekend. Bob was missing when I awoke at 2:30 AM. Sunday morning. At 4:00 AM., his car plowed over bushes and destroyed clay pots as he pulled into the yard. I confronted him in a hushed but heated tone at the front door.

"Where the hell have you been?"

Bob seemed amused to be caught in the act, a Sylvester with Tweety's tail-feathers protruding from the side of his mouth.

"For a drive," he said haughtily.

"You're going to kill somebody. Where did you go? It's four in the morning?"

"To the beach."

"Oh, that's great!"

"I wish you'd stop worrying."

"That's exactly what I should do, stop worrying," I said to myself. Sebastian was with me. I would have to find a calm place inside. Only then would I be able to see beyond the immature grin, through his red, road-mapped eyes, and past his muddled mind revved up on speed. Convincing him to stop was a hopeless endeavor. "I'm going to bed," I said quietly.

I returned to our room where I fell asleep alone. When I woke up, Bob was gone. We talked by phone a few days later, and he asked that I not pressure him about using. As hard as that was, I did as he requested.

Speed breeds paranoia. One evening, Bob accused me of having given up on him, of pulling away. He said he could sense my interest in other men. This was untrue, but I was keeping a distance to protect myself.

He called me in an agitated state one morning. He had "misplaced" his car the night before, like it was a set of keys or something. He couldn't remember where he'd been or what he'd done. He was suffering blackouts, sinking closer to bottom. We drove around that night, hoping to jar his memory, but we never found the car.

At times, he was drug free and could talk openly about his struggle. Sheepishly, he would confess dangerous behaviors or embarrassing situations while under the influence. During one of his benders, he had altered a prescription he'd gotten from a "speed doctor" by increasing the number of refills. When he presented it at CVS in Dupont Circle, the pharmacist saw through his scam. The police were called, and Bob was told to remain until they arrived. Instead, he fled the scene, a decision he later regretted. Weeks later, the police began leaving messages at his apartment, threatening him with arrest if he failed to surrender.

In July, Bob finally admitted defeat and entered a residential treatment program not far from my home. For the first time in months, I was hopeful things might change. Those hopes eroded, however, when he left the program early against the advice of his counselor. In an exit interview I attended, the counselor asked me a direct question.

"Suppose Bob used again, Mike? What would you do?" The question moved lunch from my stomach up into my throat. I had to answer honestly.

"I'd leave."

"Does that mean you'd end the relationship?" She was forcing me to be clear.

"Yes." I turned to Bob. "I love you, but I can't stay around if you go out again."

Letter from Bob—July 23, 1994

I know I'm supposed to be doing my fourth step, but this is for you.

Today was a bitch, but look at us. It's worth it to live reality, because out of all the shit and pain comes so much love and intimacy. And I feel that intensely right now for you and about life in general.

I think it's important for you to understand that my feelings about you are real! Always remember that. Even when we're having hard times.

I've never known anyone who has the capacity to love back like you, and I know I shouldn't take that for granted. Always remember how much respect I have for you. It comes in handy when you want to run.

I'm living life for the first time and, yes, it's painful. But I think missing out on it is worse. I learned a lot today. Thank you. Nitey nite.
Love,
Bob

Following the rehab program, Bob's language was upbeat and energetic. But his nonverbal behaviors were solemn. He seemed determined to project a positive attitude and override the self-hatred that festered beneath his surface. His attempts to exude confidence could have been for my benefit, or maybe he was trying to convince himself. I kept those thoughts to myself. He was too fragile.

I chose instead to support his attempts at normalcy.

I knew we were clinging to the remains of the relationship. Bob weaned himself off the Prozac he'd been taking for four years. Discontinuing the medication following a major relapse was unwise, but he insisted that he had the support of his doctor. He spoke about this choice in idealistic terms, a "throwing off of the yoke," a courageous decision that would finally make him "drug free." I thought the decision was as ill conceived and as hollow as the cheerfulness he continued to project, but potentially more harmful. Still, I said nothing.

In September, we planned a trip to Rehoboth Beach, Delaware. The week we were to leave, I knew Bob was using heavily again, but I kept that to myself. He was certain to deny using, and we'd have a confrontation. I might even be forced to play the final relationship card. Instead of risking everything, I held what I knew until a counseling session the morning of the trip.

"What's going on?" Ned began. Dismal silence. He tried again. "Who wants to start?" More silence. Resentful that Bob refused to speak, I started.

"We're supposed to go to Rehoboth today, but I think he's using again." Bob stared straight ahead and said nothing.

"Why don't you ask him?"

Tweety feathers again protruded from his mouth. I was infuriated by the grin on his puss, a look it would have given me immense pleasure to wipe off his face. And yet, a ridiculous notion was nosing its way into my mind that was impossible to disregard. I *couldn't* let go of Bob. I would be alone again. Left alone . . . again. *Again?*

My eyeballs darted up and to the left where they always go when retrieving visual memories, jittering in their sockets like a computer in search of data. When had I been left alone? The answer came swiftly on the heels of the question. It was the night when my father had spattered me with his filth and left me alone in the dark. Forty years later, my fear of abandonment was stronger than the urge I had to knock Bob off his chair for sniggering back at me.

Rather than be alone, I would tolerate his deceit.

I projected poise and control in sharp contrast to the turbulence in my gut. I addressed Bob with patience and sober-mindedness.

"You're using, again, aren't you?"

"I'm not! I'm just tired. I haven't been able to sleep."

"Are you sure?"

"YES!" I heard a strong protest in his voice.

"Okay. If that's what you say." Inside, I was gagging on that statement, gasping for air.

How sad. Both of us were lying like Sylvesters, but for very different reasons. We headed for the beach, Bob behind the wheel of my car. When I noticed he was doing ninety miles an hour along the highway, the irony that I might actually be "speeding" to a premature death could not be lost on me.

Then it hit me. I was acting like a battered spouse, wringing my hands and afraid to stand up to my man. This was not a legacy I wanted to leave my children. And I would be goddamned if I'd keep quiet like I had when my father was driving loaded down country roads thirty years earlier.

I spoke firmly but quietly to Bob, instructing him to pull over at the next opportunity. He protested mildly but did as I asked. I drove in silence to our destination.

The proprietor of our bed and breakfast was a pleasant gay man whose patience Bob immediately tested when he attempted to barter a reduced rate by claiming poverty. As evidence, he tactlessly emptied his pockets onto the kitchen counter, plinking the few small coins he had down on the Formica. Exasperated by his antics, I stepped between the two, handed the innkeeper a credit card, and made light of my partner's silliness. I scowled at Bob, cocking my head and broadcasting a stern "Would you please stop!" in his direction.

Over dinner in a dimly lit restaurant, we stared at each other in silence, two dour faces reflected grotesquely in the table's candlelight. Bob picked at his junior salad. When he blamed me for spoiling our weekend, his aggressiveness triggered a mild panic attack that rushed through me. It was a final warning that I had to disengage or risk becoming an active partner in his unreasonableness.

When we left the restaurant, the night was as sultry as an August bayou, steamy and dense, a relentless, oppressive rainfall pounding the earth.

Back at the bed and breakfast, the host was watching the Miss America Pageant, an annual "must see" for gay men. Why are we interested? Certainly not physical attraction. I think it's an appreciation of the pageantry—the talent, sophistication, and presentations. Perhaps a carry-over from the "dress up" many of us played with mom's clothes or the production numbers some of us staged for our families when we were kids. We love a parade; it's in our bones. And who ever said you had to do art to appreciate a Picasso?

But Bob was unable to sit still. He announced he was going for a walk on the beach, arguing it was a perfect night for a stroll. I knew he'd be unstoppable, so I let him leave without protest.

When he hadn't returned two hours later, I retired to our room after Miss South Carolina won top honors. As I lowered my book to my waist and floated off to sleep, I told myself to maintain my balance, no matter what Bob did that night. I felt a step closer to letting go.

Suddenly, a hellish nightmare shattered the peace. Someone was tapping on glass and calling me in a frantic voice. It felt just like the time I had been awakened from a deep sleep in 1990, and a voice called out my name from my bathroom mirror. The disturbance battered its way into my consciousness, sounding increasingly familiar the more I turned in its direction. It was my name I heard . . . louder and louder. . . . "Mike" . . . "MIKE!" And that voice . . . the person in distress . . . I knew that voice. . . . It was Bob. Where the hell was he? What was wrong? It wasn't a dream. Bob was in the alley next to the house, knocking loudly on the window above the bed and calling for help.

"Mike . . . Mike! Open the door! MIKE, I lost my key!" His rapping was incessant, annoying. "I'm locked out. Open the door. I'm cold."

"Well, that's too bad!" I barked back through the wall, thinking I should let him rot out there. But I caved in, mostly to get some sleep.

He was drenched from his escapades, clutching his muddy gym shoes in his left hand, one white sport sock stained brown in his right, and looking like "The Creature from the Black Lagoon."

I focused on not giving him a reason to be upset. A grandfather clock in the living room chimed one while Bob changed into dry clothes. His tomfoolery was not over. He was chattering about his misadventures. He'd fallen in a sinkhole on the beach, lost one sock, all his change, and his house key. He'd loitered around the arcade until it closed and lost his way back to the house.

I had to extricate myself from the conversation, my fuse getting too close to the dynamite. "I've got to get back to bed," I interrupted.

"Do you have to be like that?" He was talking much too loudly.

"Be quiet. You'll wake up the house. Let's go to bed." But Bob didn't budge.

"Why are you being like this?" He was ready for a fight.

"I'm going to bed. Are you coming?"

"No."

I closed the bedroom door and searched his waterlogged garments for the culprit making him crazy. Tucked into his jeans in a small, cloisonné pillbox, I found two blue capsules with white crosses on them. As quickly as I had opened the box, I closed it again and stuffed it back into his Levis.

With more bad news than I cared to know, I retreated to the bed and pulled the covers over my head. I whispered the serenity prayer into my chest, eager to escape the tragedy in which I was embroiled. I nodded dizzily in and out of consciousness until I sensed someone hovering overhead. I opened my eyes to see Bob hunched over me, holding a grocery bag in one hand and gripping a pencil like a dagger in the other.

"Here, I want you to have this before I leave."

It was the surly voice of a dark angel. The single frame of that image will always remain in my memory as a haunting photo of a weekend gone wrong.

Frozen with each other, unspeaking, unyielding, and unloving, Bob added another ice cube to the freeze when he dropped the paper sack on the foot of the bed and then rushed from the room with his overnight bag slung over his shoulder. Written on the exterior of the paper bag was a note in pencil, each line making its way completely around the circumference of the sack. His letter filled the entire bag, from top to bottom. It was a deranged tirade, blaming me for our troubles and listing my shortcomings. I heard the sliding glass door open and close. Bob was gone.

Walking out with his clothes was a final statement. After packing my things and leaving a note for the proprietor, I left as well. For a short time, I regressed into my desperate, needy self and set out in search of him. I drove up and down the streets of Rehoboth, working my way from the ocean westward before realizing my desire to hold onto him, given his condition, was senseless. Here I was in pursuit when I should be headed in the opposite direction.

I gave up. Within three hours, I was home in my own bed, resolved to let him travel his own path for a while. For the first time, I vowed to get on with my life.

I resisted the urge to call him, to hear his voice, to see his face, just the way I had learned to avoid a first drink. I did prepare myself for a call from him. I would keep the conversation cordial and business-like, as unemotional as possible. I would suggest that we not see each other for at least a month. I would not blame him for the breakup and explain that I needed to be away from him while he was using.

It went well during my rehearsals—until he phoned one Friday evening.

"Hi, how are you?" He had a quiver in his voice I'd never heard before.

"I'm okay. How are you?" I was eager to hear what he had to say. *He* was the one who walked out.

"I'm all right, but I feel very strange, not seeing you."

"That makes two of us. How did you get home from the beach?"

"I hitched a ride. Got one right away." He became strangely quiet. We retreated to our separate corners, the world championship at stake.

"I have something to tell you!" His voice was playful, but anxious—spooky. "You won't like it."

"Just tell me." I held my breath.

The sigh from Bob was as deep as it was long. "I . . . uh . . . slept with some guy after I got back." He waited for a response, but I was speechless, struck by the news that I feared most. The voice in my head rattled off a stream of self-flagellation.

I told you! I told you! You stupid idiot! Those words stung like a jailer's whip, flogging my backside with brutal force. What had I done to deserve this? It must have been my fault. Whatever it was, I was sorry. I would never do it again, honest! Mea culpa . . . mea culpa . . . mea maxima culpa!

But you wouldn't listen, would you? NO! You had to do it your way. And now look at you. I told you they can't be trusted.

While that clatter was being blasted from a loudspeaker into my brain—and while my nemesis railed at me for trusting another man—Bob had gone on with the conversation.

"It was really weird, man—having sex with someone else—really bizarre! It's like I wasn't there, like it was surreal. I'm so used to having sex with you, you know? It was the guy who gave me a ride back to D.C. Anyway, we got to talking and he asked me why I was hitchhiking and I told him I had a fight with my boyfriend. He asks if I want to go home with him, and I wasn't about to refuse. I mean I wasn't going to vacillate anymore, so I went ahead and did it."

A question popped into my head. I was too hot to hold it back.

"Did you enjoy it?" I asked sarcastically. It stopped his rambling.

"Enjoy it? Well, yeah, I . . . guess I did. It was OK . . . Blah, blah . . . I mean it wasn't bad . . . Blah, blah . . . It was . . . different . . . Blah, blah . . . Weird . . . Blah . . . Blah . . . Blah . . . Blah . . . Blah."

His gibberish was bullshit being cranked out by a drug-infested mind. I interrupted Bob in mid-sentence.

"You've made your choice then," I said grimly. He was stunned.

"What do you mean?"

"It's over."

"Why?"

"We agreed—no sex outside the relationship. I want a break." *Don't pussyfoot around for Christ's sake! Dump his sorry ass!*

"For how long?"

"At least a month or two. Please don't call me."

"Are you sure?"

"Yes, I'm sure. I'm done."

I was a roaming mound of guilt after calling it off, mercilessly scolding myself for failing yet another time. But my recriminations were counterbalanced by a firm conviction that I'd done what I could. Two months earlier, I was ready to walk, but I had begged Ned to help me through one more cycle before giving up. In taking that final step, I had also put myself on notice. In a session with Ned a week after the breakup, I explained every sickening detail. I wasn't surprised when he told me the pills I found in Bob's jeans were "white crosses," a potent form of street speed. No wonder he'd been so whacked out and so abrasive.

Still, for weeks, my head was filled with obsessive thoughts of him—anger, desire, remorse, jealousy, and more desire. I never stopped hoping he would call and say he had finally conquered the addiction. I yearned to be soothed by his sexy voice or supercharged by his magnetic touch. But those cravings vaporized in a second when I conjured up the image of him at the bed and breakfast, drenched and unkempt, mad-brained and ready for war.

Except for two times when he left zany messages on my answering machine sounding like Goofy on laughing gas, I didn't hear from him until one Sunday in October. From the bitterness of his opening salvo, I knew he was fired up on speed.

"I want to know why you told me not to call you." It was a challenge, not a question. Angry that he was violating my boundaries, I tried to remain neutral.

"Let's not go through this again, okay?"

"Why? You owe me an explanation."

"I won't stay around while you're using. I've had enough."

"YOU OWE ME AN EXPLANATION!" He shouted into my ear. The cork on my temper blew, discharging the rage I'd been suppressing.

"I DON'T OWE YOU SHIT! YOU'RE THE ONE WHO SLEPT WITH THE FIRST GUY WHO CAME ALONG. NOW LEAVE ME ALONE. DON'T CALL ME AGAIN, DAMN IT! IT'S OVER."

I slammed the phone down and didn't answer when he called back. Grabbing my coat, I ran out to the first AA meeting I could find. A week later, I received a conciliatory letter.

Letter from Bob—October 10, 1994

Hi Mike:

Sorry for the altercation on the phone last week. I didn't mean to provoke you into a frenzy. I remember the way you used to encourage me to talk. Not only did I not know how, it annoyed the fuck out of me. But you're right. Talking is good. What happened was not your fault or mine. Yes, I slipped and you justifiably got angry. My using was never a reflection on you.

I wish I hadn't slept with that man, but, somewhere inside, I knew we were through. I knew you wanted to move on. I felt it in your energy. I heard it in what you said. Maybe that's why our final time together seemed so bad. But I still love you.

I hope you'll come to like me one day. You were always there for me, and, as much as I was able, I was for you. I have admiration for you and all you've had to endure. You allow no place in your life for complacency, and I respect your devotion to your family.

I miss being next to you and the fun we had. Sure, you could be an asshole, and some things you allowed me to do were worse than that.

But you're also a wonderful person, very affectionate and caring. I have no resentment.

If you ever want to see me or talk, I'll be very pleased. Stay well—inside and out.

Love,
Bob

Drawing the curtain on the relationship had not been easy. Officially, I had only asked for a trial separation, not a divorce. I didn't want Bob to give up. I wanted him to fight, but I wouldn't tell him that.

I never acknowledged his letter. I lived as if we'd never see each other again, a concept as unacceptable as it was unimaginable. In conversations with Carlene and my AA friends, I'd tell them it was time to get on with my life, but that's not what I believed. While they nodded in agreement, I'd be silently reassuring the little boy squirming inside: "I know, little guy . . . You want him back."

I played the part over the next month, wearing a weathered mask of calm, acting the eligible bachelor, a man on the rise again, but privately lamenting the end of the closest human connection I'd ever known. I remained confused about what to do. How disheartening, to be a part of a production that feels like the mega-hit of all times, only to have it fall apart during previews.

Things didn't stay quiet for long. During the first week in November, a social worker called to tell me Bob was being held in a D.C. jail. He'd been arrested for altering that prescription. She asked me to post bond. Friends and family had already said no, that he'd have to accept the consequences of his actions.

I also refused. With Thanksgiving approaching, I had made plans to visit friends in West Virginia. For the next two weeks, I wondered what had happened but heard nothing until a letter arrived at my office via courier.

Letter from Bob—November 21, 1994

You know, I am so pissed at myself right now. I wrote you the best letter last night. Can you believe I left it at home? Being sober hasn't diminished my ability to be dizzy; if anything, it's worse.

First, I'm going to take some initiative here. I love you. VERY MUCH. I have for as long as I have known you. Unfortunately, my drug addiction fucked things up. But I can't let seventeen months of pain, happiness, sadness, growth, etc. go to waste. There is something worth it. I don't want to do this with anyone else. I'm not saying I want to jump into anything heavy, but I'm not prepared to give up.

Conversely, if you don't want me in your life, then I'm prepared to respect your decision. I will no longer bother you. I don't think I've ever been as direct, and this is not easy for me.

Secondly, nobody is perfect. I made mistakes, SUE ME. I didn't do them intentionally. My addiction had nothing to do with you. It was all me. I do apologize for the deplorable way I behaved. There is no excuse for it. You were correct to disconnect. But no matter what you believe, that isn't me. It's the chemicals.

Thirdly, you are not the easiest person in the world to get along with. I have the capacity to accept you as you are. I don't want you to be perfect. That's not what this is about. It's about the things I love about you. Since you've been gone, I've been really sad and empty. I miss you tremendously.

I would like to go forward at a pace that we can both handle. How do you feel about this? I'm asking you to reconsider and to take a leap of faith with me.

So, today is Monday. On Friday after work, I'm going to that park at St. Thomas Church where we used to go. I'll wait there for you until 7:00 PM., regardless of the weather. If you want to do this, then meet me there. If you don't, then don't come. I don't need any explanations—just a yes, or a no. So, yes, you come—no, you don't.

I hope you take this at face value. Don't overanalyze or complicate what is quite simple, because I mean what I say. It's just taken me a long time to be able to say it.

I will honor your decision, whatever it may be, and there will be no recriminations.
Love,
Bob

Exactly what I'd been hoping for! Exactly what I feared at the same time!

I wanted him back, but I was afraid to give him another chance. This internal conflict would require more wisdom than Solomon brought to bear on the baby problem. He had left me no room to maneuver, no way to protect myself. That was uncomfortable. Sitting with him in our park again would be nice, but starting up where we'd left off at the beach would be tough.

I called him from work the next day, knowing I was ignoring his rules.

"Hi, it's me."

"Hi! How are you?" Bob sounded cheerful.

"I'm okay. Look, I know you didn't want me to call, but I had to because I'll be in West Virginia with Elaine and Dixie this weekend. I won't be able to meet you."

"I'm glad you called then. What did you think of the letter?"

I took my time. Our futures rode on my words.

"I liked it. I'm really pleased you're sober again."

"Thank you. So am I!"

"But I'm nervous about moving too fast. I was hurt by what

happened. It's going to take time to sort this out. I hope you understand."

"I understand completely."

"I have a suggestion."

"What's that?"

"Could we just write back and forth for a while? I'm still gun shy."

"That would be fine. I'll go first. I'll write you today!"

"I'll look forward to the letter."

The weekend away provided a welcome change of pace. We did simple things. Elaine had become a dear friend after we'd worked together implementing innovative programs while I was dean of the Kendall Demonstration Elementary School. She and her partner Dixie were the perfect pair to unwind with at their mountaintop A-frame. We swapped silly stories over gourmet dinners and shared thoughts about wellness, spirituality, and recovery over dessert. We played parlor games and quibbled over the rules. We built cozy fires and gazed out through floor-to-roof-peak plate glass at the Lost River Valley below.

When I returned home Sunday afternoon, I was as relaxed as I usually am after a long run and a hot shower. I was only slightly bothered when my answering machine refused to play back its messages. After fiddling with it for several minutes, I unplugged the monster to stop its irritating whirring noise.

Had Bob called?

I retired early, thinking about him. I had reason to be

optimistic about the future. I fell sound asleep with Bud Man curled behind the crook in my knee, purring and pawing at the comforter as if he were nursing at his mother's teat. I slept soundly until my bedside phone startled me awake at 6:00 AM. Thinking it must be a wrong number, I planned to quickly dispatch the caller.

"Hello?"

"Can I speak to Mike Deninger?" A woman's voice, business-like, official.

"Speaking."

"Mr. Deninger, there's a Maryland State Trooper outside your house waiting to talk to you. Could you please go down and answer the door?"

"Why? What's wrong?"

"The trooper will explain, Mr. Deninger." She hung up. I rolled out of bed, pulled on the jeans I'd left in a heap, and grabbed a shirt from my dresser top. Descending to ground level, I envisioned myself being carted off in cuffs for unpaid speeding tickets. What else could it be?

Padding barefooted down the ceramic foyer, I could see the trooper approaching the front stoop through the window. I opened the door cautiously, prepared not to give him access without a search warrant.

"Can I help you?"

"Are you Mike Deninger?"

"Yes, I am.

"Mr. Deninger, may I come in please?"

"Have I done something wrong?"

"No, this is not about you. We need your help."

"With what?"

"May I please step in?"

"All right."

He entered the foyer, towering over me by at least a foot.

"Mr. Deninger, do you know Robert Tyler?"

"Yes. Why? What's happened? Is he all right?"

Was it another overdose? A second arrest? My god, what could it be? I had that "sinking" feeling below my navel like when an elevator stops abruptly after a long drop. When the officer was slow to respond, I knew it was serious. Good news is given quickly; bad news is held back. "Is there a place where we can sit down?"

I led him into the den and turned to face him. The room was dark and cold, the last shadows of night quivering in empty corners. I couldn't sit. I wanted to hear this standing up. "Just tell me, whatever it is."

"Mr. Tyler was hit by a car at about 1:00 AM this morning. He was running across the Beltway near the Baltimore Washington Parkway overpass. The driver of the car didn't see him crossing to the inside lane before the car struck him."

"Is he all right?! Where is he now?" I shot back impatiently. An ending was nigh. Doors were closing around me. I began to shake from my waist to my neck, muscle spasms emoting fear in my chest and arms.

"He was thrown fifty feet. They worked on him at the scene for a long time, but I'm afraid he just couldn't hang on."

"NAAHOOH!" A protest came howling out, more a groan than a scream. How could that be true? Bob *couldn't* be dead! We were just getting started! I began to pant high in the chest, as if that would erase the words. As I regained a hint of composure, I said calmly, "Tell me it's not true!"

"I'm sorry, Mr. Deninger." His final word. No changing the truth. Bob was dead.

My legs crumpled beneath me like the girders of the Twin Towers years later. The trooper pulled me upright and guided me to the black leather couch where Bob and I had spent evenings nestled under a woolen afghan. He hovered nearby, spoon-feeding me what he knew of the gruesome accident. Not wanting to hear the gory details, I stopped listening. "Blah . . . blah . . . blah . . . blah." Then I cupped my hands around my eyes, elbows resting on my thighs, and stared at my bare feet in silence. Tears trickled down my cheeks and dropped beads of sorrow onto the charcoal carpet.

I told you, man. I warned you. You just can't trust them.

15

A SEAT AT THE BACK OF THE BUS

No one could know why Bob was crossing the Beltway at that time of night. The possibility that he was moving with conviction into the stream of traffic, making it suicide and not an accident, was a consideration. I wanted to know the truth. Bob had to be on his way to see me when he was killed. Why else would he be on foot in that part of Maryland? And if that were the case, what was his purpose?

The trooper said the paramedics had detected a weak pulse just before he slipped away. I wanted to know what his final moments were like; whether he was conscious and in pain; whether the first person on the scene gave him comfort. If I had been there, I would have lifted his twisted torso onto my lap and held him like Mary held her son in the *Pietà*. I would have caressed every inch of his mangled frame, kissed every wound.

While sitting alone with the horror after the trooper left, I couldn't get the racking vision of Bob being struck by a car and catapulting to his death out of my head. That ghostly reenactment of those last few seconds played like a morbid outtake from a gory film. Its graphic nature brought on an attack of the jitters.

For the next two hours, I paced back and forth in my kitchen, as restless as a caged leopard, occupying myself with menial chores the way a mother does when she loses a son to war. I was much too resentful to seek comfort from a god who would allow him to die. Too early in the morning to call a friend, I felt locked in a holding pattern, circling in place, a captive of those unwanted images.

I finally came to rest on the top step of my first-floor landing and stewed, churning out cynical thoughts. *What if Bob's death was divine retribution for my past sins, a grueling reprisal from a vengeful God?* I recalled a moment when I was twelve years old and kneeling in church. I was about to receive the sacrament of Confirmation, a passage into adulthood during which the bishop anoints your forehead with holy oil and taps you on the cheek to encourage you to receive the holy spirit. I was in a dreadful predicament. I had cursed at my brother that morning for tackling me on the front lawn. A costly mistake. Swearing was a mortal sin, and you could not be confirmed unless you were in a state of grace.

Just before the ceremony, Sister Marie Jeanette reminded us that Father Dunn was hearing confessions at the back of the church if we needed to be forgiven. I remained in my seat. Standing up in full view of my classmates was an embarrassment I was unwilling to endure. If I stood, they would taunt me about my sinfulness. The self-righteous busybodies, the same ones whose aunts were nuns and uncles were priests, would badger me until I disclosed which of the commandments I had broken. I'd rather go to hell than expose my crime.

So I went through the ceremony in mortal sin, hoping I wouldn't explode at the altar rail. A worse offense was tacked onto my soul for receiving the sacrament in a state of sin, and I'd lose heaven if both sins weren't absolved before I died. I never did confess them. I have since hoped that a forgiving god would not harbor a grudge for that long. However, the possibility that I was finally being punished for those two sins did cross my mind as I sat on the carpeted landing the morning Bob died.

The bubble of my daydream burst like a pin through a balloon when the doorbell rang. A ridiculously optimistic thought occurred to me. *Maybe it was Bob; maybe the trooper had been wrong.*

I rose from the steps and moved slowly to the window, carefully parting the mini-blind slats with two fingers like a gangster on the lam. I peered down on the front stoop. There, rocking on the soles of their feet, were two young, strapping Mormons. Dressed in white shirts and black ties, knapsacks perched on their backs, they were ready for the umpteenth conversion of their day. In no mood to listen to snot-nosed missionaries sermonizing about ultimate truths, I skulked away from the window. I retreated to the back of the house where I paced the circumference of my cage again.

The trooper had asked for an address for Bob's next of kin. His belongings would be held for the family when they claimed the body, the trooper had said. A chill shot through me when I heard the words, "the body." He'd only been dead a few hours, but he'd already been relegated to the status of an object, a carcass without rights or persona. What they would call his "remains" would be disposed of in a manner that his biological family would determine. I had no say in the situation.

The trooper asked me not to call his parents until the police had time to notify them. I bristled at that request. Who the hell was he to tell me not to call? How did he know I was not just as much family as his blood relatives? But it never occurred to me to ignore the request.

During our first summer together, we talked about death. Bob had made me promise to have his body cremated if anything were to happen to him. He wanted his ashes spread in the waters off Bahia Honda, a beachfront park at the tip of Florida where the Atlantic and the Gulf of Mexico converge. We had discussed suicide in that same conversation. I warned him not to leave that way, or I would chase him into the next dimension and wring his neck.

Bob may not have meant to end his life, but he had at the least died a victim of his own recklessness.

I wanted to see him one last time. I waited until evening before calling his brother. I got no answer. In case he'd not heard the news, I left a vague message, asking him to call me about an urgent matter. When he didn't return my call, I left for an AA meeting. I would have to tell the story of Bob's death to a room filled with friendly faces but, still, it wouldn't be easy. My sponsor sat beside me and rested his hand on the nape of my neck as people drifted in. The room drew silent after the introductions and waited to hear what I had to say. They must have had advance word.

I struggled for control while telling the story, holding my emotions at bay. In the end, everyone in the room shed tears of their own. Losing friends to addiction is not uncommon in our circles. Another member of our group had taken his life that year, a closeted religious man who could not reconcile his desire for men with the shamefulness he had learned in church.

On the drive home, I recalled an oath Bob and I had sworn that the first one of us to die would contact the other from the afterlife. As I entered my foyer, I decided I had to get my answering machine fixed or purchase a new one. I didn't want to miss a message from his family. When I sat on the floor next to the device, I wondered whether Bob's spirit might be trapped somewhere in between dimensions. I'd heard that sometimes happens with suicide victims. With its Playback button stuck in the down position, the machine was dead, except that its blinking, green light indicated a message was waiting. Unplugging the machine, I plopped back against the wall with a thud and started to cry.

Everything was dying—Bob, the machine. What would go next? I gazed up at the vaulted ceiling and asked him, "Are you all right? Please let me know." Feeling foolish for thinking I might actually get a response, I pushed away from the wall and plugged the machine back into the outlet. The recorder jerked alive with clicks and groans.

Like a voice from a séance, Bob spoke to me through the machine. "Hello? Hello? Hello, hello, hello! Is Kyeesha there? Hello? Are you there?" As magically as the machine had come to life, it clicked dead once again, its green message light out and its Playback button stuck in the down position. Kyeesha was his pet name for me, a playful, upbeat greeting, particularly when I was down. The message had been on the machine for months and was actually recorded during one of Bob's darkest drug episodes. But what did it matter? It was his deep voice that buzzed into my skull and resonated through me like divine grace cleansing a repentant sinner. Bob had kept his promise. He was all right. I felt full of his love.

I still hadn't heard from his family the next morning. Any information I learned would have to be discovered on my own. No obituary appeared in the paper, and I saw no mention of a pedestrian accident on the Beltway. One thing I did know for certain: Bob was still being held in the morgue in

Baltimore. When I called Elaine to tell her he was gone, she reminded me that Dixie was a Maryland medical examiner, and an autopsy was sure to be conducted. They were able to keep me informed all week. Contrary to what the trooper had said about Bob having a pulse at the scene, Dixie felt certain he'd died instantly from his injuries.

Funeral arrangements couldn't be made until his body was claimed, so I still might see him before he was gone. When I reached the trooper who had come to the house, he confirmed that Virginia officials had assumed responsibility for notification of the family and gave me a number to call. The Virginia dispatcher was reluctant to release information, because I wasn't a blood relative. I had no rights. I pressed her for an exception, explaining that Bob was gay and I had been his partner. I emphasized how concerned I was that the family be notified. The woman finally gave me the name of an officer to contact. Three phone calls and hours of frustration later, I was surprised to hear that his family had been notified hours after the accident. If they knew, why weren't they returning my calls? They would be making arrangements, and I wanted to know what they were. Because Bob was Jewish, the internment could be done quickly.

For two years, I had worked as a diversity trainer with the National Coalition Building Institute (NCBI), an organization whose stated purpose is to reduce all forms of prejudice and discrimination. I had registered for a retreat for its gay and lesbian trainers to take place the following weekend, but I was reluctant to leave the house. I phoned the workshop coordinator to tell her I was canceling my attendance and explained the circumstances. In a gentle but pressing tone, she argued that the retreat might be a good place for me. I knew she was right, but I had to see Bob. I had to.

I left another message on his brother's answering machine, explaining that I understood the family had been informed and asking if someone could please call me. Bob's father returned the call. Following an extreme reaction to her son's death, Bob's mother had been hospitalized to assure her safety. We exchanged condolences and talked briefly about their final conversations with Bob. I learned he'd been evicted from a halfway house for using drugs while I was in West Virginia. His parents planned to pick him up the next morning, but he disappeared before they arrived.

His whereabouts for those next three days would never be known. As delicately as I could, I asked his father if arrangements had been made. I explained I was scheduled to attend a retreat, but I would change my plans to be part of any service they might have. No arrangements had been made because all energies were focused on his mother's recovery. Bob's body would remain in Baltimore until her condition had stabilized. His father suggested I go to the retreat as planned, promising to call if they made any decisions.

Attending the retreat was a wise decision. As diversity specialists, all the participants had been trained to facilitate intense emotional discussions at the workshops we led. But, as healers, we also needed opportunities to focus on the pain in our own lives—the oppression we faced as gays and lesbians; the abuse that some of us had experienced as children.

During the opening session, Sherry Brown, the Executive Director of NCBI, held my hands in hers as I told the group the fractured tale of Bob's death. The presentation began as a chore but turned into an experience I will always cherish. At the end, when I felt depleted, when I thought I had no more tears to shed, Sherry coaxed me to be open to the love in the room. She spoke reassuringly as she squeezed my hands.

"Mike, I want to thank you for sharing your story. I know it was hard." I nodded and sniffled in agreement. "You loved Bob, didn't you?"

"Yes, I did." Tears flowed again.

"Tell us how much you loved him." It took several seconds to get two words out.

" . . . Very . . . much."

"Yes, very much. And you're not the least bit ashamed that you loved him in the best way you knew how, are you?"

"No, I'm not." My colleagues came alive in response to my testimony. Comments were shouted from the back of the room: "That's right, Mike," and "You tell it, honey." I could feel a tingle rocket up my spine.

"And you'll always remember the wonderful times you had with Bob, won't you?"

"Yes, I will." She turned to address the group.

"In a moment, I'm going to ask each of you to make a commitment to support Mike while he's here this weekend. You will show that by raising your hand. You will be promising to hold Mike in your heart and comfort him while he grieves the loss of Bob. Are you ready?"

Heads in the group nodded enthusiastically. "All right. If you agree to support Mike during this retreat, please signify that by raising your hand and keeping it in the air for him to see." Every person in the house raised a hand high. "Mike, take your time. Look out across the room and see all the support you have this evening, all the love for you at this difficult time. Do you see the hands?"

"Yes."

"Good. Now look at each face. Can you see the love in their eyes?"

I nodded. She was right. I could see their love. "And you know you can lean on them?"

"Yes, I do."

"How does that make you feel?"

"It makes me feel good." A shy smile slowly dimpled across my face, and a single tear raced down to a corner of my moustache. The smile sparked their enthusiasm, igniting the entire group into cheers, hoots, and applause. They rose to their feet, stomping and shouting, whistling and howling exuberantly. Never before had I felt so much love.

During the break that followed the presentation, I checked my voice mail and found a message from Bob's father. The Stein Hebrew Memorial Funeral Home in Washington would handle the arrangements. The simple service the next evening would be private, with only the immediate family in attendance. He would be cremated immediately following the ceremony. What I had feared was now official. I was not welcome there.

Undaunted by the message I was certain he intended as final, I called the funeral home and asked if I could see Bob on my own before the service. The gentleman with whom I spoke sounded like "family." Although he seemed understanding and sympathetic, he said he'd need permission from the next of kin before a private viewing could be arranged. I called Bob's father again and reached him at the hospital.

When I asked for permission, he said he was not sure that would be possible. When I explained that Stein's had agreed to arrange a viewing if the family approved, he hesitated before promising to make the call.

Stein's had not yet heard from the family when I called the next morning. Reacting to my disappointment, the gentleman suggested I call again later. When a message from Stein's was delivered to me in the meeting room that permission had been granted, the workshop leaders suggested I take someone with me for support. I chose a mild-mannered southern gentleman, also named Bob. I had seen him demonstrate great compassion working with others.

I'd also been in touch with my deaf friend Carlene, who worked in the same department at Gallaudet. I trusted her more than anyone in the world. When we talked on the phone through an interpreter, she asked if she could accompany me to Stein's, and I accepted her offer.

It was Saturday, December 3, 1994, five days after Bob's death, when the funeral director greeted us in Stein's front parlor, a room thick with the fragrance of chrysanthemums and peace lilies. Dressed in a dowdy, hearse-black suit, the uniform of undertakers, and bearing a striking resemblance to Herman Munster, he recited the customary remarks designed to put mourners at ease. Formal, grisly, and too damn gloomy, I thought. "The deceased will be presented unclothed on a stainless steel gurney, covered only by a simple, white, linen shroud. The body will feel cold to the touch, because it has been refrigerated to prevent decomposition. As

Mr. Tyler's loved ones, you will have to prepare yourselves for a shocking experience, because the trauma to his anatomy was massive and severe. The room where you will visit with the departed will be well lit, but might seem unusually stark, because it's a holding area and not a formal viewing room. There is no seating for invited guests, but you are welcome to remain with the dearly beloved as long as you wish."

I struggled to interpret the language of the dead that Herman was speaking. My mind was otherwise engaged. I had disappeared inside myself to prepare for the final *tête-à-tête* with my lover. As we moved in silence down a brightly-lit corridor to what I imagined would be a dungeon in the bowels of the mausoleum, the only sound was the syncopated scuffling of four pairs of feet on tile and the whisk-whisk of fabrics brushing together at the thigh. Carlene and Bob were each hugging a shoulder.

There was no door, only a framed doorway, at the entrance to the room where the director stopped and turned to face us. With a sweeping motion of his left hand into the entryway, the man bowed his head and whispered reverently, "Your loved one is here. I'll be in the office if you require assistance."

We rounded the corner and came to a halt in the doorway, Carlene and Bob hovering so close I could feel them breathing. My head turned to the wall in discomfort at the first sight of Bob across the room. Out of concern, Carlene "spoke" gently in American Sign Language (ASL) to me. "You don't have to do this if you don't want to." I signed back. "I know, but I want to."

Gazing at my Bob, I was struck by how small he looked. Lying naked on a slab under glaring overhead lights in such a large, barren space would dwarf a giant. Stepping forward,

I paused halfway to the body. In no hurry to rush through the visit, I was vividly aware I'd never done anything remotely similar. I had to write the script and act the scene with each step I took.

Bob's body was covered neatly to the shoulders by a bleached linen sheet, looking like a breathless puppet tucked snugly into his carrying case. Only his neck and head were visible at the left end of the table. His countenance showed the pasty-faced mask of the deceased—colorless, unwholesome-looking, but finally serene. I wondered whether his ghost was hovering above his frozen corpse, a restless spirit dawdling long enough to catch the final meeting of his paramour with the shell he'd left behind.

I hadn't been that close to a corpse since my Aunt Eileen passed when I was twelve, and I felt uncomfortable then. I considered how I would say goodbye: Only look at him? Touch him? Kiss him? Kiss him . . . *Kiss him where? On the lips?* No. This was not Bob. The hulk before me was old and wrinkly, creepy, repulsive, a bad nightmare. I couldn't kiss those chilly, clotted lips. The Bob I longed for was the one who could excite me, not the one who lay stiff on the slab. I wanted him robust and manly once again.

I glanced over my shoulder at my cohorts. Carlene immediately took a place beside me, locking her right forearm inside my left and fingerspelling, "What a waste," with her other hand. Her comment evoked sadness, but I stifled the tears. When she squeezed my left hand in her right, communicating a message of support, I patted the top of her forearm and released her grip. Leaving her in the middle of the room, I approached my partner.

Standing close to the cart, I spotted a long, half-moon-shaped scar behind his right ear, perhaps an injury he sustained when he was struck but more likely an incision from the autopsy. It didn't matter. I had little interest in knowing exactly how Bob died. He was gone. Why go fishing for more information?

The chalky cast of his face and the blue tint of his lips looked no less dreadful up close than they had from a distance. His upper torso was bloated, perhaps the work of a careless embalmer. Bob would have considered this imperfection grotesque. I imagined him studying his full profile in a mirror and being thoroughly disgusted with the size of his belly. He would definitely have wanted his colorless hair dyed as well. Darker than chestnuts in life without a trace of salt, the color had gone stone gray in the few days since the accident. The traits I cherished most about him, his deep voice, his passionate kiss, and the warmth of his touch, were gone. No matter how hard I tried, I couldn't conjure those back to consciousness. The feel of my lover was floating away like driftwood on the evening tide.

The inventory of his appearance complete, it was time to say goodbye. I raised a trembling hand and placed it tentatively on his chest, afraid to touch him. The chill of his gelid flesh from beneath the linen troubled me more than his appearance. It communicated a finality that looks alone could not convey.

Ashamed that I lacked the courage to hold the corpse close, I let loose the wall of tears I'd been holding back. Involuntary contractions of my diaphragm pumped out bursts of grief and waves of regret. I wept swollen tears over all that Bob and I might have become together.

Calming myself, I moved closer in. Leaning forward with my eyes closed, I lowered my face to the shroud and gently rested my forehead on the ice-cold surface of his chest—just to feel him one last time. I was lost there for a while, dreading what life would be like without him, until I heard Bob's voice telling me not to be sad. I heard it again. Pushing myself up with the palms of my hands, the moment had come. What was left of Bob would be torched that evening and a portion of his cinders dumped into a jar.

I leaned forward and planted a soft kiss on his deeply furrowed brow. The feel of his crystallized flesh was a shock to my warm lips. I resisted an urge to recoil. Standing up, I placed my right hand on his heart and patted him gently in a final farewell. I felt ready to leave.

Carlene and Bob blurred when I turned to face them, my eyes brimming with tears. I approached their murky forms, stood between them, and placed one arm around each of their backs. They each swung an arm around me and cuddled closer until three heads joined in an intimate semi-circle. We held each other, fastened in a wordless embrace, until I felt ready to leave. Wiping away the tears with the back of my hand, I turned and glanced at Bob for the last time.

We left the chamber and started a casual pace back down the hall, my companions still close. Suddenly, the realization that I would never, ever see him again chilled me to the bone. Nothing could stop the thought that I had been abandoned yet again. The emptiness was overwhelming.

My feet stopped working. I slowed unsteadily, swiveled, and felt my back slam against the wall. I began a quick slide down to the linoleum. I hadn't fainted, and I wasn't dizzy. My body simply refused to go on. When I was halfway to the floor, Carlene and Bob caught me under the arms and lifted me back to a standing position. My feet, in a tangle, dragged behind like a drunken sailor's until I regained control and planted them squarely beneath me again.

Gay widowers know how it feels to be shunned following the death of a partner. We're often excluded from funeral services or relegated to "a seat at the back of the bus," out of sight. Even though these oversights come as no surprise, it's painful to be treated without respect. Every gay person has horror stories about exclusion following the death of someone they loved. Some are even put out on the street when covetous family members confiscate the property where lovers have lived together for years. Out of necessity, gay people have created their own ways to grieve.

I held an open house the next day for friends and colleagues who had expressed a desire to comfort me. Floral arrangements were delivered to the house, and people drifted in with bagels, cream cheese, deep dishes, and love. They huddled around the gas fireplace where I retold the tale for all who came. I stayed in "business mode" until my friend Lisa Jacobs shattered my façade. After telling me how sorry she was, she said, "You didn't need this." Lisa and I had co-taught a graduate course together at Gallaudet and she knew everything about me—my recovery from alcohol, my struggle for acceptance from my family, the incest, and the ups and downs of the relationship with Bob. Tears then flowed until the last person departed.

The next day, I was shocked to find a letter from Bob in my mailbox, written two days before Thanksgiving.

> Letter from Bob—November 22, 1994
>
> *Dear Mike:*
>
> *I guess enough time has elapsed since our phone conversation that I calmed down. At least I can type without shaking. I can't believe what a mess I was. I was really pleased you called me and that you liked the letter. I didn't know what to expect. When I heard your voice, I just knew you were going to tell me to go fuck myself. Anyway, I'm glad you didn't.*
>
> *I hope you have a nice time in West VA. Please tell everyone I said hi.*
>
> *Love,*
> *Bob*
>
> *P.S. By the way, my zip code is 20005. What's yours? Is it 20075?*

The letter had been delayed because Bob had used the wrong zip code. Skeptics would argue it was a coincidence. To me it was more. He was speaking to me from above the clouds again, keeping his promise.

I raised the letter to my face and sniffed both sides for his scent. I smiled and whispered to him, confident he was listening. "You're still here, aren't you? And this is how you want me to remember you."

I lingered by the mailbox, speculating. Friends had asked why Bob ran into traffic and whether his death might have been a suicide. No one knew. He may have feared we'd never be together again, despite the upbeat tone of his letter and our pleasant conversation before I left for the mountains. He might have been down on himself for relapsing and getting evicted from the halfway house.

Perhaps suicide became an attractive option. He might have been unable to embrace a future that included drug charges, mounting debt, disappointed family members, and a lover who was keeping him at arm's length.

On the other hand, he might have believed he could safely weave his way through traffic that night and make it to the other side. That, however, seems the least likely of the possibilities. Putting those speculations aside, I turned away from the mailbox and affirmed how pleased I was to have his last letter in hand.

From that moment on, I talked frequently with him, believing I could have his ear. And he kept talking to me.

> Dream—December 20, 1994
>
> *I'm seated on the couch in the living room on Brooks Avenue. Several men are there I don't recognize. I feel a threat of violence. A gentle, sandy blond man stands near the front door. A dark-haired man behind me pulls out a gun and shoots the blond guy, but the bullet hits him without much force. The blond guy also has a gun but has trouble getting it out. I duck down with my hands over my head. Later, when I inquire about the young man, I'm told he's dead. I get a phone call from Bob. When I answer, he says, "Hello? Is this Kyeesha?" It's nice to hear his voice again.*

The winter holidays were overshadowed by the memory of Bob's withdrawal from Valium the year before. Kurt and Renee had shared Christmas with me on both occasions. In 1993, it was with Bob while he was recovering from his first relapse. In 1994, they were helping me mourn his loss. Kurt, about to turn seventeen, was a junior in high school, already two inches taller than me and proud to let me know that. We had played a "two-on-two" basketball match in Glenarden Woods Park a couple weeks earlier against two guys his age. We were a good team, even though we lost by a hair. Renee was a senior at University of Maryland College Park, a member of the university dance team, and an officer in her sorority.

My new townhouse, a sprawling, pristine, undecorated space, had not yet become a home. Christmas decorations were left undisturbed in their boxes, because I was uncomfortable expressing joy that couldn't be sustained in my heart. I did have one glistening moment two days before Christmas, when a card arrived from my mother. The rift in our relationship hadn't been healed, so her handwritten note came as a pleasant surprise.

> Note from Mom—Christmas, 1994
>
> *Dear Michael:*
>
> *I wish you the best in this holiday season, especially since hearing about the recent loss of your friend. May God bless and keep you.*
>
> *Love,*
> *Mom*

By acknowledging the loss of my "friend," my mother had communicated for the first time that gay relationships in my life might not be ignored. Bob's violent death was the catalyst that softened her refusal to accept me fully. I phoned to tell her how much the card and her tender words had meant. Although I could tell she was still ill at ease, we had taken an important first step, thanks to Bob's untimely demise.

Mrs. Tyler and her husband invited me to lunch a few months after Bob's death and we chatted on the phone a few times. They asked me questions I couldn't answer: Why did Bob start using drugs again? Why was he running across the Beltway? Did I think he was coming to my house at the time of the accident? His mom wanted to know what could have gone wrong a few days before the accident. I had no answers.

They shared a copy of the coroner's report with me. No drugs were found in his system. That didn't make sense. Why would a man who was drug free and in his right mind risk his life by trotting across a super highway?

When she told me it was Bob's wish to have his ashes spread in the waters off Bahia Honda, I confirmed that he had made the same request of me. The family planned to wait a year before making the trip to Florida. I made it clear I felt obligated to be with them, given the promise I had made to Bob. They said they understood.

After hearing nothing for several months, I called to inquire how they were doing. I was invited to lunch again. His parents would never know how disappointed I was when they told me they had scattered Bob's ashes weeks before. They gave no explanation as to why I wasn't included. Instead, they handed me two snapshots taken that day at Bahia Honda. I studied the photos silently while Bob's mother described the exact location beside a grove of trees where Bob's ashes had been strewn in the surf. I feigned interest in what they were saying. "Blah . . . blah . . . blah . . . blah." I felt betrayed and resentful. The photos were an exclusionary tactic designed to appease me. Worse yet, I was sure they had no idea they were forcing me into a seat at the back of the bus.

After that, I fell out of touch with his family. I called them from time to time to say hello, but there was never anyone home. For about three years after his death, I talked to Bob, whenever I felt his presence beside me at home. While washing dishes one winter afternoon, I passed gas and filled the kitchen with a foul odor. I heard him chide me for farting with the words he often used: "Oh, oh, Big Bang!" I bellowed laughter throughout the house before speaking confidently to him. "I know you're here, you devil! And I'll always love you." A chill flashed over me like prickly heat, causing the hair on the top of my arms to stand. He *was* there. I was certain of that.

I craved affection after Bob's death. I hated being alone. I began to prowl in the evening for one-night stands without any expectations beyond a morning cup of coffee. I hadn't been in a gay club since I met Bob, so putting myself back "on the circuit" was discomforting. I started frequenting "leather bars" in search of anonymous sex after which phone numbers were rarely exchanged. Called leather bars because patrons will occasionally dress in black leather accouterment—belts, armbands, studded harnesses and collars—these clubs portray an image of kinky, perverted sex that, in practice, is largely untrue.

Customers mill about shirtless in those bars, some in revealing states of undress. Guys troll around the room staring lasciviously into the eyes of men they find attractive, halting a few feet in front of a prospect and staring him down in a penetrating manner. Others prop their backs against walls and mug at the passing parade. They stand with arms folded defiantly across their chests, posturing like glum-faced divas. But the leather scene is a fanciful game that lonely men play, not the menace it appears to be.

Contrary to the gruffness portrayed, many of these "leather queens" who prance and pose by night are mild-mannered, white-collar workers by day. Most are regular guys who engage in normal sex practices, not the sadomasochistic brutes their evening attire or their theatrics suggest. In reality, they're amateur thespians in an elaborate role-play. Like pompous peacocks strutting around a grungy, dimly lit barnyard, they portray exaggerated, super-macho caricatures, probably to compensate for the times they were called a milquetoast on the playground. Underneath their rough exteriors dwell kind-hearted souls searching for the same uncomplicated affection that drew me to their hangouts.

I went through a flock of peacocks in the three years after Bob died; each bird less thrilling than the one before. Always safe, so never sorry. The lovemaking was as humdrum as cattle mating in the pasture—passionless, unemotional, and unsatisfying. The encounters were devoid of substance and without wholesome futures. Each meaningless tryst had a simple, nonbinding contract lasting only a few hours; an agreement I could cancel at will without further obligation.

Although those liaisons did nothing to nurture my soul, I stayed in control the entire time, knowing I could feed at the trough and leave, no questions asked. Avoiding prolonged entanglements protected me from harm. The sex during that period was spawned by a voracious appetite for warmth, but any closeness was restrained by a fear of intimacy following

Bob's betrayals. I made sure I wouldn't be abandoned by deserting each one of them before he ever got close. Thus I became a master of the preemptive strike.

16

REBIRTH OF WONDER

I arrived in The Big Apple on my fifty-first birthday in 1997. The city was nothing like what I remembered. Not one panhandler accosted me all day. The alleys were clean; the streets bustled with energy. New York was reborn—and so was I. I was reminded of a line from a classic Lawrence Ferlinghetti poem: "I am waiting for a rebirth of wonder." I *was* waiting. And I was ready.

I had opted to retire six months earlier during a university downsizing. I was thrilled to be starting over. I had completed my graduate studies in mental health counseling and was about to accept a position as a therapist at a Miami hospital when I was offered a leading role in the premier of a New York play. I turned down the Miami job to follow a dream. Everything was about to change.

Tim McCarty, an old friend, and the genius behind an international theater group called Quest4Arts, called to ask if I would perform a staged reading. It was a new play by Willy Conley, a deaf faculty member in Gallaudet's Drama Department. Tim had cast me as Christ in *Superstar* in 1979, and he thought I was well suited for the role of Grandpop in *The water falls*. The play would be produced by the New York Deaf Theater organization in a few months, and the director came to the reading. He was impressed enough to offer me the role in the upcoming premier. Although I had not acted professionally to that point, I had frequently worked as an ASL interpreter at productions in Washington's major theaters. This invitation to spend the summer onstage—paid, even—surprised and thrilled me!

One day, while riding the subway to rehearsal at the Chelsea Playhouse, I was feeling remarkably content. An elderly priest boarded the 9 train at 23rd Street and sat opposite me, fingering a rosary. Glancing up from my script, I was startled by his resemblance to my Grandpa Mike. My mind connected the sighting of this look-alike to a rosary I'd found on a park trail the week before. I made a mental note to send the beads to my mother. She'd like that.

After rehearsal, I hopped the same train back up town to catch a commuter from Penn Station out to my place in Jersey. At 23rd Street, the first person to board after the doors slid open was the same Grandpa Mike look-alike from that afternoon. What were the chances of that? I felt a chill. My thoughts zoomed back forty years.

From the time I was no taller than a yardstick, I had great admiration for the saints pictured in prayer books, their halos floating over their heads and sunlight beaming down on them through stained glass windows. How did prayer work for them? I wanted the strength it gave them to face adversity. But I always got the same disappointing result whenever I prayed—nothing. The smallest miracle could have made me a believer, but I never felt a connection. We were always told to "practice our religion." But the word "practice" made no sense to me. From what I could see, everyone was "practicing" right up until his or her casket was lowered into the ground. And no one ever got it right.

The nuns continually told me I might be "called" to a life as a priest. I prayed for that "call," but it never came. What happened in sixth grade was certainly not a call, just a lesson in humility. Each spring, I built an elaborate shrine beside my bed to honor Mary, the Queen of May. I surrounded her statue with blue and white crepe-paper streamers, tulips and lilacs swiped from our yard, and candle stubs pressed in hot wax on saucers. Kneeling at the foot of Mary's chipped plaster figure (nothing in our house was unblemished), I prayed for her intercession. When the candles sent smoke shadows oscillating up the wall, I squeezed my eyes tight and asked for a sign. *She could make my father stop drinking.* That would be a good sign. *Anything* would be fine.

Despite building shrines for years, I never heard from her. Not once.

Sunday mornings, I always knelt erect at Mass (only sinners slouch) and clearly enunciated the prayers Sister Ignatia had taught us in second grade. When those prayers yielded no response from on high, I figured there must be something wrong with my approach. Not one to give up easily, I stopped at the side altar after Mass and dropped a dime into the brass box beside the tiers of blood-red, glass vigil lights. Using a long, balsa taper, I'd transfer fire from a lit candle to a fresh votive. After shaking the flame from the taper like fever out of a thermometer, I stared at its smoldering tip, mesmerized by the smoke rising like a genie from a lamp. Kneeling on the thick, red velvet pad at the altar rail, I pleaded for inspiration. But even that changed nothing. Self-critical thoughts flushed into my mind from a bottomless reservoir of negativity. I felt worthless and sinful.

The most highfalutin service of the year took place on Holy Thursday night. Gilded vestments (priests in high drag), opulent floral arrangements, chilling choral music, and hoards of people helped create this dramatic Mass. A blend of exotic fragrances honeycombed through the church. Incense commingled with the scents of Easter lilies and beeswax candles. The smells tickled my nose and begged me to sneeze. Each time the choir voices rose to an explosive crescendo, my senses peaked with a rush and subsided with them, too. Vibrations from the sixty-three-pipe Wurlitzer organ made my cheekbones vibrate like a tuning fork and caused the back of my throat to tingle. Our pastor, carrying the Eucharist encased in a large gold monstrance, led scores of priests, nuns, seminarians, altar boys, and flower girls down the aisles of the church.

A crowd of people, packed into the rear vestibule like sardines in a tin, peered over shoulders to catch a glimpse of the Blessed Sacrament as it floated by, like onlookers might have vied to see Jesus shouldering his cross on the way to Golgotha. Again, I waited for the miracle, but it never happened. Not even on Holy Thursday.

I stopped praying to the Roman God in my mid-twenties, and by the age of forty, I was in staunch opposition to the church's discriminatory practices. The Catholic hierarchy was not about to forgive me for lying down with men—and I was not about to give them up. But there was another reason. I resented His agents on earth, the arrogant men of the cloth who left the rectory to masturbate incognito in public restrooms; the men who abused boys, covered up these wrongdoings, and had the nerve to write proclamations condemning homosexuality as "intrinsically flawed." Such hypocrisy reached beyond the limits of acceptability, destroying the last bit of confidence I had in organized religion.

How could I pay homage to the pontiff and his legion of thugs? They have destroyed the lives of children in every corner of the world, and most of their crimes will likely go unprosecuted. As a professional counselor and a survivor of incest, I know these things all too well.

If I were to recommit to a higher power, I would have to be free of the guilt and self-flagellation inculcated in me by the dictates of Rome. Yet finding a credible replacement wasn't easy. In my observations, other traditional religions were just as pretentious and chauvinistic. Their leaders were often shamefully egocentric or full of pride and self-aggrandizement. None of the faiths I encountered actually practiced unconditional love and acceptance, although they purported to be charitable. In my search for a belief system, I found my own standards for spirituality were more humane and inclusive than the religions I studied.

Three decades after I left the church in my twenties, the pieces finally fell into place, and I achieved a level of spiritual harmony. Although I'd attained material success as a young man, any self-respect I had garnered from personal and professional accomplishments had been silenced by the homosexual curse, alcoholism, and deep-seated Catholic guilt. The glue that held my shamefulness in place for those years was an impenetrable system of denial. As they say in AA, I was as sick as my secrets. Admitting I was an alcoholic and accepting my sexual orientation had not been options. However, the day that I sat frozen in my rocker and was unable to move—the day that I have marked as the beginning of my recovery—I became ready for a call from the Universe.

From that bottom point when I was thirty-eight years old, I set out on a journey to face my denials and adopt the spiritual values that would define my life going forward.

Specifically, I went through an amazing transformation into and through the 1990s—a makeover of impressive proportions. After a few years of counseling, I shed my addictions and fought my way out of the closet. I was then forced to deal with memories of incest and to grieve the death of a lover. On the career front, I resigned my position as dean and accepted a transfer to a research and teaching position. Each was a portal through which I had to pass, prerequisites to a rebirth of wonder.

During this time, seemingly insignificant events were imbued with meaning, conveying information in mystical ways. Physical sensations—a chill, an adrenaline rush—escorted insights regarding the purpose of my existence into my conscious thinking. From an unknown source came a new and overwhelming desire for change. From conversations with friends, movies I saw, readings, and dreams I recorded, messages streamed into my consciousness.

There was only one path for me, and I was on it.

Beckoned by these tenacious calls of the highest order, I rose to the occasion, my reformation profound.

In the course of my metamorphosis, I pieced together my own view of the cosmos. I came to believe there is an order to the universe and that humans are joined with that order via the spiritual self. Through that connection, souls enjoy a union with each other and with an overarching energy, one to which no single religion can lay exclusive claim. I concluded that this connection was grounded in experience and confirmed with intuition and logic. The overarching energy is not one but many, not limited but limitless. The language of the energy is love, and providing guidance is its mission. Humans gain access to this loving network through the senses, particularly the "sixth sense"—meditations, hypnosis or other altered states, dreams, prayers, seers, chance encounters, and introspection.

I embraced a belief that each individual, each soul, in connection with a life on earth, is moving on a predestined path of his or her own in the context of the overarching energy. A soul's journey spans many lifetimes in a continuous movement toward higher levels of consciousness. There is no external regulator of these movements and, in that sense, no supreme being who determines the outcome.

Further, every thought and event in a world-bound journey is purposeful and linked to a larger plan. Each moment offers the soul an opportunity to evolve, but free will can alter the direction. With each decision, one moves closer—or farther away—to the intended purpose. One's advancement to higher levels is, in that respect, self-determined and freely chosen. Most important, each person is called to live in love. Of that, I have no doubt.

What I have come to believe makes sense to me. Each of us travels our own river. We cross and merge with other streams along the way, encountering souls who play roles in our life dramas and we in theirs. We're challenged to rise to higher levels by giving and receiving love in the context of our lives on earth. That means we choose to accept these challenges or not; we choose to walk proudly into the light or shuffle meekly into the darkness. All of it is perfectly orchestrated and precisely timed.

Song Lyrics—March, 1997

Out of the Sky Comes the Sun

Those times when you have no more faith in the universe
And answers are nowhere to be found
Look up above, because with love the cosmos is run
And out of the sky comes the sun

When drowning in fear, your world about to crumble
When nothing is left in your reserve
The earth will shift, the fog will lift, all nature undone
Then out of the sky comes the sun
How it works is inconceivable, but you will know it's all believable
As pearls of wisdom come to you from beyond

So open your heart, release your mind, begin the journey
Feel all the energy around
You'll see the light, you'll know it's right, your fears . . . you'll outrun
As out of the sky comes the sun

Yes open your heart, release your mind, begin the journey
This power is at your command
The moons divide, the stars collide, creation redone
When out of the sky comes the sun

These beliefs didn't originate with me. But having arrived at them on my own—from many sources, from the inside out, with love and with reason, and without threat of punishment—gave me confidence and conviction in my new life.

When I was forty-four and dean of all pre-university level programs at Gallaudet, I went to a psychic for a reading. Unlike the slight-of-hand trickery seen in media portrayals, this reading resembled a business meeting. Jody Hymes explained that her spirit guides had channeled the information through her before I'd arrived. Its accuracy was uncanny.

> Psychic Reading—October 25, 1990
>
> *Bragus here.*
>
> *And welcome, Mike. The turmoil that you have felt in your adult life has come from trying to be something you did not choose for yourself—expectations from family and society. You have been hard at work to clear yourself of these obligations. The theme of freedom is a strong one for you for the coming ten years. For without that, inner peace is blocked by stress and emotional pain. There is no reason for you to do other than what you choose, and that must be in your own self-interest.*
>
> *You have taken care of others for so long that you are far from knowing how to take care of yourself or to let others take care of you. You are challenged to live differently. Give to yourself first, before you give to others.*
>
> *Your life goal will be revealed to you through a path of ease and contentment. By unblocking your creativity and expressing yourself freely, you will open the doors to inner peace.*
>
> *You have taken on the burdens of others. Do a careful inventory of what is yours. Give back or say no to what is not. Determine the qualities of your own life that you wish to enhance for your own benefit.*
>
> *Bragus and Friends*

Only a few of my earthly friends knew that my climb up the administrative ranks was driven by what others expected, not by what I wanted for myself. My always choosing a difficult path—over-reaching to offset feelings of inferiority—was something I'd never told anyone. The psychic's statement that "freedom would be a strong personal theme for the coming ten years" seemed far-fetched, but I was curious about the prediction.

One year before the reading, I'd been promoted to the top job in the Pre-College Division. I'd been disenchanted with administrative work for years, but the faculty had aggressively lobbied the president for my appointment. I felt obligated to them. I had become tired of the daily grind, of people bitching and complaining about petty matters. What little excitement I still derived from my work came from experimental programs in cultural diversity that our division was implementing. One of those programs fostered greater alignment of school policy and practice with Deaf culture—and later set me on a collision course with I. King Jordan, the president of the university. (In the literature on deafness when the word "Deaf" is capitalized, it represents a cultural group and its allies that share a distinct set of values, beliefs, attitudes and a common language in the form of American Sign Language).

For more than thirty years, a civil rights kind of movement among Deaf people in the United States had slowly been developing. By the 1980s, Deaf activists were demanding more influence over the management of the institutions that served them, including Gallaudet. In 1988, when the university's board of trustees selected a hearing woman as president, the student body seized control of the campus in an organized act of defiance that the media followed from around the world. It was lauded as a classic American civil rights action. Throughout the two-week protest, I was one of a few hearing administrators granted entry to the campus by the student group, and only because my commitment to the cause was well known. As a result of that action, I. King Jordan was swept into office as the first deaf president. In the aftermath, I learned that the board, forced to meet off campus during the protest, had planned to fire me for colluding with the protesters.

> Psychic Reading—January 28, 1992
>
> *Bragus here.*
>
> *Welcome, Mike. The year ahead will provide you with many challenges, and we cannot say it will be smooth sailing. New opportunities will come gushing in, especially after mid-February. The changes are linked, and one decision necessitates many considerations. The pattern of change is all around you. The choices will touch you personally, top to bottom.*
>
> *One reason you are in the midst of so much evolution is that you are a catalyst, an inspirer of change in others. But you must stay clear about your own self-interest. That must come first. You have learned the hard way that vesting your success in others' hands does not work. You see things more clearly and make better decisions.*
>
> *A key theme for you this year is advancement, promotion, and expansion. February and March are times when your insights will be most keen. From April until July you will be bringing new balance to your activities. The fall will find you wishing for resolution, but the time is not yet right. Around year's end, the pieces will fall into place at last. Big changes are in store.*
> *All for now,*
>
> *Bragus and Friends*

In a private meeting on Valentine's Day in 1992, President Jordan threatened to terminate me from my position as dean.

Dr. Harvey Corson, the Deaf provost and my immediate supervisor, was not present. My crime was addressing a faculty group the week before in ASL without speaking the English words at the same time. I had signed naturally, the way a Deaf person would, without voice.

This manner of communicating was at the center of a controversy raging on campus. Supporters of Deaf culture insisted that signing without voice was preferred, because, when a person signed with voice, the visual aspects of ASL were distorted or eliminated entirely. The addition of voice to ASL made the communication more like a pidgin language, they argued, one that borrowed from ASL and from English, but was true to neither. Proponents of established practice favored signing with voice and in English word order, believing that to be the best approach in the schools. It was the Deaf way or the hearing way; the battle lines had been drawn for over 100 years.

The president was furious at me for not using my voice. One might think it odd that a deaf president of Gallaudet would believe that ASL should not be used without voice. The fact that President Jordan was born hearing and raised in a hearing family might have accounted for his views. He became deaf at age twenty-one in a motorcycle accident. He believed that it was better for hearing teachers and staff to use voice simultaneously with ASL, although he did not have the same expectation of Deaf professionals who had the ability to speak. He was walking a tightrope between his Deaf and hearing constituents. One thing was clear though. He viewed the fact that I had led a school-wide meeting in ASL without voice as a major threat, one he would not tolerate.

I was the first hearing administrator to challenge language

practice at the university. At the end of our meeting the president told me I would be fired or receive a strong letter of warning; he hadn't decided. We agreed to keep our discussion confidential until the matter was resolved. I made sure that I summarized his specific comments to me in a note to my file.

I found a definite irony in the fact that, four years after his ascendancy, the president was threatening a dean who had risked his career to help secure the man's appointment. I kept the silence, even later, when I was publicly chastised and called a liar by Philip Braven, the chairman of the university board of trustees at the public portion of one of its regular meetings.

I was incorrectly accused of ordering all employees in my division to sign without voice. I stood my ground, even at the board meeting. My position was that teachers and staff had only been strongly encouraged, not required, to use ASL. I also pointed out that signing without voice was allowed by the school's Total Communication Policy. On the other hand, when I chose to address the faculty without using my voice, I was taking a stand.

My run-in with the president occurred three months before an exposé about the ASL controversy across all of Gallaudet appeared in the *Washington City Paper*. The article was developed after my meeting with the president, and I was interviewed by the reporter writing the story in April. She pressed me to declare whether I had required employees to sign without voice during my welcoming address in August. I gave a politically ambiguous response with enough "spin" to avoid being pinned down. (After discussing the impending interview with the university's public relations officer, I had agreed to respond in this way.)

To avoid oversimplifying the issues of the time, let me explain where I stood with my own development: Just weeks after the president threatened my termination, I had my last drink of alcohol. My first day of sobriety had been March 21, 1992. That same month, I came out at work, announcing I was gay in a division management team meeting. I felt free for the first time in my life!

Of course, freedom is not always won with ease. I gave managers permission to confirm that I was gay if employees inquired; only asking that they be judicious with the information. I was all the way out and expected disapproval, but I was unprepared for the rumor that circulated a month later. A division director informed me that one of her staff members had been told by a teacher, with some certainty, that I had a "terminal illness." It was 1992 and an AIDS diagnosis then usually meant death. Someone was talking up my demise. What to do?

It was a teachable moment, so I crafted a meaningful response. I asked if the staff member who received the information was willing to talk to me, with assurance that I had no interest in knowing who had spoken to her. With that understanding, I explained to the staff member privately that she had my permission to communicate the following to the person: "I'm HIV negative and healthy, and I think he or she has a terminal case of unkindness for spreading that false information." I don't know whether she actually told the person, but the rumors did stop.

My experience with the Deaf culture movement was closely paralleling my own awakening as a sober, gay man. As a diversity trainer, I had helped others overcome the effects of prejudice and discrimination. Now I was *living* diversity on many fronts. Plus I understood the Deaf struggle and felt emotionally aligned with its cause.

Some viewed my actions as reckless. Complaints poured into the university from those who supported the simultaneous use of sign language with voice. Hearing parents of students, hearing faculty and researchers, even members of the U.S. Congress weighed in on the issue. In the end, I stood alone against the attacks. Those who believed as I did were afraid to speak out.

When I left for home after the "massacre" on Valentine's Day, I was aware of my predicament, but not distraught. Clear-minded and peaceful, I went inside, meditating and journaling an entire weekend before reaching a firm conclusion.

The following Monday, I requested a transfer to another position at the university. If necessary, I would resign. The president responded through the provost that they would consider the request. I was asked to continue my silence.

For two months, all communication to me was channeled through Dr. Corson who attempted to broker an agreement acceptable to both me and the president. I had made one request of the administration—that any decision be announced well before the end of the school year. I also came out to Dr. Corson, thereby putting the administration on notice that, as a gay man, I was protected from discrimination by the laws of the District of Columbia.

After three months, they'd made no progress toward a decision. So on May 19th in a confidential memorandum to the president and the provost, I informed them that, in the absence of a decision, I would independently announce my resignation at a meeting Friday, May 27th. If I weren't reassigned to a different position, I would leave. The president must have been unnerved by my audacity, but he must also have known that firing a dean who was closely tied to the Deaf agenda wouldn't be popular. On the other hand, centrists would view the creation of a new position for me as rewarding recalcitrance.

The decision didn't come until May 26th. I was called to the administration building after hours to meet with Dr. Corson, who offered me a position in the Research Institute. Because he hadn't yet received the president's approval, I agreed in principle to the transfer but heard nothing the next day. I was resolute. I would announce my resignation as planned.

Twenty minutes before the scheduled time, Dr. Corson, who was sympathetic to but cautious about the ASL issue, called using an interpreter and asked to meet me outside the high school auditorium. He rushed into the school lobby and pulled me into the boy's bathroom, so no one would see what we were about to discuss. The mood was clandestine, my boss jittery and out of breath. An observer might have thought we were dealing drugs or planning a tryst. We sealed an agreement outside an open stall while a puzzled senior student was relieving himself at the urinal.

The president had officially agreed to the transfer.

In the meeting that day, May 27th, Dr. Corson spoke for several minutes about his relationship with me and how much he appreciated all I had done in my twenty years with the Pre-College Division. Everyone knew what was coming. He announced that I had tendered my resignation and would assume a position in the Research Division. He then invited me to the stage. I addressed the group in ASL without voice.

> PreCollege Remarks—May 27, 1992
>
> *I want to thank Dr. Corson for his kind words. I would also like to thank everyone I've had the opportunity to work with in my twenty years at pre-college programs. It has been a wonderful journey.*
>
> *And now, it's time for a change. Recently, I have become clearer about my purpose in life and what I must do. There are things I could accept before that I can no longer accept. There are things I used to tolerate that I can no longer tolerate. Things that were once important to me no longer hold my attention. I'm being called in other directions.*
>
> *When I realized this, I had no choice but to move on. For these reasons, I requested reassignment and am pleased that I will continue my career with the university. I look forward to my work as a research scientist.*
>
> *I wish you all the very best.*

I was speaking in code without naming the issues, declaring my homosexuality, admitting to a loss of interest in administrative work, and signaling my refusal to support policies that I opposed. They knew little else about my journey, but they all understood what I meant. I left the auditorium with dignity. Speaking from the heart had served me well.

Coincidentally, the *City Paper* article appeared the day my resignation was announced. The reporter was unaware of the negotiations going on behind the scenes while the story was being researched and written. In her article, she ragged on me for sending "mixed messages" to employees and for not being forthright about my views.

News of my resignation traveled fast. When the same reporter contacted me for a follow-up interview, I saw it as a well-timed opportunity to set the record straight. I hadn't been free to clarify my position on the language controversy previously with her, but the situation was still tense. I might face reprisals if I spoke honestly in a second interview, and the president could rescind my reassignment.

I decided to go inside for the answer.

That weekend, I drove to Virginia Beach to visit the Association for Research and Enlightenment (ARE), a center dedicated to the works of spiritualist Edgar Cayce. I spent the first day listening to lectures, browsing through the bookstore, and silently seeking guidance in the meditation garden. Nothing came through.

That evening, while engrossed in a self-help book, the title of which escapes me, I became intensely aware of the questions before me. Was I to grant the interview or not, to speak out or remain silent? As I slipped into a slumber, Sebastian whispered, "The solution will be forthcoming."

I woke early and found a place on the beach to relax and continue reading. When I opened the book to the next passage, the first two sentences flashed up at me like fire off the page: "We have but two choices in life. We can move boldly into the light, or turn and shuffle meekly into the shadows."

I had my answer, my turning point.

In my second interview with the *City Paper* reporter, I clarified my views about the use of ASL. It had been important to me that everyone sign clearly and naturally, I told her. It was never my intention to forbid people to speak, although I acknowledged that my encouragement had been interpreted by others as an edict. I wasn't the only player in the drama; others were just as culpable. But she didn't care about them. I was more newsworthy for two reasons: I was a hearing person, and I had a high profile at the university.

She pressed for an admission that I had been forced out of my position, but I saw no purpose in confirming that. Although my job had been threatened, she didn't know that, and I didn't tell her. I clarified that I had made the decision to resign. I was protecting the president, even though in one meeting with me and three managers who reported to me, he had denied that he'd ever threatened me with termination. In truth, my loyalty was more to the institution, for which I had greater respect than the man in charge. Besides, it was intrinsically a war of ideas, not character assassination—a clash of values, not personalities. Ironically, weeks after the verbal warning, the president had even suggested through Dr. Corson that I could remain as dean if I desired.

The *City Paper* reporter missed the most important dynamic in her follow-up article. When I admitted having "lost the confidence of the administration," the reporter assumed my reassignment had been forced on me. Her story narrowly focused on the idea that I was a "casualty in the Language Wars at Gallaudet." I didn't consider myself a victim. If the reporter had asked the right questions, she would have learned that my actions had as much to do with my own journey, my awakening, as it did with the clash of opposing philosophies. I was stepping into my destiny, standing up for my beliefs, letting my voice be heard.

One could even argue that my role in the drama had been divinely engineered to foster my personal growth. That made sense to me. After all, a mystic had forecast the mid-year changes. And these events had sharpened my spiritual vision. I was clearly on my path, and I would no longer shuffle back into the darkness.

After my transfer to the Research Division, changes marched into my life from every direction. I learned how to give to myself first, making improvements in many areas. I whitened my teeth, replaced my wardrobe, and shaped my body with vigorous exercise and a low-fat diet. Muscle replaced physical frailty. Exploring the mind-body-spirit connection became my mission. Readings and meditations yielded a new awareness of my soul's purpose. Doors opened everywhere.

From 1992 until my retirement in 1997, I worked on projects that were more compatible with my interests. For example, in the spring of 1993, at the time of the National March on Washington for Lesbian and Gay Rights, I helped establish the first gay and lesbian employee association at the university. Although we were a protected class, gay employees still feared living openly on campus. A listserv was established and three of us served as monitors of the group that fostered confidential communication among members. A baby step.

In 1994, my Deaf friend and colleague Lisa Jacobs and I redesigned and co-taught a program for new graduate students called Culture and Language Colloquium. One component was a two-day NCBI diversity workshop that celebrated all differences in the new student group based on race, gender, religion, sexual orientation, class, national origin, hearing status, and other targets of prejudice.

Unfortunately, one self-identified Christian female student became angry when she had to witness gay and lesbian students living openly and telling their stories of oppression. She remained silent until two months later when she filed an anonymous sexual harassment complaint against me and the university. The complaint (which I was not allowed to read) charged that I had created an atmosphere in which gay men behaved in ways that were offensive to the complainant based on her religious beliefs. Lisa Jacobs is straight and was not named in the complaint, although we were co-teachers in every respect. The student clearly targeted me.

I was cautioned not to attempt to determine the identity of the student or engage in any discussions about the complaint. I tolerated these restrictions for a month. When administrators were unable to tell me how the complaint was being handled, I did two things: I talked to a gay employee rights attorney who explained the complaint had no merit. I then told Mr. Lindsey Dunn, the Vice President for Diversity, that I intended to file my own sexual harassment complaint against the student and the university based on my sexual orientation.

The complaint was withdrawn the following week. I concluded that the more "out" you are, the more you become a target.

In 1995, I joined a team of gay and lesbian faculty that developed and co-taught the first graduate gay and lesbian issues course offered in the School of Education and Human Services. I gave several lectures during the course, including one on the history of lesbian, gay, bisexual, and transgender (LGBT) people. The following year, I gave a campus-wide lecture during Diversity Week about Martin Duberman's book *Stonewall*, which chronicled the Stonewall riots in 1969. I also challenged the university's Diversity Day Committee when it refused to make sexual orientation a topic of its annual program.

Because of my expertise and the wide circulation of the

City Paper article, I was a frequent lecturer on cultural conflict between Deaf and hearing people within Gallaudet and at other schools and universities. I fed my gay appetite with trips to Key West, Provincetown, and Fire Island. Yes, I was as "out" as one could be and sported a diamond in my left ear. I mothballed my business suits in favor of the casual dress of an urban gay man.

When I listed my Maryland townhouse for sale and headed for New York in the spring of 1997, I felt like a new man. All my possessions were in storage, except what I had crammed into my Nissan 240sx. As I barreled up Interstate 95 Billy Joel was blaring from my car's speakers: "You've given me the best of you and now I want the rest of you."

17

FULL CIRCLE

Following the New York run of the play in 1997, I visited Mom that August in Rochester. She was still viewing me from behind a veil of disapproval, still withholding her love. We couldn't discuss my life as a gay man or the incest. She did inquire about the circumstances of Bob's death, but she offered no consolation. Our conversations were cordial but stilted and uncomfortable. I went out to the gay clubs in town without saying anything. "Don't ask, don't tell" was still the operant policy. Driving back to Washington, I decided to keep my distance. Thankfully, that changed over the next few years.

Mom passed away just before dawn on January 20, 2001, three months shy of her ninetieth birthday. She might have said that she chose that morning because she refused to witness the inauguration of another Bush later that day. I hated to see her go, but I could certainly understand that reasoning, given the mess Dick and "W" eventually got us into. As a New Deal Democrat, Republican rhetoric always soured her disposition.

Her illness had been brief, following a fall at home. The tools of modern medicine couldn't balance her body's failing systems. She was allowed to slip away without drastic, life-prolonging measures as she'd requested.

Mercifully, she and I had become comfortably close two

years before her death. As she was slipping into a coma, I sat on her hospital bed and whispered in her ear, "I'm glad we're buddies again. I love you. And if you're ready to go, it's all right." She was ready. She'd told her nurse the day before that she would soon be with her Lord.

I spoke on behalf of the family at her funeral mass, my role as spokesman still intact. It was my pleasure. My message was honest and uplifting, unlike my father's eulogy seventeen years earlier. I had no guilt, no anger, and no tears of regret. When her casket was rolled back up the aisle in transit to her burial plot beside Dad, her grandsons took the handles as pall bearers. Kurt was among them, by then a handsome, young rock-drummer of twenty-one. Renee was twenty-six and had received her doctorate in physical therapy from Slippery Rock University in 1999. She was engaged to be married to Bryan Alsop the following August and regretted that her grandmother could not be there. She and my former wife joined the procession ahead of my partner of three years and me. After a few steps, we blended into one cohesive group, moving four abreast. We walked together arm in arm, showing our love. Mom would have approved.

The two inches of snow that had fallen overnight had become slush when the temperature rose during the service. Freezing rain patted a soft tempo atop the green, canvas canopy over the plot. No organization was apparent in the family tableau. Mom's offspring and on down the line numbered almost fifty, crowding in close for a last glimpse of the coffin. They strained to hear the Prayer of the Dead competing with the din of the rain.

My eyes shifted up and to the left as I remembered my last visit to the cemetery. I could see myself on all fours in a downpour, pounding my father's grave with a balled fist and shouting obscenities. It had been seven years since I'd unleashed that anger. The priest's words called me back to my mother's internment. "The service is over. The family asks that you leave the gravesite."

Before I could pull on my gloves, the church bell tolled the hour, exactly as it had after my graveside tirade seven years earlier. Shivers launched up my spine and jiggled my shoulder blades. Gooseflesh rose on the sides of my neck and prickled down the backs of my arms in successive waves. Another cosmic event, I thought. Mom and I had achieved the ultimate closure, coming full circle.

A traditional Catholic phrase came to mind: "It is right and good."

I moved into a trendy loft apartment in Laurel, Maryland, after returning from New York in the fall of 1997. Seated next to my window overlooking Main Street, I set up a new computer and got serious about writing this book—and finding a lover. With a dial-up connection to the Internet, the world of online chatting and "no strings attached" hookups became my evening entertainment. Thanks to AOL, cyber cruising had replaced the printed personal ads.

I wrote by day and traveled the web by night with the Internet giving new meaning to the old adage that people are never who they seem. I wish someone could explain to me how guys who look like princes in their doctored online photos could turn into toads before we met for coffee. They may have thought the same thing about me!

A striking photo of a man popped up in the DCm4m chat

room on December 1st of 1997. His GQ looks and blonde moustache forced me to stop and stare. His six-foot-two frame was standing in a summer stream dressed in shorts and a white, v-neck sleeveless shirt. Tall men make me drool. His profile read, "Exceptional in every way . . ." I knew that was code; the length and girth of his manhood had to be a matter of pride. Of course, I wondered if he was really royalty or just another amphibian.

I left and returned to his profile several times, thinking he was too good for me (the voice was on me as usual), but I sent the GQ guy—Michael—an instant message anyway. His response was swift. We chatted for several minutes before I thought I should end the conversation. "This isn't going to go anywhere," I said aloud. When I wrote, "Guess I'd better go," he asked, "Do you have to . . . ?" I felt a chill. I answered soberly and with a blush of interest, "No, I guess I don't. . . ." He had raised the ante. We moved from the computer to the telephone and decided to meet for dinner that Friday, December 5, 1997.

> Journal Entry—January 9, 1998
>
> *Michael: You're a dreamboat. Dinner last night at Mediterranean Blue was the best. I love your company, your wet kisses, the way you dress, your tall, gorgeous frame. I see you like me too. You'll be here again tonight in my arms, me in yours. Will you be the love of my life? All the ingredients are certainly there. You're on my mind all the time.*

Fast forward to a fragrant mimosa morning in the summer of 2010. Michael Mayes and I had been together almost thirteen years, long enough to be selling off property, writing wills, and planning our retirement. We were running our coonhound in the open space behind our Virginia townhouse community. The dog, like Disney's "Ferdinand the Bull," was bred to hunt but born without the will. His breeder had tied him to a tree and fired a gun to test his fearlessness. The dog had failed. His disposition was as fragile as mine had once been. No surprise. We'd both been abused as pups. That made us brothers under the skin.

This one-year-old purebred "red tick" with markings like a Guernsey cow needed constant reassurance. He was already named Mikey, so Sebastian must have guided me to his photo on the Internet.

I knew what I had to do. I stroked his back gently. I massaged his floppy, hound dog ears and kissed his forehead. I spoke in whispers. I gave him three light pats on the side each time I lowered his food to the floor. I resolved never to punish him when I called him to me. He needed to learn to trust, just as I had; and he did eventually bond with us, first me and then Michael. Our love transformed him from a skittish loner into a laidback, loving couch companion. With the name Mikey, how could anyone say this dog was not meant to be part of our household? After he joined us, I started signing family correspondence "The 3M's." The Internet has been good to me. I met both of my current long term companions in cyberspace.

As for Michael, he is as sweet and gentle, loyal and loving a man as I have known. These qualities drew me to him and the same ones have sustained our relationship. He's not a bells-and-whistles kind of guy, not the one leading the conga line at wedding receptions, but he does stand out in a crowd. Elegant and refined, he's quite intelligent and not the least bit shallow. Perhaps most importantly for me, he's also constant—as constant as night goes to day and day goes to night.

When we were joined in civil union in Vermont in 2001, with our good friends Bill and Mary Ellen Robinson as witnesses, Michael told me he would never knowingly do anything to hurt me. I believe him now. But during our courtship, I was as hard on him as I had been on Bob. The curlers were in my hair again and the rolling pin at the ready. He had to do for me what we would both later do for Mikey. Because I'd been betrayed as a boy, love prospects have had to pass my security screenings before gaining access. With each new relationship, old fears have risen to a conscious level and barked warnings from a deep reservoir of deprivation. That's the way it's been for me, each and every time.

> Michael's Vow—January 2, 2001
>
> *You fill me with happiness, and I am grateful that you are here. You know what hurts and what helps, and you come to the rescue. You love me in spite of myself and put me back on my feet again. In short, the supreme spirit that guides our paths knew I needed someone exactly like you.*
>
> *But our journey is also about the support I will provide you. When I tell you that I care, it means that I will try to understand. I will never knowingly hurt you. You can trust me and tell me what's wrong. It means that I will try to fix what I can, and I will listen with my heart to what you need me to hear.*
>
> *Thank you for sharing your personal world with me and for being the wonderful, kind, giving person that you are. I love you . . . with all my heart.*

Ned Geraty, the talented therapist who guided me through my memories, once told me that intimacy grows along with mutual predictability; that couples achieve deeper levels of connectedness as they're able to predict each other's behaviors. Michael turned out to be who he said he was, and that allowed me not only to trust but to be more vulnerable.

Michael has passed each test with high honors. I love him. And I do believe the curlers and the rolling pin have been retired for good.

Rewind to the summer of 1998. My sister Ann had called to say my mother was diagnosed with breast cancer. She had encouraged me to come home, given the severity of Mom's condition. By that time, Michael and I had been living together in his Washington, D.C. townhome for a few months. I was torn between principle and compassion. I felt compelled to visit my ailing mother, but I was unwilling to dishonor Michael by leaving him at home in the closet. (At that time, I had not disclosed the details of our relationship to Mom, and I expected she'd be uncomfortable with the topic.)

My dilemma was soon resolved. My mother's cancer turned out to be slow growing, and the doctors assured her treatment was unnecessary. Then, with my sister Ann in the lead, a gathering was planned in Rochester where Michael and I would be the guests of honor. It was not billed that way, but that became the reality. Healing was in the air.

I had a healthy amount of skepticism regarding the get-together. What if, upon introducing my partner, my mother ran from the reunion screaming, "Oh shut up, Michael, just shut up!" Despite my sister's assurances that Mom was ready, I felt apprehensive. We stayed the weekend in a downtown Rochester hotel, knowing not to ask if we could share a double bed at my mother's house. I called my sister one last time to confirm that my mother was expecting us to visit. Michael remained remarkably calm, which unsettled me. He had no idea how Margaret could turn on someone!

At the appropriate time, I called her from the hotel and, without mentioning Michael's name, asked if WE could visit. Her words were guarded, her tone pleasant enough.

My mother proved me wrong in Michael's eyes that evening. She played the role of "sweet old granny good witch" magnificently, as pleasant and soft as she could be. I was relieved by her graciousness. Merely kindness to a guest or evidence of a transformation?

Only one thing soured our visit. My oldest nephew, who lived with my mother, came in sloppy drunk that night. He barged into our conversation, breathed beer into Michael's face, and spoke incoherently. I was livid but restrained myself. My mother had been enabling him just as she had my father, keeping him in suds and telling family members to butt out when they suggested she make him leave. I saw the image of Lester in the foreground, not my nephew, bending over Michael, with my mother in the background glaring at him disapprovingly. And just like with my father, she said in a disgusted tone, "Go to bed. You're drunk."

Except for that moment, the weekend turned out perfectly and proved to be a turning point in my relationship with Mom. Our family reunion took place at my niece's house the night after our visit, and Michael got properly introduced to the family. The food was much more than the usual family fare, the laughter hearty and the stories embarrassing. We did everything a family does to welcome a new member—without a hint of homophobia. The men took our relationship in stride. No one got inebriated. In fact, alcohol wasn't even served. I suspect the drunken nephew was barred from the event. By that time, most of the family members had gotten sober, all the way out to Margaret's grandchildren.

We celebrated a homecoming in so many ways!

As we were leaving town the next day, we stopped to visit Mom. I was able to share the details of my life with Michael, and she gave no indication my disclosures made her uneasy. The liberal, loving part of her shone through. If I had any doubts about whether she was a true convert, they were silenced when we departed. My mother had never been one to say she loved you or to give you an embrace. I had taught her how to do both as an adult. That morning in her foyer, she caressed my cheek and said with certainty, "Goodbye, and I love you." I held back the tears. But then she turned to Michael, reached up high to pat him on the cheek, and said, "And I love you, too."

I left a believer. Not only that, her acceptance had reawakened our closeness. When I gave her permission to "pass over" in the hospital two years later, there was nothing left to resolve . . . or so I thought.

About a year after mom's death, I got a call from a young woman with whom I had done some hypnotherapy work in 2000. She left a message that she wanted to talk to me.

Moira (not her real name) is an intelligent, grounded, sensitive woman with exceptional talents. She's had successful careers in the corporate and real estate worlds. She's also clairvoyant; although I'm not sure she would describe herself that way. Moira stayed in touch with me after our work together, because she kept getting psychic impressions about me—my health, issues in my life, the status of one of my children—that she wanted to share. She didn't know why these impressions came to her, but they were amazingly accurate, and I could usually identify their relevance to my life. I had never shared my history of sexual abuse with Moira. So when she called the year after my mother's death, I was curious to hear what she might have to report.

According to Moira, during one of her meditations she had experienced, a nearby "presence" or "energy." Several days later, the distinct image of a woman sixty years or older came through. Moira explained that whenever a presence is with her, she can feel what it's feeling and understand what it's communicating as if the person comes through her. This woman's shadowy figure was outlined from behind by a bright light. She was someone who kept a lot inside and did not reveal much to others. It was important for her to appear prim and proper, although inside she was coming from a place of shame and embarrassment. There was something she was not proud of.

The woman insisted that Moira convey a message to me and would not leave her alone until she had. As Moira told me, "She knew what happened, and she was sorry she hadn't done enough to protect you. It did get addressed some between the two of you, but she never got the chance to tell you how sorry she was and how much she loved you." Given my mother's disdain for "shrinks and psychics," it's ironic that she would forward her apology to me through an extrasensory channel.

I was stunned. She knew! But what did she know? When did she know it? Had she known it while she was alive? Had she witnessed anything? And if something got addressed between us, what was she talking about? Her version of what we said to each other had to be a lot different than what I remembered.

A deep chill went from my hips to my shoulders when the information registered. At the peak of the sensation, my head twitched to the left.

Impressions also came to Moira of a blond boy, about six

to nine years of age, and an adult male in the house with a drinking problem who was abusing him. The boy hid behind a sofa to escape the man and even slept there a number of times. A few times, the boy fought the abuse, but he was powerless to stop it.

She then saw an image of the boy being picked up by the underarms and carried to where he was molested. On another occasion he was abused by the man on a bed. Moira also got an image of another adult male who did improper things to the boy. She couldn't discern faces on the adult men, but her descriptions mirrored specific images that had returned to my conscious memory several years earlier.

"Yes" to the hiding behind the couch, being lifted up from under the arms, the man with the drinking problem, and the sexual abuse. Even the idea that another adult male had done improper things to me, likely my uncle, didn't seem startling. But one tidbit stood out like a whale in a fishbowl. *I had never imagined that my mother knew what was going on at the time.*

To make sure I understood correctly, I contacted Moira again to clarify her impression of what my mother had known and when. Her sense was that my mother had not known at the time but became aware of the molestations after she passed on, although she couldn't be sure.

While my mother was alive, I had begged her not to blame herself if she felt guilty, assuming that she'd been unaware. I gave her my forgiveness if she believed she hadn't done enough to stop it. Strangely, though, my mother's apology stirred up more reactions than it settled.

I was shocked and filled with questions. Was this realization that she had not done enough based solely on what she learned of the abuse in the afterlife? Did she have suspicions at the time? Had she not believed me when I told her? Exactly what had she known or believed in life? My friend Carlene and others held the opinion that my mother had to know what was going on. Didn't she wonder why I slept behind the couch? Come on! Was this just about cleansing her guilt? And how could she not think that he was capable of harming his children, given what she knew about him? This was the woman who denounced her sister for abandoning her kids. If Mom's children were her life, why hadn't she left her husband to keep us safe?

I believed what Moira had told me. She had integrity and no knowledge of my history. This led me to review all my previous interactions with my mother—her tirade at my house, her silence while we watched the incest movie, her halfhearted response to my family letter. "It could have happened," she had said coyly. "If you say it happened, then I believe you." However, this new information suggested that her statements were, at the least, insincere; at the worst, they could have been contrived or even deceitful.

At the same time, I had to thank my mother for this evidence, this final vindication of all I had remembered. And I realized something important. It was the first time she'd ever apologized to me. It would most certainly be the last. I was moved by her method, her intensity, and her authenticity. She had been frantic to get that message to me. Plus I believed what she said, for there must be a strict rule against telling lies across the dimensions.

Her confession and the apology carried tremendous weight. "I shouldn't be angry," I told myself. "Anger would be a useless emotion." I knew it was time to release her, lest she continue to haunt Moira, so I asked that a message be conveyed back to her if she made herself known again. "Apology accepted. I forgive you. You can move on."

Is that not what you do for a tormented soul?

Once again, I expected that to be the end of it, but it wasn't. What happened next was proof certain that the effects of traumatic memories linger. You might stay one step ahead, but you can never leave them completely in the past.

The day after I finished writing this book in December, 2010, I read the last chapter to Michael. In doing so, I wanted to convey how much I valued his support. When I was reading about accepting my mother's apology, something went awry. He seemed preoccupied or disinterested. I began to feel unsafe. Into the next morning, I remained moody and distant. A minor argument broke out and, as I tried to explain my dissatisfaction with his reaction to my reading, I realized what was bothering me. The bottom had fallen out of my mother's apology.

My head was pushing forgiveness, but my heart was bleeding. She was the mother who had admitted not doing enough to protect me; who worked to silence me about the sins of my father; who destroyed photos and handwritten evidence of my uncle's pedophilia; who was more worried about me being gay than the theft of my innocence. When she confessed from the other side, was she hoping I'd give her a pass?

Pain, not anger came rushing in. Michael consoled me on the porch of our mountain home all morning. I longed to be held but was afraid to ask him. Thankfully, he knew what to do. Waves of guttural sobs rolled out of me and punctuated descriptions of my woundedness. A flirtation with the final solution bubbled up. "Times like this I understand why people think of suicide," I said, "You want a way out. You want it to be over." When Michael begged me not to do that, I was ashamed of my grandstanding. I assured him I had no intention of hurting myself.

The next day I felt flat, spent, and dazed. Michael hovered and watched for signs of recovery. I was hungry for affection or maybe just a dietary indiscretion, reparation for the emptiness. A Big Mac and large fries would have filled the void and given me the break I deserved. But I went for a bike ride instead to sweat it out—a healthier choice.

I hadn't cried that way in twelve years, and I may not ever again. Oddly enough, I had been consoled by Michael then, too. We had been sitting on the couch in his Capitol Hill townhouse, partners for less than a year. A TV program depicting a tender moment between a father and his young son triggered a swelling of grief. Such love is something I never had.

To be sure, writing about the incest is emotionally risky, but by comparison, my mother's after-hours revelation felt like a killer ambush. I may not have crumbled if I hadn't learned she was sorry she hadn't done enough to protect me. How different it could have been if she had told me that before she died, less painful to be sure. I returned to a sense of balance a few days later, as I knew I would. One step ahead of a memory isn't idyllic, but it's all I can do.

Looking back, I don't feel angry at my mother. And refueling the dispute we had settled while she was alive would be futile. So I'm not about to go pounding on her grave; I'm done with that.

To give me peace, I choose to believe that her volatile life with Lester, her fear, and her denial of the seriousness of his problems made it difficult for her to safeguard her children. Further, if she had ever desired to make amends to me in life, it was probably overruled by her Spartan pride. I'll assume it had little to do with me.

So here's what I say to her now: "Margaret, listen up! Your forgiveness has been upheld upon appeal. And if you want to make it up to me, could you please intercede for me up there and secure some peace for me with the time I have left down here?

In the years since my mother's passing, I've worked as a licensed professional counselor and hypnotherapist in private practice. I took extensive training in Ericksonian Hypnotherapy, Neuro-Linguistic Programming, and Eye Movement Integration™ and became a certified trainer in each of these fields. I'm known as a specialist in the treatment of trauma and post-traumatic stress, working with clients as varied as 9-11 first responders, policemen, and firemen; Vietnam, Iraq, and Afghanistan vets; and victims of childhood sexual abuse, incest, rape, and physical assault. I have made numerous presentations, taught classes and conducted workshops on Eye Movement Integration™, a technique for healing the effects of trauma and am considered an expert in the use of this approach. In short, I have found meaning and experienced exhilaration in helping individuals recover the way others once helped me.

That's what you do when you find an answer—you pass it on.

I've learned to manage the depression and anxiety that have been with me since adolescence. Antidepressants have kept the symptoms of social anxiety in remission. With Trazodone, I can sleep at night. Without it, I cannot. The phobias that were once so crippling are now only memories. But no medication has ever lifted the moderate lethargy and somatic symptoms of depression that are with me more days than not. I've tried them all and have seen every kind of doctor. I stopped the search for a medical messiah in my mid-fifties. The goal then became *acceptance* rather than outright cure.

Mikey has become part of my therapy. Instead of staying under the covers, I rise with him at 6:00 AM. I take no mental health days because I know a loving partner, two great children (and now two dear grandsons), a coonhound, and many people depend on me. I let Michael know when the depression is getting me down by speaking in code. Saying "this is not a good day" warns him that my energy is low and I may be tearful or grouchy. "I'm really struggling today" tells him it's much worse. I'm not asking him to do anything about it, just keeping him informed. When he says, "I'm sorry" (as he always does), his kindness motivates me to get going. I never liked being coddled. And I trust only Michael with this level of information. It serves no purpose to share it with others in my daily life. That would give it too much attention, and talking unnecessarily about depression can burden others.

By exercising, doing projects, and staying busy with clients, I lose awareness of dark thoughts and pressing feelings. Without a preoccupation, I'm alone against the pain and susceptible to thought obsessions. Pushing through and being outwardly focused helps drown them both out.

But, more than that, I have embraced my purpose in this

life, and I do what I can to live it every day. I am a catalyst for change and an agent of growth and renewal in others. Nothing is more certain. Jody Hymes' reading of my tea leaves was on target. I find meaning in helping others heal and teaching other mental health therapists how to effectively use the healing techniques I have learned. I've found my voice and I'm speaking out.

Sometimes I look back. I realize that until the memories came up for resolution, I'd been running fast, always a few paces ahead of my history, and unaware of the damage enfeebling my life. I had instinctively numbed my disturbance with work and alcohol, two addictions in a symbiotic relationship that masked the origins of my discomfort. Today, the thoughts that were repressed and shielded by screen memories are conscious. I can explore them without the anguish that ushered them in. I can explain them to others casually, without tears, without rancor. I recall them just as they first came back to me in the therapist's office, on the massage table, or in my lover's arms. They're as clear as any past visual memory. They were bubbles that needed to burst. And burst they did.

Naturally, some questions will never be answered. If my Uncle Vin was indeed a pedophile, as his photos and note proclaimed, have I remembered everything that happened during my visits? I did recall a time when he carried me down into his basement, and my head got banged on the open milk-box door as we rounded the turn in the stairwell. I was limp in his arms. I could have been sedated or asleep. I recall being abused one time on a bed in his room. But I never saw the face of the man who did that to me. I had always assumed it was my father. If it was my uncle, there must have been a Mr. Hyde to his Dr. Jekyll.

> Dream—June 26, 1998
>
> *I'm talking to a 12 year old boy who is withdrawn and afraid of expressing himself. When I encourage him to speak, he confides in me that he shouldn't. Vincent wouldn't like it.*

I no longer lie awake at night ruminating about these things. The eruptions have subsided, I've learned many lessons, and my life is on a corrected course. It actually feels right. I experience joy now in ways that suit me—through the lives of my children and grandchildren; when I'm cooking a meal for my family or friends; when I'm chatting with Michael in the morning; when I'm teaching other therapists healing techniques; when I'm writing or speaking as an agent of change.

Frankly, I have no desire to know what else might have happened to me. If there's more, and it's important, I believe it will come up for review. That's how it works. Repressed traumatic memories don't rematerialize when you're taking a pleasant stroll or staring up through the trees on a gorgeous summer day. Mine were given birth in the midst of pain after a hard, extended labor. Think twelve-pound baby!

In my experience, going in search of memories is counterproductive. When it's time and if it's meant to be, they will come.

But there is one last piece. It's about reaching closure with my father. My mother and I finally settled everything after her wild pitch in extra innings, and I now believe we're at peace. My father died in 1984. I already beat him up at his grave in the early '90s, but I want more than that, something different. There has to be a better ending for us.

If I could bring him back and have that last chat with him like Kevin Costner did with his dad in *Field of Dreams,* what would I want from him? What would I say? . . .

Mike: *DAD! HEY DAD! CAN YOU HEAR ME? . . . Dad! DAD! Answer me. I know you're out there.*

Lester (waking up, sound of bottles clanging in background): *Oh shit! What's that? Is someone calling me? Jesus, I was having the worst drunk dream. What a freakin' nightmare! Now who's there? Who wants me?*

Mike: *It's me, Dad, Mike.*

Lester: *Mike? . . . my son Mike?*

Mike: *Uh yeah, your son Mike. We need to talk.*

Lester: *About what?*

Mike: *You know what.*

Lester (uneasy): *Uh . . . I'm . . . um, kinda busy. Can it wait?*

Mike: *No, we need to talk now.*

Lester: *Oh man! Do we have to? Can't we just let it go?*

Mike (firmly): *Easy for you to say. No, Dad. We're not putting it off any longer. We're going to talk now.*

Lester (protesting, then accepting): *All right already! Damn! OK, OK. What do you want to know?*

Mike: *I want to know why you did it.*

Lester: *Did what?*

Mike: *You know what. For Christ's sake, why did you mess with me?*

Lester: *Aw, come on now. Jeez. That was a long time ago, and in another life. I don't know why.*

Mike: *There must have been a reason. Did you hate me?*

Lester: *Hate you? No! Wait. How could you say that? I loved you! Well OK, I didn't show it, but I did. You were my boy, my son.*

Mike: *Then why?*

Lester: *I couldn't stop him.*

Mike: *Stop who?*

Lester: *The monster. He would seize control of me. I'd see the whole scene through some other pair of eyes, not my own. Some crazed maniac was in control of me.*

Mike: *I'm supposed to believe that?*

Lester: *No, really! Afterwards I'd feel awful. I'd vow never to do it again, but it wouldn't last. I drank to deaden the pain.*

Mike: *Why do it if it made you feel that bad?*

Lester: *You have to understand. It had a life of its own.*

Mike: *How did it all get started?*

Lester: *Don't ask me that. It stirs up too much.*

Mike: *I'm sorry, but I deserve some answers. I want to know what made you do those things to me.*

Lester (searching for an answer): *Like I said, I was messed up. . . . It uh . . . it was the booze. It wasn't me. It was the booze.*

Mike: *Don't give me that shit. And don't hide behind the booze. There had to be a reason.*

Lester: *There was no reason. Would you stop asking these questions? It's making me very uncomfortable!*

Mike (angry): *Uncomfortable! God no! We don't want to*

make YOU uncomfortable. Well what about ME? Do you have any idea what it did to me?

Lester: *Yes . . . I do . . . I do know . . . I mean . . . it must have been terrible . . . for . . . for you. Terrible. I was a jerk, OK? A real jerk.*

Mike: *That's it? You were a JERK? You're going to have to do better than that.*

Lester: *What are you getting at?*

Mike: *Look, I know about this stuff. Guys aren't born pedophiles. There's no handbook with instructions on how to molest children. It's learned in other ways. Secretive ways. Tragic ways. Hurtful ways. They learn it in the streets and in closets and bathrooms. They learn it in parks and behind school buildings, in rectories and basements. And it's taught by creeps—creeps disguised as babysitters and scoutmasters, teachers and pedophile uncles and coaches and priests and bishops and . . . fathers. They back you into a corner, yank down your pants, and . . . force themselves on you. They do horrible, degrading things to you. They devour your innocence. They rip out your soul . . . They take advantage of you because . . . well, because it does something for them, or, maybe, just maybe, because it's what they know. It's what they've learned. It's infectious. It's passed from one generation to the next like a ravenous social disease that feeds on the young. . . .*

Mike (pointedly): *Do you see what I'm getting at now?*

Lester (resigned): *Yes. I get it. But why are you doing this?*

Mike: *It's simple. I want to let it go. I want my freedom. I want to forgive. I've been trying to do that for a long time. I didn't think I could. But I knew if I didn't forgive you,*

I'd remain a victim of my own rage, unable to break free, a prisoner of my resentments.

Lester: *I wish someone had explained it that way to me.*

Mike: *Did someone mess with you when you were young?*

Lester: *You don't need to know that, and what difference would it make anyway?*

Mike: *It would help me understand. It would give me a reason not to blame myself for what happened.*

Lester: *No, you got it all wrong, son. You were a great kid! An amazing kid. It wasn't you. It was me. I never found the way out.*

Mike: *Yes, but if there were a reason. If you had a reason, it would be about you and not about me.*

Lester (with emotion): *All right. Look. This is hard for me. Suppose someone did mess with me. Now I'm not saying he did, and I'm not saying he didn't. But suppose someone did . . . when I was young . . . and he . . . he . . . shit* (breaking down, then recovering). *So would that make you feel better?!*

Mike (consoling his father): *I'm sorry, Dad. I'm sorry someone did that to you. Yes, it would give me a reason. It would help me understand.*

Lester: *Please don't blame yourself. It's just like you said. That's how it works. First, you're the kid, the one they prey on. At some point, and it's not too far along, the roles get flipped. You become the beast and not the prey. Then it gets all convoluted . . . So . . . suppose someone did . . . uh . . . mess me up. You know what I mean.*

Mike: *That doesn't change what happened.*

Lester: *I know. I know. Could you ever forgive me?*

Mike: *Maybe.*

Lester: *Really? You mean it? If you forgive me, then maybe . . . maybe I could . . . learn how to forgive myself. Maybe I could move on. . . . You know, I haven't been the same since you pounded on my grave that time. I know I deserved it. I'm so sorry, son. Will you forgive me?*

Mike: *Yes, I forgive you.*

Lester: *That's terrific. Maybe I'll find some peace now. Wouldn't that be great?!*

Mike: *Yes, that would be great for both of us.*

Lester: *Thank you.*

Mike: *You're welcome.*

Lester: *I love you, son.*

Mike: *Well, that's a first.*

Lester: *It's about time, isn't it?*

Mike: *Yes, it is about time. I love you too, Dad.*

Lester: *Thanks. I do have to get back now, but if you ever need me, you just give a holler, and I'll be there in a jiff. Better late than never, huh?*

Mike: *Yeah. Better late than never. Bye Dad.*

Lester: *Bye son.*

Dream—May 4, 2006

My Dad appears a few feet in front of me, dressed in his blue retirement suit. His cheeks are rosy and full. His radiant smile is sending me love. He looks much happier and healthier than he ever did in life. He approaches and plants a buss on each cheek—like a Frenchman. A nice sixtieth birthday gift for me!

ABOUT THE AUTHOR

Born into a large working class family in Rochester, New York, Dr. Mike Deninger rose from humble beginnings to a leadership position in the education of the deaf. By the age of 33, he had completed his doctoral studies and been appointed Dean of Kendall Demonstration Elementary School at Gallaudet University. In 1989 he became Dean of Pre-College Programs at Gallaudet. His name in the field of deafness became associated with microcomputer technology innovations, k-12 curriculum development, school improvement, and cultural conflict in schools and programs serving the deaf.

Dr. Mike now enjoys sharing his skills, knowledge, and wisdom in his current role as a mental health therapist and through his writings, workshops, and presentations. He understands from the inside out what it's like to suffer from tragedy, and he's keenly aware of the renewal that's possible when one frees the mind, relaxes the will, and cultivates the inner spirit. His book *Snakes in my Dreams: A Mental Health Therapist's Odyssey from Hardship to Healer* poignantly conveys the truth he feels obligated to share "before my time is up."

Dr. Mike received a BA in English and a MS in Special Education from Canisius College. He earned his PhD with distinction in Special Education Administration and a MA in Mental Health Counseling, both from Gallaudet University. He is also an accomplished American Sign Language interpreter who worked for 25 years at Gallaudet before launching his current career as counselor, writer, trainer, and specialist in the treatment of trauma and post-traumatic stress.

Licensed as a Professional Counselor in Virginia, Dr. Mike holds certification from the National Board for Certified Counselors. In 2000 he attained certification as a clinical hypnotherapist from the National Board for Certified Clinical Hypnotherapists. In 2007, he received advanced certification as a trainer of Eye Movement Integration™. In 2009 he was certified as a trainer of Ericksonian Hypnotherapy, and Neuro-Linguistic Programming from the American Hypnosis Training Academy.

During his prestigious career, Dr. Mike has been a teacher, principal, graduate professor, university dean, and researcher, as well as a counselor and trainer of mental health therapists. Dr. Mike is also an equity actor who has performed off Broadway in New York and at the Kennedy Center and Arena Stage in Washington, D.C.

CPSIA information can be obtained at www.ICGtesting.com
Printed in the USA
BVOW021119030912

299438BV00001B/82/P